UNMASKING AGE

The significance of age for social research

Bill Bytheway

First published in Great Britain in 2011 by

The Policy Press
University of Bristol
Fourth Floor
Beacon House
Queen's Road
Bristol BS8 1QU
UK

Tel +44 (0)117 331 4054
Fax +44 (0)117 331 4093
e-mail tpp-info@bristol.ac.uk
www.policypress.co.uk

North American office:
The Policy Press
c/o International Specialized Books Services (ISBS)
920 NE 58th Avenue, Suite 300
Portland, OR 97213-3786, USA
Tel +1 503 287 3093
Fax +1 503 280 8832
e-mail info@isbs.com

British Library Cataloguing in Publication Data
A catalogue record for this book is available from the British Library.

Library of Congress Cataloging-in-Publication Data
A catalog record for this book has been requested.

ISBN 978 1 84742 617 8 paperback
ISBN 978 1 84742 618 5 hardcover

Cover design by Qube Design Associates, Bristol
Front cover: image kindly supplied by www.alamy.com
Printed and bound in Great Britain by Hobbs, Southampton
The Policy Press uses environmentally responsible print partners.

In memory of Mike Hepworth – a great gerontologist and a good friend

Contents

List of figures and tables

Figure

Tables

Acknowledgements

This book has been written in the first year of my retirement following a career of 46 years in social research. During that time I have learnt much from many colleagues in the universities of Aberdeen, Keele and Swansea and elsewhere, working in gerontology and medical sociology. In particular I wish to acknowledge the guidance I received during the1960s and 1970s from Raymond Illsley, Gordon Horobin and Roy Mapes. As I indicate in Chapter One, I draw on material collected for a number of research projects and I am particularly indebted to the following colleagues: Chris Harris, Jean Cleary and Billie Shepperdson (*Retirement through Redundancy*); Julia Johnson, Tom Heller, Rosemary Muston and Sam Marshall (*Long-term Medication and Older People*); Richard Ward, Caroline Holland, Sheila Peace and Irene Paton (*Research on Age Discrimination*); and Joanna Bornat and Karen Francis (*The Oldest Generation*).

Over the last 15 years I have been a member of the Centre for Ageing and Biographical Studies at the Open University, and this has been a particularly exciting time: CABS has provided much practical and collegial support. In particular, I have also used material collected for the project entitled *'The Last Refuge' Revisited*, and I learnt much by following this innovative and revealing study, undertaken by Julia Johnson and Sheena Rolph, along with Randall Smith of the University of Bristol.

I appreciate the funding for the projects listed in Chapter One, variously from the Economic and Social Research Council, the Department of Health, the Joseph Rowntree Foundation and the Big Lottery Fund. In undertaking them we have collaborated closely with colleagues from a number of other organisations: Gillian Crosby and Angela Clark at the Centre for Policy on Ageing, Dorothy Sheridan and the Mass Observation Archive, Tom Owen and Help the Aged, and Bren Neale, Libby Bishop, Ros Edwards and Susie Weller of the Timescapes study based at the University of Leeds. Also the conferences of the British Society of Gerontology have provided regular opportunities for much exchange of stimulating ideas and the discussion of research findings; likewise the International Symposia in Cultural Gerontology (and Lars Andersson, Pirjo Nikander and Brian Worsfold in particular).

In drawing on various non-research sources, I am grateful to Tony Benn, Ken Blakemore, Moira Chadwick, Margaret Goodchild, Hazel Nixon, Jennifer Powell and Anita Rogers. I am particularly indebted to a number of anonymous participants (see Appendix). Others have assisted me by providing evidence or comment: Amanda Grenier, Leonie Kellaher, Richard Rose, Andrea Russell, Anthea Symonds and Oliver Tatum.

I am grateful to Emily Watt, Leila Ebrahimi, Kathryn King, Jo Morton, David Simmons, Charlotte Skelton and Laura Vickers at The Policy Press for much advice and assistance, and to the anonymous reader of the final manuscript.

Finally, I could not have produced this book without the support and encouragement of Joanna Bornat and Julia Johnson. For five years Joanna and I have collaborated on the Oldest Generation project. Research based on the collection and analysis of longitudinal data generates a very different perspective on age and ageing, and I have been lucky to have worked with Joanna, not least through her experience and expertise in oral history. Julia, my partner in life, has been my collaborator on a series of projects over the last 23 years. She has patiently tolerated my various preoccupations and has been an invaluable sounding board in the writing of this book. I hasten to add that the various opinions that I express and conclusions I draw are all my own.

ONE

Introducing age

Age is a simple word that really shouldn't need any introduction or explanation. Consider the following. It is the entry for 31 October 1965 in the diary of the British comedian and writer, Kenneth Williams:

> Read the new Carry On, 'Screaming', & wrote to Peter
> Rogers that I didn't want to play another 'old' character. If
> he offers to make the age younger, I'll do it, not otherwise.
> I'd rather play my own age. (Davies, 1994, p 265)

There is nothing exceptional about this extract; quite the opposite. I could have chosen any number of examples of people talking or writing about age and about the impact that age has on their lives.

Williams died in 1988 after a long career that included acting in many of the celebrated *Carry On* films. This diary entry is representative of a certain characteristic bitterness that he felt about his public persona. What it also indicates is that age was a matter of concern to him: he wanted to 'play [his] own age' and to appear younger than the 'old' characters he had previously been given.

Diaries that are published are, of course, edited, and editors often include footnotes to explain details for the reader. However, there are no such footnotes attached to the above entry, and this confirms, should this be needed, that readers are assumed to know what is meant by the word 'age' and how it relates to a sense of personal identity. It is not difficult to imagine the conversation that might have taken place between Williams and Peter Rogers and the ways in which the actor might have insisted on playing his own age.

Typically actors are made up, sometimes to appear younger and sometimes older. Williams was 39 when he wrote the above entry, and it is possible that he was made to appear older in his earlier films: lines drawn on his face or a greyish wig placed on his head, perhaps. Sometimes, in extremes, actors wear masks in order to appear very much older. The concept of 'the mask of age' has been much discussed in social gerontology and I consider it again in Chapter Five. It represents the popular complaint that 'I feel younger than I look': the implication being that 'the mask of age' determines how one appears to others. It conceals 'the real me' and 'the age that I feel'. Did Williams feel younger than he looked? A few months later, on 22 February 1966, and now on the set of *Carry On Screaming*, he celebrated his 40th birthday. The entry for the day concluded:

> I suppose it was my best birthday ever. Well, I've been waiting a long time to be forty. I'm certainly starting to look it, I think. (Davies, 1994, p 273)

One of my aims in this book is to consider in detail how people age, what they say about how they look and what they think, how they spend their time and how they measure it, what they choose to do and what to avoid, and how they value experiences, positively or negatively.

Background

There is a long history to this book: it draws on my career as a researcher undertaking funded social research. My interest in age started with a decision in 1968 to undertake postgraduate research on the impact of mortality on the social networks of older people. At that time, with a degree in statistics, I described myself as 'a statistician working in sociology' and my primary interest was in the relationship between chronological age and mortality and the ramifications of this in the lives of older people. In 1971, I became a member of the first committee of the British Society of Gerontology, and in 1974 I undertook research for Age Concern. This led to a continuing collaboration with campaigning organisations. I began to appreciate the power of ageism when Maggie Kuhn of the Gray Panthers visited the UK in the late 1970s (Bytheway, 1980), and this encouraged me to examine further the language of policy and practice. It was in this way that I drifted away from research based on analyses of statistical data. However, although I had been involved in small-scale qualitative research during the 1970s, it was only in 1983 that I embarked upon a substantial project that required me to 'enter the field' and undertake interviews myself. Later in this chapter I describe some of the funded research in which I have been involved since that time.

In addition to age I have had three other continuing preoccupations: time, analysis and fieldwork. I became interested in *time* when I learned about stochastic processes as an undergraduate student studying statistics. I have been intrigued ever since by the ways in which histories unfold over time, how social institutions such as the family either disintegrate or expand through regeneration, and how historically significant events and personal experiences can coincide, seemingly randomly but with very real consequences. I realised in the 1960s that this view challenged the deterministic models of the family life cycle that were then dominant in sociology and so, in 1971, I embarked upon postgraduate research in which I analysed the occurrence of intra-family events. How did sequences of births, marriages and deaths occur characteristically within families, and how might these be interpreted as time passes and one generation follows another? The analysis I undertook confirmed for me not only the impact of war and ill-health, but also the internal uncertainty of family histories, particularly towards the end of life, and I began to think of ageing as an ongoing private struggle to maintain order and to make sense of the seemingly random events that complicate our lives.

During the late 1960s, as a statistician in the MRC-funded Medical Sociology Research Unit, I became interested in the organisation of data *analysis*. Much of the Unit's work was based upon the cohort of babies born in Aberdeen between 1951 and 1955. Dealing with large-scale longitudinal data (just before the ready availability of computers), I realised that it was helpful to adopt a two-stage approach. The first stage entails extracting and preparing data in ways that ensure that the resulting data will meet the aims of analysis. This started in my case with the Aberdeen Maternity Hospital records which were being collated with paediatric data and primary school records. At the end of this stage, there is, somewhat metaphorically, a pile of data on the table awaiting analysis. The second stage, the actual analysis, entails recognising that what we are searching for, at least initially, are 'findings' from within the assembled material. Put bluntly, it is the material on the table that is being analysed, and not 'the real world' it is there to reflect. As a statistician at the time, rather than a sociologist or paediatrician, I was more concerned that the findings should not misrepresent the data, rather than that they should uncover the truth 'out there'. An important element in this was not just an appreciation of how a concept or variable might be defined, but also how it should be measured and coded for the purposes of research.

Analysing statistical data is an absorbing challenge and it was my main concern for many years. It was only in the early 1980s that I began to think of undertaking original *fieldwork* myself. As a gerontologist I became interested in exploring the ways in which redundancy towards the end of a working life might be re-interpreted as premature retirement. With funding, I began interviewing men who had been made redundant from the steelworks in Port Talbot, South Wales. I visited them to carry out these interviews at the time of the national miners' strike, and I vividly remember driving along the M4, overtaking long convoys of armoured lorries transporting Polish coal to the Llanwern Steelworks near Newport. Having turned off the motorway, located a prospective interviewee's address on the local street map, parked my Austin Metro and knocked on the door, I often found myself being told the latest early morning news about the strike and the struggle of the miners. Ever since then, I have been excited by the prospect of the 'journey of discovery' that constitutes fieldwork, and the opportunity it offers to see familiar worlds from different perspectives.

A career in funded research is driven primarily by empirical objectives rather than theoretical concerns, and I have often been stumped by the question: 'Yes, but what is your theory?' Researchers are often expected to find a theoretical anchor in a specific academic literature around which they organise their fieldwork. While I would agree that research reports should include references to relevant theories, this often results in these theories being challenged and an alternative interpretation of the meaning or significance of data being developed. I was excited in 1990 when Jaber Gubrium and Brandon Wallace published a paper titled 'Who theorises age?'. They argued:

> ... not just professional social gerontologists theorise age; we all do to the extent that we set about the task of attempting to understand the whys and wherefores of growing old. It is argued that when the proprietary bounds of gerontological theorising are set aside, striking parallels can be found between the everyday theorising of ordinary men and women concerned with ageing and their more celebrated gerontological peers. (Gubrium and Wallace, 1990, p 132)

In this book I draw on various research projects in which I have been involved (listed later in this chapter), in which a common concern has been with 'the everyday theorising of ordinary men and women' and the impact that this has upon their experience of ageing. More generally I have been attempting to develop a more fundamental understanding of how people come to grow older. I describe the strategies adopted and the strengths and weaknesses of the research methods employed and how such research contributes to the development of theory in relation to age.

I will also include extracts from literary sources: novels, biographies, published diaries and correspondences, and it may be helpful if I comment here on the value of such evidence. In 2004, Julia Johnson wrote a timely review of the 'cultural turn' in gerontology pioneered in Europe in the 1990s by Mike Featherstone and Mike Hepworth, and more recently in North America by Margaret Morganroth Gullette and Anne Basting. Relating fiction to social research, Johnson wrote:

> Novels, of course, are valuable as sociological data, they possess cultural interest as purveyors of collective and subjective experience and symbolisation [...] Novelists, and indeed auto-biographers, are able to write about ageing and later life as they observe and experience it, unconstrained by the disciplines of empirical research. (Johnson, 2004, p 2)

It is this experiential aspect of ageing that is so difficult to document through empirical social research: we are all well practised in describing age in familiar clichés rather than in ways that describe how we actually find it, and many interviews about age draw heavily upon such clichés. Successful novelists have the knack of uncovering what we feel about life but have never managed to recognise or articulate. I remember the shock, for example, when starting May Sarton's novel, *As We Are Now*. The protagonist is Caro Spencer and her opening words are:

> I am not mad, only old. I make this statement to give me courage. To give you an idea what I mean by courage, suffice it to say that it has taken two weeks for me to obtain this notebook and a pen. I am in a concentration camp for the old, a place where people dump their parents or relatives exactly as though it were an ash can. (Sarton, 1973, p 9)

I was familiar at that time with the idea that old people's homes were seen by many as places where old people are 'dumped'. What shocked me was not just reading what this might entail for the person being dumped, but also what might be involved in articulating and writing such an account. I was also taken aback by the idea that being 'old' could be mistaken for being 'mad' and that engaging in such writing might require very specific kinds of courage. I was also struck by the power of the writing, articulated grammatically as it is in the first and second persons: seemingly May Sarton is writing as an old person, specifically for me, the reader. At the time she wrote this she was in fact about 60, long before she was struck by the chronic illnesses that feature so prominently in her celebrated journals. It was, presumably, through observing the experiences of others that she was able to construct such a vivid account of institutional living.

So an important aim of this book is to explore ways of capturing the lived experience of life at different ages. In the Appendix I list all the people whose experience I have drawn on, including the anonymous participants of various research projects.

Although the focus of much of this testimony is on later life, an important supplementary aim of the book is to consider the significance of age *throughout* the life course from year zero onwards, and thereby to bridge the gap between gerontology and research into earlier phases of life. 'What is your age?' and 'What is it like to be growing older?' are questions that can be asked of anyone regardless of age. I have no doubt that research that contributed to an integrated theory of ageing from cradle to grave would be both challenging and revealing.

Much of what I am able to call upon in this book reflects my own biography and my experience of the worlds I've lived in: those of a white male born in the UK in the middle of the 20th century. Moreover, much of my research experience, as is the case with all post-war British gerontology, relies heavily upon the testimony of the survivors of those generations whose early life was dominated by the dangers and exigencies of the 1939–45 war (including the steelworkers I interviewed in 1983).

The concept of 'age'

This book is essentially about the concept of age, so let's return to the word itself. As a noun, dictionaries make a distinction between age defined as the length of time a person has lived, as the length of time that other objects (animate and inanimate) have existed, and as a historical period. In this book, I am concerned only with the first of these. But is age no more than 'the length of time a person has lived'? Often dictionaries include a secondary definition, specifically of the derived term 'old age', and it is interesting and perhaps significant that there is no corresponding term 'young age', either in the dictionary or in everyday talk. Possibly this is because, as a verb, 'to age' is defined as 'to grow old', and the past participle 'aged' is often used as a noun or adjective to identify those who have lived a long time and 'grown old'.

What these complications indicate is that although age may be defined in terms of time, it is more than just a way of measuring time: age is about the experience of growing older. So there is a tension here between two radically different meanings, one a seemingly static characteristic of the individual (typified by the question 'What is your age?') and the other, a more dynamic phenomenon ('What is it like to be growing older?'). The complex relationships within the vocabulary of age are discussed in more detail in Chapter Four.

In thinking about the concept that is represented by the word 'age', two elements are dominant: time and identity. Age is about time, but it is also about individual identity. This is most clearly apparent when we consider the ways in which age appears in 'ordinary' everyday speech and writing. So Kenneth Williams writes both about 'the age he looks' and the length of time he has waited to reach the age of 40. The age he looks is an important element in his wider social identity based on visual recognition. In contrast, his 40th birthday is a temporal milestone in his unfolding biography.

This individualistic conceptualisation, however, excludes the way in which age is a structural component of organisations and institutions. It is not just that many bureaucracies use age in regulating access to resources; age itself is an institution that features prominently in many structures and practices. Consider two examples: the Office of National Statistics (ONS) and Age UK.

The ONS is the most authoritative source of social statistics in the UK, and its publications demonstrate well how social research takes account of age in surveying the population. In introducing 'some of the individual demographic variables', the ONS lists sex, age, relationship to household reference person, marital status and ethnicity.[1] So there it is: number two in the pecking order. Here age is conceptualised as a variable, comparable with the other standard variables: sex, marital status and ethnicity. Each variable is made up of a set of mutually exclusive categories whereby each and every member of a population can be classified. They differ in the number of categories and in the ways in which categorisation is achieved through a series of interview questions. But the critical feature that ensures that each functions satisfactorily as a 'variable' is that every interviewee is categorisable. On the basis of responses to questions the interviewee ends up in one and only one category of each variable.

The age variables are based upon the interviewer first asking adult respondents aged 16 or more for their date of birth. If this is refused they are asked 'What was your age last birthday?', and if this in turn is not answered the interviewer makes a 'best guess'. This results in age being measured by 'years lived'. Given this is a number that can range from zero to over 100, various categorisations are derived, the most concise being made up of six categories, namely:

- 16 to 24
- 25 to 44
- 45 to 54
- 55 to 64
- 65 to 74
- 75 and over.

Had the ONS interviewed Kenneth Williams in 1965, he would have been placed in the second of these categories. This then illustrates how age features in the routine practices of organisations such as the ONS.

How might age function in the context of organisational *structures*? Consider the titles of UK campaigning groups. In 1971, the National Old People's Welfare Committee was renamed 'Age Concern' and then, in 2009, Age Concern merged with Help the Aged to form 'Age UK'. So, taken literally, age has replaced 'old people' and 'the aged' as the focus of a continuing campaign. The title 'Age Concern' implied that age was the focus of *concern*; in contrast the title 'Age UK' carries no such implications. The promotional literature being published by Age UK focuses heavily upon 'later life' and 'older people'. It 'celebrates' ageing and sets out a positive vision for 'our ageing society'. So, to date, it has avoided addressing the tricky question of what age is.

In this book, my primary concern is with how age is used both in everyday life and in official systems, to inform and structure actions and expectations. In both contexts, I see age as having three distinct roots.

The first, echoing the biology of age, is *the body*. The human body is an organism that is evidently, in the experiential sense, subject to certain universal biological processes. We are able to view our bodies in mirrors and photographs, and we interpret many slow changes in their appearance as being due to age. We see what age is doing to our bodies and thereby to us. We view others and perhaps compare notes on the changes we observe. From time to time, we find ourselves forced to accept that there are actions that we are physically no longer able to perform. In this context, age is *of* the body.

The second root is the *documentation of chronological age,* resulting from a wide range of social and bureaucratic practices that begin with birth and continue throughout life. As a consequence, chronological age can be, and is, marked and frequently celebrated (and sometimes resisted or denied), and the individual can be located against a timescape of biography and historical circumstance. The chronologisation of history and of the individual life course ensures that we are made aware that only those over a certain chronological age are able to share personal experiences of historically specific and temporally located events.

The third root is *relational* and, more specifically, *generational*. Starting with the parent/child relationship, reproduction maintains a growing network of social relations that serves as an alternative indicator of age status. Claiming to be old enough to be someone's parent, for example, is an unambiguous indication of a generational difference. There are social worlds that survive and maintain a continuing identity because of regeneration, one generation of participants succeeding another: 'The King is dead, long live the King!'

Two arguments flow directly from this approach to the conceptualisation of age. The first is that age and many age-related concepts are social constructions: even though the body is indisputably changing with time in ways that seem inevitable and predictable, encapsulating this in one explanatory concept ('age') is a linguistic and thereby cultural act. Adapting W.I. Thomas' famous proposition (Thomas and Thomas, 1929, p 572), age is real in the sense that if people define age as real, then age is real in its consequences. The second argument is that people become old largely as a result of the institutionalisation of age. This is accomplished by: (a) the dating and certification of birth, (b) the inclusion of date of birth and/or age in the bureaucratic processing of individual persons, (c) the formal constitution of generational relations, starting with the legal specification of parental responsibilities, and (d) the use of chronological age in the formulation of policies and regulations that restrict access to rights and resources.

Featured research

My interest in age originated in my postgraduate research. My primary objective here was to study how births, marriages and deaths punctuate the unfolding experience of family life. I attempted to develop contrasting perspectives that uncovered shared rather than individual experiences. The only adequate source of data available to me was *Burke's Peerage* (Burke, 1955). From within this detailed compendium of the genealogies of the British aristocracy, I extracted large samples of differently defined 'family structures' and with these data went on to write a thesis titled 'The Dynamics of Family Structures'. Although this was never published, a paper presented at the 1977 colloquium of the European Social Research Committee on Ageing was included in the subsequent publication (Bytheway, 1979a).

In this book, I feature the projects described below. All were supported with funds from bodies outside the host universities. Such resourcing imposes a temporal structure on research and, in particular, all fieldwork has to be undertaken within time periods that are, in relation to whole lives, relatively brief. Moreover, in order to secure the funds, certain compromises have to be made. Simply studying how people grow older is insufficient; there have to be more immediately 'useful' objectives.

I was centrally involved in each of these projects, undertaking fieldwork and analysing the resulting data. Despite the constraints of limited resources, they all provided me with a 'real world' gerontological education and a richer understanding of the later lives of the people around me.

The use of the concept of old age

This 18-month project was funded by the Social Science Research Council in 1980. The objective was to study 'the ways we write and talk about old age and the things we are liable to hear and read'. Drawing upon Berger and Luckmann (1967), I attempted to address the fundamental question 'How does old age exist at all?' by focusing on the literature readily available to people involved in 'the old age industry' who in one role or another had dealings with older people.

I drew a diverse sample of 21 documents, beginning with three examples of basic linguistic handbooks: a dictionary, a thesaurus and a library classification system. The documents were analysed using a set of seven keywords and their derivatives, and the analysis of these three demonstrated how age comes to be represented in the organisation of knowledge. The other selected documents ranged from a government White Paper to Aesop's Fables and from a report on an Age Concern survey to a book of cartoons (with captions). Rather than follow any prescribed analytic procedure, I simply identified every appearance of the keywords and derivatives, and then developed categories reflecting the ways in which they were used.

In conclusion I identified five themes: the use of the concept of generation, the significance of location, the perspective of the author, the stigmatisation of old age, and concern for the reality of the ageing process (Bytheway, 1982). There was no immediate follow-up to this study, but subsequently I drew on it in writing about ageism (Bytheway, 1995).

Retirement through redundancy and Early retirement and the care of older relatives

In 1981 the Economic and Social Research Council (ESRC) funded a study of the impact on the local economy of Port Talbot of 'Slimline', a redundancy plan implemented in 1980 by the British Steel Corporation (Harris, 1987). Slimline offered older workers, aged 55 years or over, a deal that was specifically intended to discourage them from seeking any further work. As a consequence, the study was based on a large sample of 752 workers in which younger workers were deliberately over-represented. Nevertheless, it still included 121 men who were 55 or over and, as a result, in 1983 I was able to propose to the ESRC a supplementary project, *Retirement through Redundancy,* which examined the consequences of redundancy for these older workers. The basic question I addressed was whether their redundancy was their retirement. I was interested to know what had happened since they had left the steelworks, and how they described their current status with regard to work and the labour market.

In the summer of 1984 I interviewed 108 of these men. They had had very different careers. Some had worked in the metal industry before the Second World War; some had been part of the massive expansion of the Port Talbot plant following nationalisation in the late 1940s; others were miners who had moved to work in Port Talbot in the 1960s when their mines had closed; and there were a few who had joined the workforce much more recently having been made redundant by other employers in the 1970s. Despite this variety, my basic strategy was based on four questions: what they did immediately after the war, when they joined the steelworks, how they felt about being made redundant in 1980, and what had happened subsequently (see Bytheway, 1986, 1990). I was able to transcribe details obtained from an earlier interview (undertaken for the research on the impact of the redundancies on the local economy) on to a proforma. This meant that the course of the interviews was dictated by these details rather than a fixed set of questions.

The following year I secured funding from the Joseph Rowntree Foundation to return to some of these men in order to study the care of older relatives in their families. This project, *Early Retirement and the Care of Older Relatives,* was a more complicated one, in that the plan was to interview other members of the family as well as to revisit the steelworkers. I began with interviewees who had mentioned at least one older relative (often a parent) and, after recounting what had been learnt from the ESRC project, I would ask about the possibility of meeting this person or, possibly, someone more closely involved in providing family-based care. It became a more ethnographic study and I found myself describing my method as 'taking a walk around the family'. In many instances I had *conversations* with people rather than engaging in interviews, and sometimes several members of the family were involved in such exchanges (Bytheway, 1987, 1989a). In Chapter Nine, I present a case study of one of these families. Tom Wilson was the former steelworker and the focus is on his widowed father, Martin.[2]

Between 1987 and 1997 I worked on a number of projects. Although none produced data that I could draw on in writing this book, two are relevant to the study of ageing. First, between 1990 and 1993

I was employed on *Teamcare Valleys*, a major project funded by the Welsh Office that had the aim of promoting teamwork in primary health care in the South Wales valleys, a large deprived area. This work reflected my continuing involvement in medical sociology, but it also complemented the steelworker study in providing a contrasting perspective on migration and employment careers (Bryar and Bytheway, 1996, pp 54-8). Also it informed our bid for funding for the medication project (described in the next section). Secondly, my collaboration with Julia Johnson on ageism (Bytheway and Johnson, 1990) contributed to the Open University course *An Ageing Society* (K256), and eventually to the publication of a book (Bytheway, 1995) and then the RoAD project (described below).

Long-term medication and older people

This project, a collaboration with Julia Johnson and Tom Hellen, was funded by the Department of Health and undertaken between 1997 and 2000. It was planned to inform the National Service Framework for Older People and for this reason it was confined to people aged 75 years or over (Bytheway et al, 2000; Bytheway and Johnson, 2003).

The main study was conducted in eight diverse general practices in England and Wales. The aim was to recruit randomly from each practice 10 patients aged 75 or over who were living in their own homes and had been receiving medication for at least 12 months. Of those approached, 54 (41%) were unable or refused to participate, and we ended up with a sample of 77 participants, who were each interviewed three or four times. In addition, they were asked to complete a semi-structured two-week diary that included a record of social contacts as well as symptoms and medicine taking. The participants agreed to information concerning their medicines and contacts with health professionals being abstracted from records held by the practice, and, when they were interviewed, all the medicines that they had at home – prescribed or purchased – were logged. Thus we obtained very detailed information about the participants' use of medication, both from their own perspective and that of the practice. Following the completion of our fieldwork, we fed initial findings back to the practices through a series of local seminars. Some of the patients who participated in the study took part in these, along with GPs and practice nurses.

More generally, the diaries generated evidence of the enormous diversity in the everyday lives of older people. While some were very ill and dependent on others, the sample also included two who were still gainfully employed, and others who had substantial responsibilities in caring for others. One man, for example, still visited his mother, well into her 90s. Another participant was caring for her seriously ill daughter. We concluded that it is dangerous to make broad assumptions about the needs of 'the elderly' or about how their medication 'should' be managed. It is all too easy for policy and practice to be based upon stereotyped images of frail, older people with bottles of tablets tidily placed on their bedside tables.

In Chapter Three I introduce Jane Neal, a participant whose diary was particularly interesting in revealing the impact of changes upon the routines of everyday life. And then in Chapter Eight I describe the situation of Eric Farmer. He lived on his own and was heavily dependent upon support services. As such this case study raises important questions for how we think through the consequences of an ageing population.

Birthdays in adult life

This project started in 2002 with a collaboration between the Open University and the Mass Observation Archive (MO) based in the Library of the University of Sussex. Subsequently, between 2004 and 2005, it was supported by a grant from the ESRC. The overall aim was to collect and analyse evidence about the social significance of birthdays in adult life and, in particular, how birthdays contribute to a personal sense of ageing. It drew on two sources of data: the ongoing MO project, started by the Archive in 1981, and a survey undertaken by the Office for National Statistics (Bytheway, 2005, 2009).

In 2002, 186 members of the MO panel of 'ordinary people' submitted accounts of the significance of birthdays, for them and for their family and friends. In particular, they had been asked to comment on how their previous birthday had been celebrated, and contribute their thoughts on how the event relates to the experience of growing older. Of these writers, 120 had responded 12 years earlier, in 1990, to a similar request for thoughts about celebrations including birthdays and again, in 1992, on the topic of growing older.

About one in four of the MO writers played down the significance of their birthdays and reported that their previous birthday had not been celebrated. Most of the other accounts, however, were positive, and many features of childhood celebrations had survived into adulthood. However, the emphasis was placed not on parties and presents, but rather on being remembered on the day itself through the receipt of cards and phone calls.

Some MO writers commented on changes in how birthdays are celebrated, to some extent as a result of increased commercialisation. Many of these comments focused on decennial birthdays, the 'big ones'. Predictably, in comparing how specific contributors had written about their birthdays in 1990 and 2002, there was evidence of changes in family relationships. Looking back on their own childhoods, many of those who were parents commented on how things had changed for their children and grandchildren.

The responses illustrated how the age number is itself a universal element of individual social identities: 'Today I am 50'. Using simple arithmetic, MO writers made much of the 'facts' of chronological age in writing about how birthdays are viewed in the context of family and social relationships. At another level, however, they recognised that birthdays are milestones in life's long journey.

Each MO panellist is anonymously coded by a unique number, and this appears at the top of every response that they submit. I have used these numbers when quoting extracts in Chapters Five, Six and Nine.

RoAD

Between 2004 and 2007 I directed RoAD (Research on Age Discrimination), a two-year project funded by the Big Lottery Fund and undertaken by a team at the Open University in collaboration with Help the Aged. We examined the impact of age discrimination on the lives of older people. Involvement of older people was at the heart of the RoAD methodology, with over 300 older people from across the UK working in a collective effort to grasp the reality and significance of age discrimination (Bytheway et al, 2007).

The aim was to point to ways of achieving a more age-inclusive society; more specifically to uncover forms of exclusion, to describe the experience of being – or feeling – excluded, and to identify ways in which such discrimination might be challenged. The intention was to focus on actions rather than attitudes.

As it was a national study we needed to recruit 12 fieldworkers from across the UK, and for these we specified two primary requirements: some relevant experience of research and to be an 'older person' themselves. Although not implementing any age bar, we expected the fieldworkers to be willing to identify themselves as 'older people'. The 12 ranged in age from 44 to 71. We saw them as 'co-researchers' and the working relationship as collaborative rather than one of 'them working for us'. The main task of each fieldworker was to support and interview three older people in their area who had agreed to keep one-week diaries for the project. At the end of the week the fieldworker interviewed them, focusing on specific experiences, 'things that happened' in the course of the diary week. The interview then moved into a less structured phase when fieldworker and diarist discussed the issues that had been raised, exchanging accounts of similar experiences.

Through selection, we endeavoured to ensure that the diarists were a diverse group, but achieving this was not straightforward. Anticipating that some potential diarists might have sensory impairment or limited dexterity, or might be people whose first language was not English, we indicated that they could ask someone to act as a 'scribe', writing entries into their diaries. We also offered a small payment to diarists. As the project progressed, we realised that the goal of 'representativeness' opened up complex questions of how lived experiences are captured and expressed as stories, and the importance of understanding how different aspects of identity – of who we are and are judged to be – overlap and intersect.

A total of eight men and 29 women kept diaries, and they ranged in age from 60 to 97 years. For the most part they were unknown to the project prior to volunteering. Thus they were freely identifying themselves as 'older people', sometimes seeing their role as that of searching out evidence of age discrimination as it affected other older people. In designing the diary, our intention was to provide sufficient space for those 'with a lot to say' or with complicated experiences to recount, while at the same time indicating that all we wanted was a record of things that 'actually happened'. We did not ask the diarists to check that specific criteria were satisfied before including notes on a particular experience, and the fieldworkers explained that we would not be disappointed if spaces were left blank. Having described the purposes of the diary, the fieldworkers made arrangements to return to review and collect the diary. They sought permission to record the interview on tape.

Through the project, we uncovered clear and stark examples of age discrimination. In addition to discrimination in employment, we came across experiences that are part and parcel of everyday life. Reinforced by mundane and commonplace practices, the discriminatory elements are often invisible, even though they result in older people being excluded from public spaces and social activities.

In this book, I present three case studies from this project. First, in Chapter Three, there is Daphne Smith, whose diary provided evidence of how daily activities were threatened by risks posed by teenagers. In Chapter Five I enclose extracts from a report on a case study on how older women used their local hairdressing salon, and in Chapter Nine

I describe an exchange between Anna French, an interviewer, and a diarist that demonstrates how age can constrain everyday relations.

The oldest generation

Finally, between 2007 and 2011 I have been working with Joanna Bornat on *The Oldest Generation* project (TOG), part of the ongoing *Timescapes* programme of qualitative longitudinal research funded by the ESRC. TOG has focused on the dynamic nature of older people's relationships and identities, set in the context of changing structures of intergenerational support. Our aim has been to explore how and why certain family relationships endure or change over time and how these processes affect the lives of the oldest generation. A particular focus has been on the marking of relationships and identities through key events such as birthdays, marriages and deaths (Bornat and Bytheway, 2008; Bytheway and Bornat, 2008).

We recruited a diverse sample of 12 families through the UK-wide Open University network and followed them over an 18-month period. In each family we recruited one member of the oldest generation, someone over the age of 75 years, who was interviewed in 2007 and again in 2009 (referred to as 'the senior'), and one person who kept a diary and took photographs ('the recorder'). The diaries were returned each month and this created a routine which extended over the 18-month period.

Initially around 40 people volunteered their families to take part and this enabled us to select a diverse sample of 12. Certain minimum specifications were met; for example, the sample included one senior who was over 95 years of age, and another who was not born in the UK. One family dropped out when the recorder decided she had not fully appreciated what was expected of her. This family was replaced. There were three others where the recorder did not keep a diary for the whole period and another two where the senior died within the 18 months. In both cases, interviews were carried out with proxies – a son in one case and two daughters in the other.

Through life history interviews, diary entries and photographs we have collected and collated a substantial amount of retrospective as well as current and future-oriented information. Two diaries, for example, include more than 50,000 words, and in total there are diary entries for nearly 4,000 days.

A number of the seniors and their families feature in this book. In Chapter Two I include extracts from the diary of Josie Shaw; in Chapter Three I feature an interview with Angela Rammell and the diaries of Adam Arthur and Alice Watson; in Chapter Five I use the diary of Daniel Cole to illustrate some aspects of the impact of bereavement; and in Chapter Seven there is a long account of 12 months in the life of May Nilewska, aged 99. I have also drawn on a Timescapes project involving TOG that focused on siblings, and the contributions of two participants in that project are included in Chapter Six.

It sometimes seems that it is only the middle third of any project that is adequately funded and resourced. Prior to the start there is all the work entailed in preparing and submitting applications for funding, and then, after completion, publications, presentations and other dissemination work follow over several years thereafter. I see this book, for example, as an important opportunity to disseminate conclusions from the above projects.

Other sources

One other source of research data upon which I draw in Chapter Three is the diary material collected for *'The Last Refuge' Revisited*, a project undertaken by Julia Johnson, Randall Smith and Sheena Rolph (Johnson et al, 2010).

In attempting to consolidate my arguments, I have supplemented the above sources with other kinds of material. In particular I have drawn upon a number of publications in the field of literature: fiction, biographies, diaries, correspondences and journalism. In particular, in Chapters Two, Five and Seven I make use of the diaries of Frances Partridge (1990) and Anne Chisholm's biography of her (2009). Similarly, in Chapter Five I draw on Tony Benn's celebrated diaries (1995, 2003). I include brief extracts from a number of novels and autobiographies, most notably perhaps in Chapter Nine from Julian Barnes' *Nothing to be Frightened of* (2008) and Tom Courtenay's reminiscences of his mother (2000). In order to examine how published collections of photographs are used to portray age, I have used a collection from the celebrated American photographer, Imogen Cunningham (1977), and, as a case study of the importance of returns in later life, I quote extracts from some unpublished autobiographical writing by Margaret Goodchild.

I have adopted a serendipitous strategy: some of this material dates back a few years when I had earmarked it for inclusion in a book such as this; other extracts, however, have come to hand as this was being written. I have not gone out of my way to find material that supports a particular argument, and because of this I feel I can claim such material to be more 'representative' of ordinary experience than might otherwise have been the case.

A third source, one that raises difficult questions about generalisability, is that of testimony and personal experience. While the RoAD project was running we maintained an open website and invited people to submit examples of their own experience of age discrimination. We received many responses, and it has occurred to me subsequently that such testimony is a neglected tool in social research. I have not set up a similar website for this book, but I have talked about many of the issues with friends and relatives and occasionally asked about their own experiences. Not unlike more standard interviews, these exchanges have been revealing, and in places I refer to them and occasionally include quotes.

This kind of evidence is often dismissed as 'anecdotal'. I've always thought this an arrogant reaction. The fact is that courts of law rely heavily upon such evidence and social researchers could learn much from how it is tested and examined by the forces of law and order. It is of course inappropriate to claim that anecdotal material represents what is 'typical': I would agree that good sampling is needed if the aim is to draw general conclusions about collective experiences. But anecdotal evidence is much more relevant and legitimate in marking out 'the possible'. In undertaking fieldwork for the steelworker project, I came across several examples of people living in extreme circumstances. After one interview, for example, I came away amazed at what I had been told and thinking 'he's one in a million'. I reflected on this, realising that actually he was one in only 108. Given a population of 50 million, this implied that he was representative of somewhere between 50 and 500,000 other residents of the UK. While not being very helpful statistically, what this argument establishes is a conclusion that he was almost certainly not alone: there would have been other people living at that time in similar 'extraordinary' circumstances.

The chapters that follow

In Chapter Two I review classic approaches to research in social gerontology and, in particular, four strains which have featured in its history: the relationship with clinical practice, the study of needs in old age, the distinction between old age and ageing, and the development of theory. Some of the problems encountered in tapping into standard sources of data are considered: interviews, observations and documentation.

I discuss alternative research methods that might uncover the ways in which age figures in the course of life, paying particular attention to the use of diaries and correspondence, and the abstracting of material from literature. It is important that all types of documents are considered as potential sources of data. How is the question of how old someone is raised or resolved in bureaucratic settings and in informal conversation? How is age revealed in conversation? How is chronological age calculated, marked and celebrated? And, in particular, how is date of birth used as a check on age? These questions are discussed in the final section of Chapter Two.

In Chapter Three I turn to how the passage of time is theorised and how this relates to age. Once chronological time is set to one side, it becomes possible to locate age in the context of different temporalities and contrasting images of time. One particularly fruitful concept is that of 'timescapes'. This enables links to be drawn between age and the three roots detailed earlier: body, documentation and interpersonal relations. Also distinctions can be made between linear and circular time. I consider how age and time are theorised in everyday life, drawing on case studies (already introduced above), paying particular attention to daily routines and how these might change with time. In contrast to daily routines, biographies are typically made up of sequences of events. These create a temporal order that is tied to personal history rather than chronological time. Circular time is evident in the annual cycle of the seasons and the weather. The consequences for older people can be substantial, and data are presented from the TOG project. A third temporality is that of return: with age, people may return to locations experienced earlier in life. The consequences of this in later life are considered and, in particular, I examine one example of an older person returning to a location last seen over 50 years previously.

In Chapter Four I begin by arguing that, while interviewing people is essential to the development of a sound basis for research into age, it is not in itself sufficient. The analysis of language and image and of how they are used to represent age and ageing in the wider cultural landscape is just as important. They generate models of age, and of how people of different ages are and 'should be'. There is a full and complex vocabulary of age terms in the English language. I contrast how 'old', 'older' and 'elderly' are used as adjectives, and this leads to an examination of how historical trends in vocabulary use reflect changes in state policy and ageist prejudice.

With regard to visual images of people, captions and accompanying text often serve to consolidate the images and what it is to be of a particular age. The mass media and advertising make heavy use of visual images and, while older people are rarely used in mainstream marketing, the older consumer is attracting increased attention. What kind of images result? How are older people portrayed and what kinds of products are being targeted at them?

There are more general issues about how older people are represented. Language and picture tend to be individualistic. How are older people represented 'en masse'? And for social research are there alternatives to population sampling? These questions are discussed with reference to the Birthdays project.

In Chapter Five I first discuss the concept of 'lived experience' and its relevance for research into ageing, and then a range of operational questions facing empirical research in this area. I draw on past research and theories of how people interpret the ageing of their bodies, including 'the mask of age'. I discuss how the mirror and old photographs help to determine how people recognise and respond to signs of age and other personal characteristics. Birthdays are central to the ways in which age is marked and celebrated. Examples are presented from the MO and Timescapes Archives, and from published diaries. A key element in theorising the experience of growing older is that of 'life transformations': ranging from bereavement to moving house to falling ill, this concept directly reflects the idea of life starting anew.

Relative age has been neglected by gerontology. Early in life, we learn the distinction between childhood and adulthood and as we pass through the former, and through educational institutions in particular, we learn to appreciate and accept the distinctions that are associated with age status and chronological age. In Chapter Six I first discuss the parent/child relationship and how this institutes a sense of generation and the age differences that help to differentiate generations. I then present evidence relating to siblings to discuss the significance of relative age in determining the character and course of interpersonal relations among people of similar age. I present and analyse evidence of social networks in later life, and how changes affect the experience of older age. Finally I discuss how some older steelworkers accepted redundancy in order to make way for younger men, thereby representing the notion of succession. In all these different contexts, age relations are often based more on seniority than chronological age.

In focusing on the processes and experience of 'becoming old', gerontologists risk neglecting great age. All too often, the oldest generation are being looked after in the security of care homes: out of sight and out of mind. Researchers only encounter them in studies of specific settings or conditions such as Alzheimer's. In Chapter Seven, I present two detailed case studies of people living to a great age. First I draw upon the published diaries and biography of the celebrated writer, Frances Partridge. Secondly I turn to a case study, drawn from the TOG project, and a diary detailing the 12 months leading up to a 100th birthday.

In Chapter Eight, I turn to the broad, societal issue of 'an ageing population'. It is, and has often been, a popular concern of politicians and the media. The concept is not straightforward, and so I review problems in defining age groups and generations. Age is a key variable in demographic and epidemiological research, and large surveys of populations have revealed strong statistical relationships between age and many other variables. To illustrate how age is 'controlled for', I describe the use of age-specific mortality rates in the analysis of cancer statistics. Perversely this has led to a neglect of the ways in which age is associated statistically with mortality.

The images that demographic analysis has developed in presenting statistics on chronological age can raise concern and anxiety over the ageing of the population. What impact does this have on the organisation of care services? I present a case study of one old person whose daily life is intricately tied in with the provision of such services. Bureaucratic responses to the ageing population can both sustain and constrain the lives of older people, and the chapter ends with an analysis of how chronological age figures in the management of breast cancer screening.

Arguably all research about people's lives is participative. And it inevitably follows that researchers will talk about 'them' and what 'we' have learnt from having interviewed or observed them. Recently there have been efforts to overcome this clumsy and restrictive relationship. In Chapter Nine I begin with an account of how, in undertaking gerontological research, I have found myself more engaged with older people than I expected. I also review issues associated with age prejudice and discrimination and how, in the RoAD project, we attempted to overcome the gulf between researchers and older people. The chapter ends with the case for gerontologists learning from their own experience of age: the timescapes of their own careers, gatherings, reunions and reflections.

In Chapter Ten, I conclude that getting real about age entails recognising that ageing is constant, complex and slow. And that it does make a difference to our lives and our relations with others, despite the unchanging continuity implicit in our fixed personal identities, and the apparently constant regeneration of many of the social worlds we live in. We have to learn to cope with the idea that each of us is still and, at the same time, no longer the person we used to be. It is through sensitive and imaginative social research that we will gain a better understanding of this conundrum.

At the end of each chapter I include a handful of questions. These are intended to prompt thought and discussion, and some relate specifically to the case studies presented. All those whose ageing experiences are drawn on in the book are listed in the Appendix. They are, if you like, the 'sample' upon which the book is based.

Questions for discussion

I Do you feel age masks 'the real you'?

2 When did you last take a hard look at yourself in the mirror?

3 Do you look your age?

4 Do you feel your age?

TWO

Researching age

In this chapter, I consider ways of researching age. I start by discussing well-established strategies, before developing the case for alternatives. There are two key issues to bear in mind: how we as researchers collect or generate data that might cast light on age, and how we secure the necessary resources and then the relevant opportunities to achieve this. In particular, a critical question is how access is gained to older people, and the extent to which access may be biased towards particular categories. There is a constant risk that we end up (a) tackling questions set by funding agencies, or other stakeholders, who may have their own particular interests in the results of the research, and (b) engaging with people who want to participate in research in order to unload their grievances or the benefits of their own experience of surviving into later life.

The aim of much gerontological research is to understand the lived experience of growing older and being old. An obvious way of pursuing this is to talk to people, but conveying any kind of lived experience is difficult since it involves skills in articulation and performance. Here is a first-hand account of one such attempt. My aim was to capture my first experience of fieldwork in a seminar presentation in 1986. This had entailed interviewing men about working in the steel industry and, in particular, their recent experience of redundancy. This started in the summer of 1984, 19 years after I had left university and become a researcher. As I have explained in Chapter One, I was 'piggy-backing' a larger study of the impact of the 1980 redundancy programme of the British Steel Corporation on the local Port Talbot economy. I had become somewhat embarrassed that it had taken me so long to undertake any fieldwork myself, and, although the project was funded for only 12 months, something like six had passed before I embarked on my first interview. At the time I denied that I was putting it off, but looking back I am now willing to admit that I was apprehensive and uncertain as to how to start. Once I had dived into the deep end, however, I quickly became accustomed to the heady excitement of fieldwork. During that summer I interviewed 108 men, and now, more than 25 years later, I have just spent 10 minutes discovering that I can recall something of the individual detail of at least 35 of them.

I called the seminar presentation 'Sociology in an Austin Metro'. I modelled it on traditional theatre, distributing, for example, a programme sheet listing four 'Acts'. I attempted to convey something of the excitement and logistical challenge of fieldwork by re-enacting a typical day. The first Act had me sitting in the university common room browsing through a book I'd just taken out of the library (literally). I read out a couple of randomly picked paragraphs and posed questions about how they might relate to the real lives of researcher and researched. For Act Two, I imagined myself in my Metro, parked outside the home of a steelworker – someone I had actually interviewed. I talked my way through a summary of what I already knew about him (suitably anonymised), trying to anticipate the interview to come. The third Act was easy: I simply read out the transcript of the real interview that had followed. And finally, in the concluding Act I returned to the common room keen to talk to anyone – in reality, of course, the seminar audience – about what I had learnt from that particular day undertaking interviews in Port Talbot.

I was attempting in the presentation to relive my own experience of fieldwork, while simultaneously uncovering the steelworker's lived experience of redundancy. As I described in Chapter One, the fieldwork coincided with the miner's strike and some of the men I interviewed had themselves been miners before transferring to the steelworks. They had vivid memories of mining and some took advantage of my visit to talk passionately about the latest news on the strike. And so, between interview and seminar – and now my recounting the story in this book – there is a complex pattern of experiencing and reliving life in the real world.

There are now many published accounts of the confrontation between the miners and the government, and many of these feature images of the impact it had in South Wales. As witnesses often say of such historical moments, I can say that I was 'there', at least on the periphery. Even now, as I write 25 years later, my mind can easily drift back to those heady days.

Research in gerontology

Historically, research in gerontology is rooted in the scientific method. As Stephen Katz has noted:

> ... gerontology in its short history has attempted to stabilize itself with a positivist narrative that ultimately reflects not

the past but the present preoccupation with scientific progress. (1996, p 29)

Much of this narrative has drawn upon clinical practice whereby doctors and biologists have studied the bodies of 'the aged'. Katz identified the French doctor Jean-Martin Charcot as one of the most influential in the 19th century. Charcot declared that his attention was focused on women:

> who are, in general, over seventy years of age – for the administrative statutes have so decided it – but who, in all respects, enjoy an habitual good health, although misery or desertion has put them under the protection of public aid. Here ... is where we shall find the materials which will serve us in making a clinical history of the affections of the senile period of life. (Charcot and Loomis, 1881, quoted by Katz, 1996, p 81)

Thus 'public aid' at that time enabled research to be based on a specific age group within the population of destitute people, and to characterise them as being in 'the senile period of life'. Despite this, as Katz comments, there was a contradiction in the suggestion that doctors should practise medicine on people enjoying 'habitual good health'. Charcot resolved this, he suggests, by assuming that senility, even if it coexists with 'good health', generates bodily problems: old age is both 'the simultaneous enfeebling of function' and 'a special set of degenerative diseases' (Katz, 1996, p 81).

The American psychologist G. Stanley Hall is often accredited with separating gerontology from this clinical tradition (Ross, 1972). He achieved this in the early 1920s by demonstrating how religion, the humanities and autobiographies were sources of insight into later life that extended the knowledge gained through medical research. In particular, he was keen to promote scenarios that could be viewed more positively than those presented by clinicians. This, he argued, was possible when a more subjective perspective on old age was incorporated.

There can be little doubt that in many western countries the 1939–45 war had a major impact on state policies and attitudes to the health and well-being of national populations. Arguably the US led the way. Ziman (1994, p 93) demonstrates how the part played by the American government changed radically after 1939, and Achenbaum (1995) describes the enormous expansion in the American government's commitment to research and development:'No history of gerontology can stress enough the critical role played by the federal government in shaping the emergence of this scientific field of inquiry' (1995, p 187). To a large extent, this investment determined the character of the methods used. Nathan Shock, for example, appointed to lead the programme on ageing at the US Public Health Service, immediately established the Gerontology Research Center in 1941 and, over the following 35 years, he promoted the development of 'well-documented observations and good scientific data' through cross-disciplinary work, but only insofar as it advanced experimental, empirical science (Achenbaum, 1995, pp 95-7).

The history of gerontological research in the UK is less substantial, relying heavily upon the empiricist traditions of Victorian philanthropy associated with the work of Henry Mayhew and Charles Booth. Blaikie argues that, with regard to published information during most of the 20th century, ageing remained a 'socially opaque issue', overshadowed by concerns regarding unemployment and the labour market (1999, p 36). At various points the government and the popular media were triggered into a panic over the ageing of the population (Shegog, 1981, for example) but it is only recently that this has led to a coordinated approach to research (Walker, 2009). Peter Townsend is the most widely celebrated British social researcher on the subject of later life. His first study, *The Family Life of Old People* (Townsend, 1957), was located in a working-class community in the East End of London. It built upon earlier research by Sheldon (1948) and Young and Willmott (1957) into urban community life. These early studies, escaping from the confines of hospital and workhouse, focused on the position of older people in families. Townsend, however, recognised the importance of not neglecting residential care. On the basis of his next major project, *The Last Refuge* (Townsend, 1962), he advocated a radical change in government policy, shifting priorities towards sheltered housing and away from institutional care.

Psychological research on age and ageing has become a distinctive field in the UK, closely associated with biological research and clinical practice. Bond et al (2007) include a number of chapters that review research on such topics as cognition, emotions, personality, adaptation, wisdom and dementia. There has been a notable emphasis upon longitudinal research, following the pioneering work of the Berlin Aging Study (Baltes and Meyer, 1999), and this has fostered interest both in ageing as a lifelong process and, in contrast, processes associated with great age.

Jamieson and Victor (2002, p 2) have noted an expansion of methodologies used by British gerontologists in more recent years.

Some of those they mention feature in this book: in particular, the use of cultural products such as literature, diaries and visual images.

What this cursory review of the history of gerontology demonstrates is how the discipline has developed primarily on the back of (a) clinical practice with older people needing, or seeking, assistance of one sort or another, and (b) surveys based on samples of people over a certain age located within various kinds of disadvantaged urban communities – surveys that entailed both interviewing and observation.

In 2010, the International Association of Gerontology and Geriatrics has rules based on five main purposes. The first of these is:

> to promote gerontological research in the biological, medical, behavioural, and social fields by member organizations and to promote cooperation among these organizations.[1]

Thus gerontology is described as an activity undertaken within a series of 'fields' by various 'organizations'. Inadvertently, perhaps, this illustrates how it has not yet established a clear location of its own on the academic map. It is frequently described as an area of study supported by various 'disciplines'. Bengtson et al (2009, p xxi), for example, in introducing theories of ageing, refer to the recent growth in 'cross-disciplinary studies concerning the mechanism of aging', and the disciplines that feature prominently in their handbook include biology, sociology and psychology, but not gerontology itself. Similarly, Johnson (2005, p xxii) describes gerontology as a 'field' rather than a discipline.

Thus a number of strains are evident. First there is the difficult relationship that gerontology has had with geriatric medicine and, more generally, clinical practice. Through its many links with the pharmaceutical industry, medical research has always been comparatively well resourced but oriented towards particular forms of intervention. Often this has led to a gross imbalance when academics, researchers and clinicians have sought to collaborate equitably. Johnson (2005, p xxiii) puts this cogently. Despite the growing importance of social research, he argues that:

> These studies are overwhelmed by the sheer weight of inquiries about illnesses – physical and psychological – and the interventions which might ameliorate their consequences.

While tensions with medicine tend to influence the development of gerontology at the level of resourcing, similar but more mundane strains surface when researchers endeavour to collaborate with local practitioners or policy makers. When it is so painfully evident that many older people have serious needs demanding urgent attention, it is difficult to propose or disseminate research that appears to achieve little more than a demonstration that later life is complicated, and that needs might not be met by a simple change in policy or practice. Inevitably much social research has been channelled into problem-solving activities and researchers are often expected to come up with 'practical solutions'. Townsend (1981) refers to this tendency as 'acquiescent functionalism': explaining problems in terms of individual difficulties in adjustment rather than structural inequalities.

A third strain that has bedevilled the development of gerontology has been the question of what we should be studying. Is it how we grow older – and are growing older at all ages – or is it about being old? The former is less presumptuous and constricting but it can lead to a neglect of the lives and circumstances of people of great age. I was struck by the critique of Andrews (1999) of those gerontologists (myself included) who, she alleged, were promoting the concept of agelessness:

> Ironically, this denial of difference, the erasure of the years
> lived, further entrenches the barrier between us and them,
> as it strips the old of their history and leaves them with
> nothing to offer but a mimicry of their youth. (1999, p 316)

I disputed this critique at the time, pointing out the way reference to 'the old' and 'their history' set them apart from the rest of 'us' (Bytheway, 2000). However, I realised that gerontology had begun to neglect those older people who were difficult to access, including the very oldest. Partly as a consequence, I advocated a shift in gerontological research towards 'extreme age' (Bytheway, 2002, p 74; see Chapter Seven).

In recent years, there has been some notable investment in the UK in longitudinal research (such as the *Timescapes* study), and this has brought into focus the question of whether gerontology is about growing older or being old. My view is that, regardless of the expressed aims of research, the latter option will unavoidably sustain the ageist distinction between 'us' and 'them', drawing upon an unresearched assumption that people somehow or another 'become old'. Through longitudinal research, a different timescape develops in which dates of life events and interviews are basic items of information, reducing the emphasis that cross-sectional research tends to place on age.

Lastly, a fourth strain is that between theory and data. The suggestion that gerontology is 'data rich and theory poor' has become a well-worn cliché. Having started life as a statistician, I have never been persuaded that the study of ageing is particularly 'data rich'; quite the opposite, in the sense that much of the data we have are limited to narrowly defined cohorts living in only a few countries. Perhaps the underlying argument is that research should be led by theory, and that data should be collected that tests and develops theory. I would go along with this, since it is an indirect way of indicating that data, as much as theory, are an essential element of research. That said, one of my aims in this book is to promote the development of more effective research methods and the collection of a broader range of data.

Between 1997 and 2001 I was editor of the journal *Ageing and Society*. In Bytheway (2002) I revisited all 117 papers that had passed through my hands (see Table 2.1). A total of 47 (40%) were based on theoretical discussions or secondary analyses of pre-existing data. Of the other 70, 43 reported findings from samples or surveys of older people, and 13 were studies of particular settings related to later life (for example residential homes). Thus four out of five empirical studies were based on samples or settings in which people were defined in some specific way as 'older'. Of the 43 studies, 34 defined 'older' chronologically, with an age criterion that was at least 50 years; the most common being 65 years, the standard age for defining the dependency ratio (see Chapter Eight).

Table 2.1: The empirical base of papers published in *Ageing and Society*, 1997–2001

Empirical base	Number	%
None	47	40.2
The general population, or samples that were not age specific	8	6.8
Samples of older people	43	36.8
Age-specific settings	13	11.1
Carers of older people	6	5.1
Total	117	100.0

This heavy reliance on age-specific samples and settings is typical of much gerontological research and Table 2.1 provides striking evidence of the close link between gerontology and the categorisation of older people on the basis of chronological age. This is a feature not just of survey research; qualitative research in gerontology often draws upon fieldwork with samples of people drawn from a specific age category. Confining research to specific categories is defendable. It enables studies to be systematic and replicable, and it may be a realistic way of making best use of limited resources. Regarding the research I feature in this book, the Medication project and the TOG project both used the age of 75 as a selection criterion. Likewise, when we were concerned that the RoAD project might be neglecting the oldest, we commissioned a participatory sub-project that was limited to people aged 85 or more.

In preparing the ground for a more focused discussion of how age might be researched, the idea of models is helpful here. Over the years there has been much criticism of 'the medical model': the ways in which medicine has developed a staged strategy for understanding how illnesses unfold and how doctors might use their expertise to best effect (Bury, 2005, p 2). It is a model that makes various general assumptions about the course of illness. Similarly, various models have been brought into play in the development of gerontology, both positive and negative. So, for example, 'successful ageing' is popular because it is a model that offers a positive prospect for later life. A report on a recent study, for example, begins:

> Successful ageing may not only be about escaping illness but also of having a positive attitude towards one's life despite poor health. The literature tends to define 'successful ageing' as the absence of physical and cognitive impairment, usually neglecting the possibility of positive adaptation or resilience in the face of health related adversity. It is not surprising then, that younger age is the most consistent predictor of successful ageing. Older adults commonly stress that social engagement and positive outlook towards life are more important than physical health status, but these are often not considered at all, or are not viewed as equal facets. Thus the dominant model of successful ageing is deficit based, and does not include older people who may be living 'successfully', with some degree of impairment. (Livingstone et al, 2008, p 641)

The implied model here is that – despite the presence of poor health or other deficits – adaptations, resilience and social engagement can still lead to successful ageing, defined as having a positive attitude.

A good example of a negative model is that of malignant social psychology (MSP: Kitwood, 1997). What Kitwood proposed was a process that explains how the personhood of someone diagnosed with dementia can be undermined. MSP is conceived as a set of 17 behaviours ranging from treachery to disparagement, and the process takes the subject through a series of stages, each transition triggered by a combination of neurological impairment and MSP. Kitwood illustrated this with a diagram representing a particular case history and the subject passing through 21 stages (1997, p 52). This is arranged in a spiral, possibly to imply that the personhood of the subject is lost as she 'descends' three-dimensionally towards a point in the middle of the diagram marked 'death'. The assumption of loss and decline dominates many models of the ageing process and this is echoed in many popular aphorisms such as 'first sign of dementia' and 'losing your marbles'. Even positive clichés such as 'she still has all her faculties' are based on the assumption that decline is the norm.

A basis for many models of ageing is the concept of 'stages': the life course being made up of a series with the individual passing inevitably through from one to the next:

> The model of the human life span divided into 'ages' or 'stages' has a long history which continues to influence our imaginings and expectations of the ageing process. (Hepworth, 2000, p 119)

One consequence of this model is that it legitimates the categorisation of the population according to 'stage'. In particular, old age as a stage generates a category of 'elderly' people. Insofar as there is unease with the ways in which 'old age' homogenises and stereotypes those categorised as being in it, there have been frequent proposals to distinguish between 'the young old' and 'the old old' and between the third age and the fourth age (Weiss and Bass, 2002). Regardless of where or how one draws the boundaries, the consequence is still a staged model of the ageing process.

Research methods

Social research draws upon a number of methods. Essentially all are based on three primary sources of data:

- spoken exchanges (including interviews and conversations)
- observation (possibly recorded through photographs or film)
- documents (personal and official, private and public).

Researchers may also use secondary sources such as the transcriptions of interviews or the observational notes or diaries of fieldworkers. With all data there is accompanying metadata: name of researcher or fieldworker, time and place of recording, source, labelling, etc.

Interviews

Referring back to the projects listed in Chapter One, in addition to the interviews I undertook myself for the Port Talbot studies, I worked with fieldworkers on the Medication and RoAD projects and this included interviewing older people. The TOG project also relied heavily upon interviews, undertaken by Joanna Bornat.

An obvious strength of interview-based research is that the researcher is in control, initially at least, and can focus the interview directly or indirectly on the questions the interview is intended to address. So, from the very outset, when an interview is sought, the researcher has to introduce the purpose and the broader aims of the project. This of course 'sets an agenda' and, arguably, invites particular kinds of response ranging from outright refusal to extended interviews in which a wide range of topics are covered in depth.

Unlike other kinds of interviews (for example, by the police or prospective employers), the research interview is heavily dependent on the interviewee voluntarily agreeing to participate and answer questions. Typically researchers hope to achieve this through general sensitivity and empathy, and assurances of confidentiality.

A large literature has developed that seeks to promote a sophisticated approach to interview-based research (Gubrium and Holstein, 2001; Silverman, 2005). Much of this is oriented to an interpretivist analysis in which both the interviewer and the interviewee (the research subject) are recognised to be actively engaged in the production of data. In this sense, they are 'co-researchers' and, prompted by the ways in which the interview develops, the interviewees may volunteer their own stories or opinions addressing their own rather than the researcher's questions. As Graham (1984, pp 118-19) has observed:

> Story-telling offers advantages over traditional interviewing, more effectively safeguarding the rights of informants to participate as subjects as well as objects in the construction of sociological knowledge.

But, perversely, this may also be seen to be a weakness: the data are 'infected' with the prejudices of interviewees, and the assumptions they might make about what the researcher wants them to say. One way of reducing this is to see the interview as an opportunity to observe the life of the interviewee. After all, the exchange does take place in real time and it might be interrupted. In a discussion of how my interviews in 1984 might be interpreted as acts of participant observation, I have posed the question:

> What do I make of the experience, in interviewing a
> woman, 75 or so and living on her own, of another woman
> walking straight into her house, warming her hands on the
> fire, listening to us but not being introduced or joining in,
> walking out and then returning twenty minutes later cursing
> that 'it' hadn't opened yet? (Bytheway, 1989b, p 123)

I answered this question by suggesting that it was entirely inappropriate
to describe her as 'living alone'. This and other examples led me
to become interested in the concept of the 'extended household',
recognising that any household may provide privileged access to
people who do not routinely live there. It was evident that while
my interviewee might be the only person who routinely slept in the
house, others had privileged access. I offered another example of how
interviews are embedded in the ongoing lives of the interviewees:

> One morning I attempted to obtain an interview from
> a steelworker who had been repeatedly refusing on the
> grounds that every day he and his wife had to visit his sick
> aunt in the hospital. It seemed that they were spending
> most of each day out of the house and they had neither
> time nor energy to spare. On this occasion I was politely
> refused once again but as before I was given some doorstep
> information about the aunt's progress. An hour later, I was
> interviewing another steelworker who happened to be a
> Borough Councillor and, in the course of this, he received a
> phone call from the first seeking his assistance in having an
> inspector check on the house of the sick aunt. (Bytheway,
> 1989b, p 125)

I recognised that it would be inappropriate to record what was said in
the course of the phone call, but the simple fact is that the unexpected
coincidence confirmed the fact that the first interviewee had real
concerns about the welfare of his aunt. In Chapter Nine, I include an
extended case study of another Port Talbot family that shows how I, as
the researcher, unexpectedly had the opportunity to observe significant
real-life events unfold. It is an example of how interviewing can be
interpreted as a more active form of participant observation than is
suggested by many handbooks on interviewing.

Letters

I first appreciated the potential of correspondence for the study of ageing when reading the correspondence and diaries of Bernard and Mary Berenson (Bytheway, 1993). The potential of letters to cast light on the experience of age is evident in the comments of those who have published edited collections. Caroline Moorehead, for example, writes:

> all her life [Martha Gellhorn] used letters as a prism through which to filter what she saw and heard, and as a way of keeping close to her friends. [...] Because there was seldom a significant stretch of time when Martha was not moving around, letters were what held her life together [... she] wrote letters every day, often describing the same particularly significant episodes to several people. When troubling things happened, she wrote them out, in long, anguished passages, as if only by writing could she lessen her own sense of grief. (2006, p 1)

Peter Sussman similarly describes Jessica Mitford's commitment to a daily correspondence with her friends. More generally, he warns that:

> Collections of letters have a biographical fascination about them, justly, but built-in distortions of the genre limit their significance. As an editor, I cannot find letters that don't exist, but I can and hereby do warn the reader of the limitations of what they're reading. The letters *do* tell an important story – or many important stories – but they cannot be expected to be the whole story. (Sussman, 2006, p xx)

These editors comment on the decline in letter-writing and express doubts about the potential of email as an alternative source for biographical research. However, there has been a growing interest in the use of electronic communications as a source of research data. Certainly we found email invaluable in the course of the TOG project, supplementing and occasionally substituting for the diaries we were collecting.

Letters are a tricky source of data because, by definition, a letter is what we write and send to another who, regardless of whether or not they reply, is free to keep or destroy the letter we sent. Normally senders do not keep copies, and so it is only when letters are routinely kept and preserved, that it is possible to compile an archive of correspondences. Collating letters from different sources is often a demanding task for those who hope to see them published. In the case of the Berensons only a small proportion of their letters have survived, and only a small proportion of these were subsequently published (Bytheway, 1993, p 162).

Very occasionally, however, two correspondents do preserve what each has written and posted to the other, and their correspondence has been combined in one archive. So, for example, Joyce Grenfell and Katherine Moore maintained a friendship – through correspondence alone – that lasted over 22 years (Grenfell and Moore, 1981). It started in February 1957 when Moore, aged 58, wrote to Grenfell, then a successful entertainer, aged 47. Grenfell's last letter was posted less than three months before she died in 1979. A year previously Grenfell had returned to Moore a packet of Moore's letters so that her grandchildren might have them. Moore says she was subsequently persuaded to publish a collection of their letters as a 'complete record of this invisible friendship'. They rarely mentioned age in their correspondence but an exception was in 1968 when Moore wrote:

> Yes – my year has had a great deal of happiness and fulfilment still, thank you. I am past my seventieth birthday now, and my husband had his ninetieth in January, and we had a lovely family party of children, grandchildren and our two refugee children (now grown-up) and a cake (made by me) with ninety candles and special odes and music (composed by the grandchildren). (Grenfell and Moore, 1981, p 112)

As with many of the descriptions of birthdays in the MO Archive, this is a positive, family-oriented account, but aspects of age can be noted: the numbered birthdays, the grown-up children and performing grandchildren and words such as 'still', 'now', and 'past'. The published volume includes a touching exchange prompted by the death of Moore's husband four years later in 1972. Moore conveys the news with the following opening sentence:

> We have been friends for so many years that I feel I must write and tell you of my *great* loss since I last wrote to you. (Grenfell and Moore, 1981, p 179)

It may be that there are many more such collections of correspondence that have been preserved but not published. If traced they could provide invaluable insights into the changing significance and meanings of age in the context of long friendships.

Fiction

There have always been lurid stories of questionnaires being filled up by interviewers using their own imagination rather than a real-life interview. So not surprisingly the use of fictional material is widely seen as inappropriate for research. At most a few quotes may be used to 'illustrate' a report. Vignettes, however, are often used by psychologists in attitude research, and for the RoAD project we extended this practice by writing vignettes that amalgamated incidents and experiences recorded in the diaries of older participants. When we set this against the continuing debates in literary studies regarding the relationship between fiction and 'real life', we realised that in producing these vignettes we had stepped over a certain threshold. Novels, despite being products of the imagination, are often based on real life and intended to reflect the author's own life experiences.

Mike Hepworth introduced many of us to the idea that fiction might be used as a resource 'for understanding variations in the meaning of the experience of ageing in society' (2000, p 1). His pioneering work was celebrated in the Sixth International Symposium on Cultural Gerontology, held at the University of Lleida, Spain, in October 2008 (Worsfold, 2010). Papers were presented there on how a wide range of novelists had written about age: Oscar Wilde, John Updike, George Eliot, James Joyce, Ellen Glasgow, Penelope Lively, Doris Lessing, Julian Barnes, Kingsley Amis and Philip Roth.

Some fiction is specifically intended to literally reconstruct a particular lived reality. Margaret Forster's novel *Diary of an Ordinary Woman* (2003), although entirely fictional, was inspired by a request that Forster received to edit the lifelong diary of a 98-year-old woman. She responded positively to the request and met the diarist, but the project floundered when a granddaughter claimed that she had been promised the diaries. Forster decided to withdraw at this point, but she continued to write a fictional account of the what-might-have-been, imagining what a 98-year-old diarist might have written. This is what Helen Falconer wrote in a review for *The Guardian*:

> It could be argued that all novels written in the first person
> are fictionalised memoirs, yet somehow *Diary of an Ordinary
> Woman* is not simply a traditional 'novel in diary form', but
> more like the incredibly detailed forgery of an unlived life.
> Not only is the background of social and political change
> meticulously accurate – unsurprising, given that Forster is
> the forger – but there is everything one would expect from

a well-kept diary: the periods of apathy, the minor grievances that crowd out great events, the desultory attention to detail, the silly prejudices, the gradual shift in character as Millicent [the fictional diarist] grows old. Strip out the words 'a novel' from the cover, and Forster could have fooled the world.

Yet, though Millicent never lived, this diary is an authentic record of how a century of English women were shaped – or, rather, distorted – by war. Anyone who cannot understand their mother or grandmother's generation can discover here what caused their emotional restraint, their passion for collecting short pieces of string, their chronic inability to cook, and above all their commitment to us, our families and our children's futures. This is fiction; yet this is true. (Falconer, 2003)

I can confirm that I remember my mother, of the same generation, collecting short pieces of string, etc. In a subsequent interview, Forster commented:

Ordinariness does fascinate me. It fascinates a lot of people. You're going on a train and you're passing all those dreary backyards, mile after mile, and you can't help looking at them and thinking, 'what lives, what's going on there?'[2]

Arguably this represents well the aim of many novelists to capture and recount the lived experiences of the 'ordinary people' they meet or pass in their own everyday lives.

Diaries

There is a long history of diaries being used in social research (Thomas and Znaniecki, 1958; Townsend, 1962; Robb, 1968). We all know what diaries are, and researchers are urged to keep diaries themselves, recording their activities and observations. Many people keep a diary to note appointments and other kinds of information, believing them to be essential for a well-ordered life. And there are people who write up their experiences and feelings every day. Whatever our inclinations, we can purchase a diary from any corner shop and use it as we choose. So, asking potential research participants to keep a diary is not difficult, and researchers have often solicited or commissioned diaries, typically as a source of insight into the details of everyday life (Plummer, 2001).

The Medication project was my first experience of commissioning and analysing diaries (Johnson and Bytheway, 2001). Diaries were also acquired for the RoAD project, and they are frequently solicited by the MO Archive: for example, a one-week diary in which contributors noted mentions of birthdays was added to the 2002 birthday directive. My main experience of the value of diaries for research, however, has been through the TOG project. Through this I have come to appreciate the value of supplementing interview and observational data with documentation that comes from the research subjects themselves.

In practice most diaries are deficient and researchers need to be alert to the implications of this. Some, for example, may include only occasional entries, with large gaps perhaps of several weeks remaining undocumented, and others may include entries that are undated or out of sequence. And it may be that the diarist has amended entries at a later date with insertions, deletions or 'corrections'. Some entries may be 'non-entries' such as 'too tired today to write anything in my diary'. Despite these possible failings, the ideal, with which both writer and reader are familiar, is that the diary should be a series of distinct, bounded entries written by the one person and covering a continuous period of time, each entry having a clearly marked beginning and end, and each being written on a particular indicated date. Where a diary falls short of this ideal, then writer and reader will work separately at developing ways of overcoming the shortcomings.

It is important to distinguish diary-writing from other forms of autobiography. Alaszewski (2006, p 2) identifies four defining characteristics:

- regularity: a sequence of regular and dated entries;
- personal: one identifiable individual who records it and controls access to it;
- contemporaneous: entries made at a time close enough for the record not to be distorted by problems of recall;
- a 'time-structured' record of 'events, activities, interactions, impressions and feelings' that the diarist considers relevant and important.

I would add to this that one aspect of 'regularity' is that ideally diaries should include entries for every day, thereby offering a *continuous* record of events. Regarding the third characteristic, despite Alaszewski's optimism, there can still be problems of recall with contemporaneous writing. What is more important, I would suggest, certainly for the study of ageing, is that as a form of contemporaneous writing each entry in a diary is written in ignorance of the entries that follow. In this way, diaries offer a continuing commentary on life as it unfolds.

This characteristic of diaries became vividly evident in a TOG diary which features a family's deliberations over a possible house move. Alan and Beat Shaw, both in their 80s, live in Essex, approximately 100 miles from their daughter, Josie, and her family, in Leicestershire. When Josie started her TOG diary at the beginning of October 2007, Alan and Beat are visiting and they have firm intentions to move to be nearer Josie. They want a bungalow because they both have difficulty with the stairs. On 3 October, Josie writes:

> Before they went we spoke at length about their plans to move to Leicestershire. I hope it is what they want. To Dad it seems to symbolise getting old & dependent on others. Mum just wants to be near us. Must get on with the search for bungalows for them.

Back in Essex, Alan and Beat's house is on the market. Someone views it on 7 October while, on the same day, Josie is 'trawling the local estate agents' in Leicestershire. She views two bungalows on 8 October and 12 October. Josie notes that Beat 'doesn't want to get rid of some furniture' and she is struggling to find a bungalow that is big enough. At the beginning of November, Josie is looking at more bungalows. Not many are suitable: 'Lots don't have separate dining room & living room & lots have steps going up to the house, which would defeat the whole point of the exercise' (3 November). Another is up a long drive and another is 'cut off': 'Mum likes to watch the world go by'. On the 10th, Alan and Beat have an offer on their house but it is 'too low'. That weekend, Josie views two more bungalows but both are 'terrible'; the same the following weekend; one needed 'a lot of redecoration' and another is next to a 'huge factory'. At the beginning of December they decide to leave 'bungalow hunting' until after Christmas.

On 19 December, Josie writes that she worries Alan will miss his friends at the golf club if he moves. On New Year's Eve, there is another phone call and talk about starting to look again. Josie views more bungalows on the weekend of 5 January. She finds one she likes but Beat disagrees since it would involve 'downsizing'. Josie writes:

> Still not convinced moving is the best thing for them when they are both well. Discussed putting in a stair lift as it is the stairs they struggle with. Both appalled at the suggestion! Anyone would think they are old.

She views three more on 11 January, all with slopes or steps. Meantime some people viewing Alan and Beat's house 'seemed to be implying the house was not sound'. Josie is anxious that Alan and Beat's presence might be putting prospective purchasers off.

Alan and Beat return to Leicestershire on the weekend of 19 January. Josie books three bungalows to be viewed. None are acceptable. They 'talked at length about moving. Not at all sure they really want to do it but at the end of the day it is their decision & I can only support whatever they decide.' Another is viewed on the Tuesday: it is unsuitable and it 'seems like we will never find anywhere'. At the same time, Josie notes how frustrated Beat gets that she cannot get up and down the stairs. At the end of January, things come to a head. These are Josie's entries for that long weekend:

> THURSDAY 31st
>
> [...] Really not sure what to do about Mum and Dad moving. Seems a huge upheaval for them when they have a settled routine they are happy with. I am sure they will make up their own mind in time. All I can do is to try & support them.
>
> FRIDAY 1st
>
> T/c from Mum asking me to find some more houses for them to look at.
>
> Grabbed ½ hr to arrange to book to see 3 bungalows over the weekend. They are having 2 sets of people looking at their house over the weekend so I think this has triggered them to look again. [...]
>
> SATURDAY 2nd
>
> [...] Agent phoned me after workshop to tell me Mum & Dad had a full price offer on their house.
>
> Rang Mum & Dad to let them know. They agreed to phone back. When they did they had decided that when faced with it they really did not want to move. Both well & Dad has his golf so why put themselves through it. So no more house hunting – agents not happy, Mum & Dad very happy!

SUNDAY 3rd

Mum & Dad rang. Sounded really relieved but worried they had upset me! Typical.

We would really like them closer but would all miss the connection with [Essex] if they did move. Maybe they will get a new kitchen now. Mum has wanted one for years but feels it is extravagant. There is something about their generation that sees spending money on extravagances (as they see it) as completely irresponsible. Suppose we could all learn something from them.

MONDAY 4th

Feeling less stressed that I no longer have to look for bungalows for Mum & Dad. I think they are equally relieved. [...]

The house in Essex is taken off the market and there is no more bungalow-hunting in Leicestershire. Subsequently in her diary Josie occasionally notes their refusal to discuss a stair lift and once again writes: 'At the end of the day it is their lives & all I can do is support them. I am sure I will be just as stubborn if not worse when I am their age' (2 March).

This story illustrates something of the complexity of families adjusting to changed circumstances. Given her parents' declining mobility, Josie recognised the sense of them moving to live in a bungalow and, if they were to move, it would be good for family life if they were to be nearer Josie and her family. Nevertheless she realises that Alan would miss the golf club and that Beat would find 'downsizing' difficult. She supported them by viewing many bungalows and discussing the pros and cons, while at the same time allowing them to reach their own decision. When Alan and Beat finally reach a decision after at least four months exploring the market, they are all relieved. Nevertheless a question mark still hangs over the possibility of adapting the house in Essex with a stair lift or some alternative. It is important to recognise that Josie might have found the 'ideal' bungalow and that Alan and Beat might have made the move, selling their home in Essex and embarking upon a new domestic adventure. Their story contrasts with that of another TOG family in which the senior in her 80s did move a similar distance, to live with her daughter and family having accepted that she could no longer manage a house on her own (Bytheway and Bornat, 2011).

Frances Partridge is a celebrated diarist, and in this book I use her diaries for various purposes. Here I want to consider what she wrote about the diary itself: why she kept it and what that involved.

Her life extended over the entire course of the 20th century (1900-2004) and she maintained a personal diary over most of her adult life. A series of diary-based memoirs were published between 1978 and 2001, followed by a detailed biography (Chisholm, 2009). The basic demographic dates are as follows: born Frances Marshall in 1900, she married Ralph Partridge in 1933 and became a mother to Burgo in 1935. Ralph died in 1960 and she became a grandmother to Sophie in 1963. She was bereaved again when Burgo died unexpectedly just four weeks after the birth of Sophie. Frances herself died in 2004. With the exception of the tragic loss of Burgo (and her own longevity), this is a fairly ordinary biography: many other women born at the beginning of the 20th century would have married in their 30s, become a mother, and then, later in life, been widowed and become a grandparent. In other ways, however, she was exceptional: in her 20s she was heavily embroiled in the social world know as 'Bloomsbury', she was a committed pacifist and a talented writer, and compared with many she led a privileged life untroubled by financial worries. Also she maintained an extensive network of friends up until the end of her long life.

Chisholm includes detailed information about Frances' diary-keeping practices. In addition to one kept for appointments, Frances kept a second from 1927 onwards, 'her diary proper, in which she wrote freely and at length about her thoughts and emotions as well as her doings' (Chisholm, 2009, p 44), in A4 notebooks (p 360). She was 'not inclined to use her diary as an instant outlet for bursts of emotion or anger' (p 159) and it was never 'a catalogue of her ailments and problems' (p 360). Rather she wrote with a 'delicate balance of humour, reflection and precise observation' (p 111). However, in 1944, Frances expressed doubts about the diary:

> Perhaps because so much that had gone into it was painful, Frances wondered, as the year turned, whether her diary was worth keeping at all. 'I don't believe I shall ever read this one through again ... As for the war, there can hardly be anyone in England who is less affected by it than I am, so I am the last person who ought to keep a war diary.' But the habit of diary-keeping, founded as it was on her determination not to let life drift by unobserved, and her need to shape and control her thoughts and her reactions, proved stronger than her misgivings. (Chisholm, 2009, p 191)

There were breaks in the diary. Around 1947, for example, she was too busy coping with Burgo's problems at school (p 219). Also, regarding Burgo's death, not one letter about it survives and she removed almost all traces of it from her diary, although 'among the few surviving fragments of diary from those weeks are some desperate lines' (p 277). Thus there is clear evidence here that diarists may choose not to enter descriptions of particularly demanding or distressing events.

It was in 1976 that Frances first began to consider publishing her diaries: 'Her diary-keeping was both a pleasure and a necessity for her, but she had never thought of publishing it, or of herself as a real writer' (p 316). Although, she was encouraged by friends, two years passed while she decided what to do.

> In the process though, she reread her old diaries, the incomplete, episodic ones from the late 1920s and early 1930s and then the ones from the war years, when she began to keep them regularly. She had never shown her diaries to anyone, not even to Ralph. Now, prompted not just by Janetta [A long-time friend who was 'like a daughter' to Frances, p 170] but by the increasing flow of Bloomsbury's private papers towards publication – including Virginia Woolf's diaries, which Olivier Bell was editing – she began to wonder what to do with them all. Was the diary even worth preserving after she was dead? She was already starting to cut and prune it herself, discarding material she thought boring or hurtful or too intimate. (Chisholm, 2009, p 317)

She also began to write about being a diarist:

> 'I've been pondering my diary and my wild ambivalence about it. Here have I been writing for thirty-six years, and I think in a sense it has seemed like my main occupation. Tragedy has struck, travel has whipped through, but there it has been as the thread on which my experiences and thoughts are strung. If I look as coolly as possible into my heart about it, one side of me must rate it quite high ... Yet there is another side which is horribly unconfident. These last days since it took shape and was in the hands of Robert, my chosen arbiter, I have been positively quivering with strange agitation, and I still find the extremes of depression and elation I have been through thoroughly disturbing.' (Chisholm, 2009, p 321)

> 'I do it [...] because though I can never invent or imagine anything, I have a passionate desire to describe what I've felt, thought and experienced, for its own sake – to express, communicate or both? And I can hardly now bear not to pin down the fleeting moments: it's an activity that has become central to my life.' (Chisholm, 2009, p 324)

Chisholm comments: 'Writing her diary was a way of validating her continuing existence; gradually, publishing it was to become a lifeline' (p 324) and, during the 1980s and 1990s, publishing became one of her primary occupations. Although she kept her diary going, by 1997 there were often long gaps between entries. She doubted the value of what she was writing and her handwriting, although still clear, was smaller and shakier (p 360). With the turn of the millennium, she reached her 100th birthday and her diary-keeping 'began to dwindle to almost nothing' (p 361).

So, for Frances Partridge, diary-keeping was a key activity in her life, not only in her everyday routines, but also in how she managed age and experienced growing older. I consider what there is to learn about age from her diaries in Chapters Five and Seven.

How old are you?

This simple question is easily understood but not necessarily easily answered (Chudacoff, 1989). In being taught to speak English, we learn that the way to ask about measurable quantities is to formulate a question using the template 'How much is it?' So we ask 'How tall are you?', 'How far is it?' and 'How many people are there?' Each such question links a dimension – age, height, distance, number of people – to a standard indicator that signifies opposites – old/young, tall/short, far/near, many/few – on an enumeration of standard units – years, inches, miles, people. Despite quantification being implicit, these questions can be answered non-numerically. How old am I? I'm getting on a bit. How short am I? Fairly short. How far is it? Oh, miles! How many people are there? Not that many. Also there is an anomaly in that one acceptable answer to the question is to be found in the question itself: How old am I? I'm old. So, despite a strange and potentially confusing logic, the question conforms to a wider pattern of everyday communication. 'How old are you?' makes sense to anyone who speaks English.

In contrast, the same question in Spanish is much more focused: *¿Cuántos años tienes?* Translated literally this reads: how many years have you? It directly measures age in units of chronological time and, seemingly, denies the acceptability of a less revealing alternative. The expected answer is a count of 'completed years' lived and so this is equivalent to the question asked by the ONS (described in Chapter One): 'What was your age last birthday?' Despite being unambiguous, this may still be answered in more than one way. Here is a moment in L.P. Hartley's story *Eustace and Hilda*:

> "[...] And Hilda's only – only how old?"
>
> "She's nearly fourteen," said Eustace, as Hilda did not speak.
>
> "Nearly fourteen, that's only thirteen [...]" (Hartley, 1979, p 179)

Note how Eustace assumes the question refers to chronological age, even though this is not directly implied, and note how there is no reference to the units being enumerated: the number is sufficient. Kathleen Woodward recounts a similarly telling experience:

> A few weeks ago I visited the Helen Bader Center, a residence for women with Alzheimer's Disease that is part of the Jewish Home for the Aged in Milwaukee. As I was being shown around the facility, a young-looking woman with long, straight black hair and a short skirt kept coming up to me and asking in a somewhat vociferous tone, "What's your number?" The first time I didn't understand the question, so she plunged ahead in the conversation without waiting for my reply. "Mine's fifty-one," she said, matter-of-factly but with punch. It was her number. It was her age. The next time she asked me, I knew how to answer. "Fifty-two". (Woodward, 1997, p 15)

The above are examples of how age is revealed through verbal exchanges. Two important studies of age disclosure are those of Nikander (2002) and Coupland et al (1991). Both are based on empirical research with samples that are age-constrained, but in different ways. The Coupland study is based on 40 videotaped interactions between pairs of women, one in her 70s or 80s, and the other in her 30s. Each pair had never met previously, and they were asked to 'get to know one another' through conversation (1991, p 57). Three categorising mechanisms related to age were identified: (1) the explicit disclosure of chronological age; (2) the use of a label ('old' or 'pensioner') or a reference to roles ('great-grandmother'); and (3) mentions of 'health, decrement or death'. Coupland et al contrasted these processes with those of temporal framing that locate the narrator in a particular position in relation to life or history. For example, one woman introduced herself with the following biographical detail:

> I retired in 1974. I'd been nursing for forty-six years ... came down to Cardiff in 1952 and I was at the CRI [hospital] until I retired ... my mother died when she was forty-five in 1933. (Coupland et al, 1991, p 63)

This is a good example of how information based on dates and intervals, can locate a speaker biographically within a particular time frame. Although she does not actually disclose her age or date of birth, it is not difficult to deduce that she would be about 80 when interviewed.

Coupland et al offer a series of examples of negative and positive processes of age disclosure. In the first of these, the older person complains that younger people (represented by a nephew) "don't want to know you", before commenting "I'm not very well these days too. I'm seventy last October ... so I find I can't *do* it so good" (pp 137-8). This comment, Coupland et al argue, is evidence of how age in years can be used to rationalise immobility. This contrasts with another example in which the older person differentiates herself from her age peers. First the younger woman describes being a mother to children at school, and then the older woman responds: "I lead quite a busy life although I'm eighty-six. I'm not young" (p 139). By implication, she is busier than most people aged 86, that is, 'not young'. These examples illustrate how, although the older participants were, in the main, more willing to reveal their chronological age than the women in their 30s, there had to be a rationale for the disclosure of chronological age. This typically leads to some kind of explication whereby circumstances are explained by age or, alternatively, used to deny or challenge age expectations. These participants had volunteered to take part in recorded conversations involving 'people of different ages' (p 57) and so it may be that they felt prompted to discuss age. It is important to recognise that some people prefer not to think about their age and that they would be unlikely to volunteer for such research: the MO Archive, for example, has accounts of how people ensure that their birthdays are not celebrated. They are concerned that people do not know their age; indeed they themselves find it difficult sometimes to remember precisely how old they are.

Coupland et al concluded that whereas chronological age is rarely disclosed by middle-aged people in everyday conversations, it 'resurfaces from its underground life' among older people (1991, pp 133-4). So it is interesting to consider how 22 Finnish men and women, all close to their 50th birthday, handled age when interviewed by Pirjo Nikander. She points out that:

> It is worth remembering that the interviewees were approached as members of a particular age group and that chronological, or clock age as such was built into the topic of discussion. So the 'speaking identity', or the category assigned to the participants from the outset was that of a 'person around fifty'. (2002, p 62)

Nikander (p 76), in discussing how age is disclosed in everyday conversation, used the following exchange taken from Harvey Sacks' seminal lectures:

> "How old are you, Mr. Bergstein?"

> "I'm 48. I look much younger. I look about 35, and I'm quite ambitious and quite idealistic and very inventive and conscientious and responsible." (Sacks, 1992, Vol 1, p 44)

Nikander was interested in how Mr Bergstein sought to pre-empt any negative assumptions about his age by describing his appearance and character. The fact is, however, that his immediate answer was simply a number (echoing Woodward's experience). We can presume that Mr Bergstein assumed that his response would be understood, particularly given the immediate follow-up regarding how he looks. In claiming that he looks about 35, he implies not only that he knows how men of a particular age look, but also that there is a standard against which appearance can be judged.

Nikander contrasts the response of Mr Bergstein with the following comment from Anssi, one of her interviewees: "I have said that I accept that I'm fifty years old" (p 143). Anssi was describing his cultural tastes and felt that these might not be thought appropriate for a man of 50. He did not seek to deny his age but, like Mr Bergstein, he was concerned to dissociate himself from any assumptions that might follow when his chronological age was revealed. He ends his commentary on his tastes and interests with: "one isn't necessarily into the kinds of things that a fifty-year-old petty bourgeois should be into but nonetheless one is fifty" (p 144). Nikander concludes from her analysis of this interview that mathematised descriptions of time and age provide speakers such as Anssi with the means to generalise the importance of age while, at the same time, playing down its personal significance for themselves (p 214).

In two publications, I have felt obliged to reveal my age. First, in *Ageism,* at the age of 51, I wrote:

> Some would argue that I am far too young to understand
> the power of ageism in the lives of people in their seventies
> and eighties and that the battle against ageism should be
> led by those of pensionable age. Perhaps I am, and perhaps
> I should have waited. (Bytheway, 1995, p 2)

In the RoAD report, 12 years later, I wrote a brief 'personal testimony'
in which I recounted three experiences of what I had perceived to
be age discrimination against me as an older person. The first arose
from being made to feel old and incompetent having missed a train
in a crowded station, and the second from feeling abandoned outside
the radiography department of my local hospital. The third was more
directly related to chronological age and did not arise from any possible
misinterpretation:

> While working on this report, The Open University decided
> to impose a retirement age on all its employees. RoAD
> became implicated when the project was mentioned in
> the January 2007 edition of *The Oldie*. As I wrote a reply,
> I realised that the week before I too had reached the age
> when I should expect to receive a letter from the university
> informing me that I was about to be retired. (Bytheway et
> al, 2007, p 90)

I return to this experience in Chapter Nine.

Any research intended to be limited to a certain age group needs the
ages of potential subjects to be revealed. Even though the researcher
may have prior access to official records such as those of a local health
centre, someone must acquire the information in some way. So, as a
researcher or clerk, how do you establish the age of someone you've not
met before? You can ask the simple question, of course, but do you get
an accurate reply? There are people who routinely claim to be older or
younger than they are. For example, in his diaries, the politician Chris
Mullin describes how, when attending the funeral of the MP Audrey
Wise, he discovered a 'little-known fact':

> She was 68, not 65, having shaved three years off her age in
> order to improve her chances of selection at Coventry and
> never adding them back on. (Mullin, 2010, p 127)

It is also a fact that your date of birth can have bureaucratic consequences
for your immediate circumstances or prospects. A difference of one
day can place you in different categories. There are many stories for
example of how schoolchildren can be disadvantaged by such rigid
age grading. Similarly, note Ken Blakemore's comment:

> I am a child of the welfare state – in a rather literal way. I was
> born on the very day that the sun rose upon a new National
> Health Service and other innovations in welfare. The day
> before, my mother cut a cartoon out of a newspaper. It
> depicted a worried looking father-to-be pointing a shotgun
> at a hovering stork (with baby), trying to keep it at bay
> until the fateful day (5 July 1948). (Blakemore, 1998, p xi)

It would be interesting to know more about the ramifications had Ken
been born on 4 July 1948 rather than on the following day, the 5th.
Dates of birth are also critical in the management of many sports and
sporting records. I notice that professional cricketers, for example, have
their ages updated not annually but daily. As I write this, the *Cricinfo*
website informs me, for example, that Ryan Sidebottom is aged '32
years and 293 days'.

Requesting sight of someone's birth certificate is the obvious way
for the researcher or clerk to minimise the risk of error or deception.
Universal birth certification only began in England in 1837, and
subsequently 'individuals were only gradually required to know their
own exact ages as society became bureaucratized' (Thane, 2000, p 19).
Regarding the registration of births in the UK in 2010, parents are
legally required to register births within 42 days of a child's birth. Given
this, it is clear that parents can still exercise a degree of discretion, and
it is undoubtedly still the case that a small number of children will
not be registered.

As a rule, we rarely have to produce our birth certificates, and as
a result we do not carry them around with us. Indeed, we may have
trouble finding them, but, if necessary, copies can be purchased from
the Registrar's Office. For a few people this is the moment when they
discover their 'true' age. A friend, for example, spent the first 41 years
of her life believing she was born in April, as recorded on her baptism
certificate. It was only when this was stolen and she had to obtain a
copy of her birth certificate that she discovered that she was born
two months earlier and that her birthday was in February, not April.
The explanation for the 'error' lay in a complicated story regarding
her parents' marital status and, for her, finding out the truth resolved
certain mysteries about her origin: 'It felt like the puzzle pieces had
clicked into place', she told me.

A more important consideration for researchers trying to establish
someone's age is that of deliberate deceit. There are many jokes about
people lying about their age, and much anecdotal evidence of people
living the lie. For example, I have another acquaintance who, following

marriage at the age of 35 to a man 12 years her junior, spent her entire married life claiming to be 10 years younger than she was. It was a shock when her real age was revealed when her husband died at the age of 70. The point is that when we are asked our age, there is some latitude in how we might answer it. Sanctions against deceit are not strong.

As researchers we do not wish to embark upon an interview only to discover, 10 minutes into it, that the interviewee is not 'old enough'. Be that as it may, what this discussion has revealed is how the question, when asked directly, raises a number of potential difficulties.

In this chapter I have reviewed how age has been and continues to be researched. Simply asking someone about 'their age' is not straightforward. So studying how we experience age and how age restricts our unfolding biographies is a major challenge. I have argued that diaries and similar accounts and records provide readily accessible longitudinal data, evidence that, potentially, will help us unmask age.

Questions for discussion

1   Are you persuaded that it is important to know something of the history of gerontological research in order to understand its role in developing government policy and clinical practice?

2   Think of someone whose diaries you have read or would like to read. In the light of what we know about Frances Partridge's diary-keeping, what do you imagine you might learn from her diaries about the experience of growing older?

3   You are researching some aspect of later life that interests you. You have just knocked on a door. All you know is that Mrs Smith lives there, someone you have never met before. She answers the door. What do you say?

4   You've spent 30 minutes talking with Mrs Smith. Unexpectedly, she turns and asks how old you are. What do you say? What would you feel?

THREE

Age and time

Clocks and calendars provide a scale against which temporal change can be plotted. However, Jan Baars (2007) warns that 'a large part of the gerontology community' is still under the 'spell' of predictions based upon chronological age (p 2). His concern is that gerontology should focus on the causes of ageing rather than the correlates of chronological age:

> While it is true that all causal relations are *also* temporal relations, or relations working 'in time', it would be wrong to identify causality with time or to reduce the process of aging to the causal effects of time. (Baars, 2007, p 4)

In his paper proposing a 'triple temporality' of ageing he begins by noting how:

> The identification of aged research populations [...] builds on chronological age and presupposes an organization of the life course in which chronological time has become an important instrumental perspective. Concepts such as age groups, age norms, or age grading presuppose chronological age as the typical instrument to regulate many transitions or entitlements. (pp 16-17)

He goes on to argue that:

> We are getting older with every tick of the clock, but this 'older' has a precise meaning only in a chronological, not gerontological sense. (p 17)

Nevertheless, he acknowledges the power of age norms and age regulations, and so his triple temporality brackets chronological age with personal experience and narrative articulation. He develops the case for a subjective time perspective:

> What we tend to think of as our *selves* has a lot to do with the ability to situate our lives in the interrelated temporal dimensions of past, present, and future. (pp 28-9)

Baar's third temporality, narrative articulation, is based upon Ricoeur's emplotment and the reconstruction of personal experiences as stories to be shared. Contrasting the grand narrative of the anti-ageing industry with that of care providers, he suggests that in both contexts narratives are not intended to be listened to; rather they are there to keep older people 'buying and busy' (p 36). Advocates of anti-ageing treatments would have you believe that by buying their products, you can 'turn back the clock', and the providers of care services aim to 'keep you independent for as long as possible'. In other words, these industries, in their different ways, have developed stories for older people to live their lives by (McAdams, 1993; Randall, 1995).

Timescapes

The word 'timescapes' was devised by Barbara Adam when she matched her ideas about time with images of landscape, cityscape and seascape (Adam, 1998, p 11). 'Scape' itself barely exists as a word or concept and yet, in its semantic associations, it invokes a sense of space, scale, distance and perspective. Typically scapes are expansive: broad and complex rather than narrow and focused. Most examples are spatial and visual: the eye travels from one extreme to another and from the near to the far. Indeed, as the eye scans the horizon, the viewer can take in a 360 degree panorama, one that has no edges. Nor need a scape be tied to one particular location: it might be a moving or changing image, one that takes time to take in.

We are perhaps most familiar with 'landscapes': we use the word in everyday conversation when describing visits to the art gallery or walks in the country. A landscape is a view; an image of land stretching to the horizon. One landscape includes rugged mountains and steep valleys; another rolling hills, trees and rivers. A landscape might be the backdrop against which action unfolds: the farmer and his tractor, or a family with a picnic. Art students are taught how to paint landscapes or how to 'capture' them in photographs, and gardeners are trained to 'landscape' a park or an urban space. Land is in itself a complex phenomenon, the alternative to sea, an unbounded canvas conveying ideas of soil, rock, earth and territory, upon which other phenomena – mountains, valleys, cities – can be located and mapped.

Both Neale (2008) and Adam (2008) imply that timescape is a metaphorical concept: it is to time what landscape is to land. So it follows that a timescape is a broad perspective on the complex temporalities of the world around us. The acts of viewing and scanning are replaced by those of recalling, experiencing and imagining. A timescape is, by definition, a view of time.

Adam (2008) identifies seven 'irreducible elements' of a timescape: time frame, temporality, timing, tempo, duration, sequence and temporal modalities. She illustrates each of these with a series of terms and words. For example, the first, time frame, is followed by: 'bounded, beginning and end of day, year, life time, generation, historical/geological epoch' (p 7). In elaborating upon this, Adam anticipates the time frames of the research that the *Timescapes* study might undertake. So she contrasts the stable, fixed, externally located and socially constructed frame of calendars and clock time with the relative, mobile and personal frames of life time, family time and illness. Within the latter frames, 'their implied past and future expands and contracts as people move along their life course' (p 8).

This approach to constructing a timescape is inevitably wide-ranging and fluid. In applying it to the concept of age we can be a little more focused. Perhaps the most important point to make is that age is essentially monotonic in the sense that we grow older not younger. This claim is of course challenged by acts or processes of 'rejuvenation', but what does the idea of rejuvenation imply? The 're-' prefix is extremely relevant to the study of ageing. After all, older people are popularly associated with remembering and reminiscing, and I discuss the implications of return at the end of this chapter. The prefix implies a sequence of equivalent experiences. Birthdays are a fine example: 'many happy returns!'

Rejuvenation is widely defined as the *reversal* of ageing, and in biology it is associated with the repair of age-related damage or with replacement with new tissue. Replacement implies the introduction of new parts and, as such, it implies that the 'patient' can be thought of as an aggregate of parts, parts obtained from different sources and of different ages. This interpretation of the consequences of biological intervention may indeed be justified if there is evidence of a significantly increased life expectancy. With a new heart, for example, a person who had been close to death might expect a return to a normal expectancy for a person of his or her age. This is perhaps a special case. For most people, their sense of self, including all their primary body parts, originate in just one event, their birth, and at present there is no prospect of this changing. For most of us, rejuvenation is a word that we might use positively but metaphorically in describing a reviving experience.

What gerontologists like Baars argue is the need to free the conceptualisation of age from chronological time: there are complex processes of change involving the organs of the body, the sense of self, interpersonal relations and the individual's position within various social worlds. We can only gain a better understanding of these processes if age is no longer defined chronologically. But if we do that, does age become nothing more than a synonym for personal change? My answer to this would be negative: we can change in all kinds of ways and in diametrically opposite directions, but we age only as a result of becoming older. Through rejuvenation we may feel younger, but we have not literally become younger.

Another way in which a linear, chronological model of age can be challenged is through the concept of circular time. We often live life in a routine, *every*day way, and the seasons are often used to portray the life course. However, insofar as personal biographies appear to be circular, the wheel returns to its starting point only as a result of having moved forward, returning to a place that we had occupied some time in the past.

The concept of timescape is fundamental to the theorisation of age in a number of ways. First, and most obviously, numerical indicators of the passage of chronological time facilitate the process of measuring and recording temporal change, and this invites all sorts of arithmetic deductions in assessing prospects and in characterising personal relations. Hartley (1970, p 189) once again provides a comic example:

> "If we each had a thousand pounds a year, how many years would sixty-eight thousand last?"
>
> "Divide by a thousand," said Hilda.
>
> "How do I do that?"
>
> "You ought to know. Cut off three noughts."
>
> Eustace took his spade and unwillingly put a line through each of the last three figures, leaving the number 68 looking small, naked, and unimpressive.
>
> "Sixty-eight years," he said doubtfully. "How old would you be then, Hilda?"
>
> "Add fourteen."
>
> Eustace put 14 under 68 and drew a line.
>
> "That makes eighty-two. And how old should I be?"
>
> "Subtract four from eighty-two. You're nearly four years younger than me."

"What a lot of figures I'm making," said Eustace, his lips following the motions of his spade. "That comes to seventy-eight. You would be eighty-two and I should be seventy-eight, or seventy-eight and a half. After that we shouldn't have any more money, should we?"

"We might be dead by then," said Hilda.

Second, timescape is fundamental because of our contrasting view of the past, the present and the future. We can look back and reminisce about past events and shared experiences, and argue about the truths of what happened and regret our individual failures of memory. And as we look back, the view of the past extends before us, some experiences being close and others more distant. As we view the past in all its detail, we are aware that there is a future 'behind us', and if we turn to look to the future we may remember the futures that in the past we had thought about and perhaps planned. We can ponder over questions concerning the realities of the past, the present and the future and how our view of each changes with time.

It is not difficult, in thinking about such timescapes, to recognise parallels with how we see shifting landscapes. Walking around a hill and setting it in a landscape typically entails matching the features of the hill against those laid out on a printed map or an earlier photograph: the hill remains the same hill. Setting the same walk in a timescape, however, involves mapping what one sees against what one has seen previously and what one imagines one might see some time in the future. With time it becomes evident that the hill at the level of rocks and organisms is constantly changing and so the issue of whether it remains the 'same' hill becomes problematic. When the hill is replaced by a social phenomenon such as 'the family', setting them in a timescape is particularly challenging since it implies an ongoing interaction between actors, agencies and changing social environments. Events and circumstances are experienced against a shifting backdrop, rather than a static one.

Everyday life

So the concept of timescape is helpful in understanding how we view and interpret age, not just in the grand perspective but also at the more mundane level of day-to-day living:

In everyday life, we do not usually move and act in the awareness that we are twentieth-century human beings.

The temporal horizon in which we are active is much more modest: the next hour, the morning, the working day, the weekend. Most things we deal with occur with the framework of everyday time. (Alheit, 1995, p 306)

Alheit contrasts this narrow and cyclical experience of time with life time, a linear perspective that:

activates a more distant horizon and stands for the 'sequentialization' of separate actions and experiences, for subjective 'continuity' and 'coherence'. (p 307)

His research relates to young people and their experience of vocational training, and his focus is on biography and career rather than age: he talks of how young people 'consider themselves to be at the mercy of a particular life career' (p 312). In similar ways, orientations to the future and the past in later life can consolidate stereotyping assumptions about older people: with time, the question 'What do you do?', for example, is replaced by 'What did you do?' Similarly, reminiscence and reunions become more common activities or, to be more precise, activities assumed to be more common as we grow older. Towards the end of life, we may reflect upon the details of our particular life career.

In more general discussions of how life is experienced, the word 'everyday' is often used to refer to inconsequential or mundane details, contrasted with rather more transformative events or with structural circumstances that are comparatively fixed. The importance of 'the everyday' in the rather different sense of 'day after day' became clear to us when Philomena Essed's description of everyday racism (Essed, 1988) helped inform our study of age discrimination (Bytheway et al, 2007). It was not that the experiences that had gained our interest were 'relatively minor' but rather that they were experienced repeatedly, seemingly day after day. It was by documenting such repeated recurrence that we sought to demonstrate that far from being trivial and inconsequential, they constituted a major element in the ways in which older people are discriminated against and excluded from wider society. One RoAD diarist (Daphne Smith), for example, wrote the following three entries in her seven-day diary:

Mon pm: Local walk with spouse on canal path; encountered 3 cyclists who showed no consideration – e.g. no bell or voice in spite of my white stick. Riding at great speed.

Thurs [visiting her sister]: After lunch husband, sister + self walked on the coastal path. We jumped a number of times, as cyclists whizzed by; me because I can't see properly, my husband because he is deaf, my sister because she is 73 and of a nervous disposition. I ask myself have bicycle bells been abolished. (Same thing on canal path near our home.)

Fri: Walked with husband on canal path near home (we try to walk every day) really enjoyed the walk except for usual cyclists riding too fast – no warning bells.

Note Daphne's plaintive claim: 'we try to walk every day'. When we are faced with such evidence of how certain threatening experiences recur day after day, the term 'everyday' takes on a rather different significance.

'The Last Refuge' Revisited project (Johnson et al, 2010) returned to Townsend's celebrated study (Townsend, 1962). A total of 20 homes that were still functioning as care homes 50 years later, were revisited in 2005-06. Like Townsend, seven-day diaries were solicited from residents, and in these diaries each day was divided into 19 boxes starting with one for the midnight to 6am period. Marie White was a resident who agreed to keep one but she did not complete it. She included brief entries for the first day (Monday), including 'Sleep I hope' in the *Midnight to 6am* box, and 'Sleep?' in the final two boxes (*10pm–11pm* and *11pm–midnight*). The other entries for that day similarly appear to detail hopes rather than actual experiences; for example, in the *6pm–7pm* box she noted: 'watch television if anything worth watching'. On the following day, there is 'same as Monday' (along with just one further entry: 'service' in the *10am–11am* box). On Friday, she wrote:

The pattern of my life is much the same. I'm not able to get about except in my room and have to go in a wheelchair downstairs etc. But I'm happy and thankful for all that is done for me and no complaints. I occupy myself with reading & tapestry, writing letters. I'm afraid I haven't been much help.

Thus she thought of each day as following a standard pattern, one that was largely confined to her own room and her chosen occupations. She appears to have decided that she only needed to record the details of one typical day, and this was what she entered on the first two pages. She appreciated the support she was being given and was apologetic for being unable to produce a more eventful diary.

The Medication project produced similar examples, some participants thinking that noting all the events of each and every day over a 14-day period was an unnecessarily tedious chore. Here is an extract from one fieldwork report:

Mrs Owen had some difficulty filling in the diary. She did not fill in days 2, 3, 4, or 5 because she said that everything was the same as the first 24 hours that we filled in together so she could not see the point. I helped her fill in day 6, explaining everything again, and encouraged her to do her best with the rest of the diary, which she did.

These examples suggest that many older people have routines in their daily life with which they are happy in that, potentially, they sustain a strong sense of continuity. These routines are ideals in that the diaries we have collected indicate that they can easily be upset or threatened. But they generate expectations about what happens every day and when. For some, life unfolds predictably as the hands of the clock rotate.

The complex way in which linear and circular patterns of time jointly affect everyday life is well illustrated by the medication diary of Jane Neal. She had poor eyesight and had to use a magnifying glass to read the labels on the medicine containers. She kept the pain relief tablets she was using, along with her anti-hypertensive medicine, in a cabinet drawer in her living room. She took these out of the drawer every evening and put them on top of the cabinet so that she wouldn't forget to take them the following morning after breakfast. The not-yet-started stocks were kept in a cupboard in the same cabinet. She used a prescribed gel to counter inflammation and swelling and kept this beside her bath. She kept eye drops on the bedside table and also in her handbag as she needed them frequently during the day. Her supplies of eye drops and gel were kept in the cupboard of her bedside table. Her diary indicated that she went out most days to shop or meet friends.

Figure 3.1 presents her consumption of these medicines (according to her diary). She was instructed to take her anti-hypertensive medicine once daily and initially this was A. On Day 9 this was changed to D, a different anti-hypertensive. B represents her eye drops (one drop to be used as necessary) and C her pain relief tablet (two to be taken up to four times a day).

Figure 3.1 reveals that at the beginning of the fortnight Jane applied drops to her eyes when washing at 8 o'clock in the morning, took her anti-hypertensive medicine routinely with her breakfast, and took tablets for pain relief at 9 o'clock in the evening. In the early hours of Day 5, however, she noted in her diary 'pain in neck and head' and she sought relief after her breakfast. This pain woke her again at 4am on Day 9. She went to see her doctor after breakfast that day. He decided to change her medicine and gave her a new prescription (D) for her blood pressure problem. She took her first tablet that evening and repeated this at roughly the same time over the following days. She had noted on Day 1 that she always had Shredded Wheat, tea and biscuits in the evening, and this had coincided during the first week with her routinely taking a tablet to control her pain. In the second week, however, this pattern was unsettled. Also she began to alleviate the pain during the day and twice she took a tablet at night. Despite this upset, her basic routines were unchanged and on Day 12, despite having taken a painkiller at 3am, she went into town at midday to shop and have lunch. In our report, we used Jane Neal's diary to demonstrate how a change in prescribed medication can unsettle other daily routines (Bytheway et al, 2000, pp 99, 104). But her diary also shows how everyday life can be dominated by certain routines.

Figure 3.1: Medication as recorded in Jane Neal's diary

Hour	Day													
	1	2	3	4	5	6	7	8	9	10	11	12	13	14
1														
2														
3												C		
4									C					
5														
6														
7														
8		B	B	B	B	B	B	B	B	B	B	B	B	B
9	A	A	A	A	A	A	A	A	A			C	C	
10					C					C		C	C	
11														C
12														
13														
14														
15														
16														
17														
18														
19														
20											C			
21	C	C	C	C	C	C				D	D		D	
22							C	C	C	C	D	D	C	D
23														C
24														

A change in one routine can have knock-on effects for other habits and familiar arrangements.

Biography and history

Chapter Two included Ken Blakemore's description of how the day he was born was the first day of the new National Health Service. A link between birth and a historical event also figures in the opening of Salman Rushdie's classic novel, *Midnight's Children*. Saleem Sinai is the protagonist:

> I was born in the city of Bombay ... once upon a time. No, that won't do, there's no getting away from the date: I was born in Doctor Narlikar's Nursing Home on August 15th 1947. And the time? The time matters, too. Well then: at night. No, it's important to be more ... On the stroke of midnight, as a matter of fact. Clock-hands joined palms in respectful greeting as I came. Oh, spell it out, spell it out: at the precise instant of India's arrival at independence, I tumbled forth into the world. (Rushdie, 1981, p 9)

Both authors were making a precise temporal link between birth and a much broader historical event, a link that in retrospect became personally important. Even though the two events were, by implication, purely coincidental, there is a symbolic significance. Both accounts include a date of birth – to the day (although Rushdie entertainingly leaves the reader uncertain as to whether Saleem was born at the very beginning or the very end of 15 August 1947) and they are keen to allude to symbols of the daily cycle: the sun rising, the hands of the clock joining together at midnight.

Do we change as we age and as historical events come and go? Barbara Adam has argued that we are resistant to the idea that we change in the sense of becoming different people with time:

> Despite the fact that nothing in our body, our physical appearance or our knowledge has remained unchanged, we think of ourselves as the same person now as the one that was born many years ago. (Adam, 1995, p 18)

I became interested in sequences of events, largely as a result of learning about stochastic processes as an undergraduate studying statistics. Through these processes it is possible to predict outcomes given various assumptions about age-specific fertility, marriage and mortality rates; the predicted outcomes can then be compared with the empirical reality. But in thinking about how people experience growing older, I realised that it is not possible to extricate family life from the wider historical context. Relying solely on current demographic rates reduces an analysis to the level of a board game. I wanted to know how age might be interpreted in the context of real, lived histories. This was the basic idea behind the research I undertook for my doctorate in the early 1970s.

My thesis began by focusing on 'the family life cycle' and I discussed how it had been formulated by researchers promoting a 'developmental approach' to sociological studies of the family (Rowe, 1966). I noted how this approach invariably generated a series of stages, typically defined by various key events. Rowe, for example, identified five stages. Many of these models referred to the average ages when key events occurred, and it was Uhlenberg (1969) who argued that this produced a sequence of stages that potentially only few families might experience in its entirety. In my thesis I quoted the description of the 'normal and universal familial process' that Rosser and Harris (1965, p 164) defined in terms of domestic groups, marriage, birth and death: 'Here', they claimed, 'in this endless process are the essential dynamics of family life'. I commented:

> Whilst the process is indeed endless given the ideal model wherein all children marry and all marriages produce children, the human situation falls a little short of this ideal. (Bytheway, 1973, pp 3-4)

As examples of the latter, I listed 'the prematurely deceased, the childless couple, the one-parent family, the unmarried parent, the middle-aged never-married (homosexual and heterosexual), the divorced, the young widowed, the stepchild, the orphan, the married couple of very different ages and the old parent of the new-born infant' (p 4). I emphasised that these were all examples of 'the consequences of *normal* patterns of family development'. In effect I sought to challenge the sociological presumption that an ideal model might be perceived to be 'normal'. I preferred a probabilistic alternative that incorporated empirical evidence of the statistical uncertainty associated with the formation of domestic groups, arising from variations in the chances of fertility and mortality and historical circumstance. Without appreciating the fact, I was attempting an interpretivist analysis of the data I collected: to understand how the histories of family events might have been interpreted by those involved. For example, drawing on Hughes (1971), I argued that a person's moving perspective on his whole life 'affects his interpretation of his past career, his present position, and the formulation of his future actions and expectations' (Bytheway, 1973, p 80).

For the TOG project, Joanna Bornat undertook life history interviews with 12 seniors: people aged 75 or over. These provided detailed examples of how biographies can be represented as linear sequences of events. Here, for example, are some extracts from an interview Joanna undertook in 2007 with Angela Rammell, born in 1928. She began by asking Mrs Rammell to "just talk a bit about your circumstances today [...] how things are for you":

> "Well I've been a widow for just 17 years. I'd been married for 41 years and my husband died. I have a daughter who is mentally handicapped and lives in the community. I had a son who died and I have two daughters who live in London and I spend a lot of time with either one daughter or the other. And I've been in this house for 47 years and I lived in the village before that."

This is a straightforward account of her current situation regarding marital status, housing and parenting, one which is heavily referenced to the past and in which time intervals are measured chronologically in numbers of years. Joanna remained focused on Mrs Rammell's current situation, before asking her about her parents. Here she replied:

> "my mother had previously, she'd lost her first husband when my brother was a baby. He was 8 years older than I am. And then she remarried and then I was born obviously. She'd be about 38 I think then. My father was in his forties. And my father came out of work when I was six, which everybody did in Wigan really. And he didn't work again until 1939 and jobs became available."

Again this provides a number of time intervals, linking age with historical events. The interview then focused on her parents' families, moving on to the world she grew up in. The sequence of where she had lived was obtained through questions such as "So you said you lived in one place and then you moved to somewhere else. Was that a big move or?" And an account of her father's search for work led to her remarking "And then my mother took ill." At this point, Joanna asked when that was, and Mrs Rammell replied:

> "1940. We realised afterwards she was ill at the end of the war – '45 – well before the end of the war because she was operated, had her operation in '45 and she died in '46. I

was 18. And she was ill for a long time. And we had to pay the doctors and the visits."

This illustrates how one development, illness, can overshadow another, the search for work, and how the family was 'unlucky' in that the doctors' visits had to be paid for; this just two or three years before the introduction of the NHS and the provision of free healthcare. Another complex sequence of events started to unfold with her father's failing health:

"I had to work because we needed to live because my father finished work during the war. He started to ail. So my brother got demobbed. We had to bring him back on compassionate leave when she was in hospital. And we needed, like, his wage. I mean you can imagine what I was earning at 17 and 18, not a lot. And, you know, we sort of lived. There was never any money."

At this point Joanna took the interview back through these wartime experiences, focusing more now on Angela's own experience: night school, getting a job, and then her mother's funeral. Eventually Joanna asked the question that led to the next stage in Angela's life: "So at some point along the way I suppose you must have met your husband?" This led to a new sequence of age-related events:

"He'd been demobbed. And we just drifted into it really."

"I suppose he'd be a bit older than you, would he?"

"Yes, five years older."

"And what kind of work was he looking for when he was demobbed?"

"Well he went working, he went ... He'd applied to go to college whilst he was waiting to be demobbed. He was late being demobbed. [...] And then he got a job with another building firm [...]"

"So did he eventually go to college?"

"Yes."

"When was that?"

"A fortnight after we got married."

"And were you courting for long?"

"I started going out with him when I was 19 and I got married when I was 21. We got married a) because he'd got word to go to college, whether he thought I wouldn't wait I don't know. And my father had died in the meantime. So that, you see, ... I couldn't have got married while my father was alive. Well, you were brought up to think you were supposed to look after them. My brother had got married. So they lived at home with us."

"So, there was, after your father had died, then you were living with your brother and his?"

"His wife, yes."

The interview moved on to Mrs Rammell's early married life: her husband being trained, her first child being diagnosed as mentally handicapped, and the fact that they had lived in a caravan for nine years. Further information followed regarding her other children, the death of her son and the births of grandchildren. Thus, in a complicated way, the interview generated a detailed chronology of the key events in a long and difficult life. These basic facts create a backdrop for a more nuanced analysis of the interplay between Angela's life and family and wider social and political histories. In particular, it illustrates well the importance of the war in determining how a particular generation entered adulthood: there are many similarities between her experience and that of some of the steelworkers I interviewed in 1983.

This example also illustrates how, in addition to providing details of dates, interviewees can describe a sequence of events. Overall, a detailed linear biography can be abstracted, which can then be plotted against age. The interview itself is structured around a series of familiar life course stages, each progression achieved through a prompting question, but generating a unique series of biographical events.

The seasons

The impact of the weather on everyday life has been neglected by social scientists, including gerontologists. Matthewman (2000) has called for a sociology of the weather, there has been some historical research on the subject (Golinski, 2000), and some psychologists have investigated its significance for mood and behaviour (for example Cunningham, 1979). Similarly, epidemiologists have long recognised the correlations between climate, health, risk and age, but there has been comparatively little research into how the weather affects the ways in which people organise themselves and regulate their lives.

I became particularly interested in the weather in 2006, when investigating the consequences of Hurricane Katrina for older residents of New Orleans and the scandalous loss of life that they suffered (Bytheway, 2007a). Since then there has been some discussion in the UK about responses to similar environmental disasters but this has tended to overlook the more general impact of bad weather on everyday life.

The one issue that has been the subject of extensive research in the UK is that of seasonal variations in morbidity and mortality. Statistics show a persistently high rate of winter deaths in the UK (ONS, 2009) and this has led to a number of policy initiatives, such as winter fuel payments for older people and the flu vaccination programme.

The standard indicator of excess winter deaths, the EWM Index, compares the number of deaths in the four winter months (December to March) with the number that would be expected given mortality rates in the rest of the year. Research published in 2010 shows that of 14 European countries, the UK has the fourth highest rate (Healy, 2003). Healy suggests that the explanation for the high rate in the UK may lie in poor housing and, in particular, in low thermal standards.

Regarding variations by sex and age, Table 3.1 is based on statistics for the winter of 2007–08 (ONS, 2009). It was a mild winter and there was proportionately less mortality among people under 65 than in the non-winter months, indicating that, for middle-aged people, winter was a comparatively safe time. In contrast there were more than twice as many deaths in the winter months among those aged 85 or over. Regarding cause, Table 3.1 shows that deaths due to respiratory diseases are most likely to occur in winter months. Young people (aged under 65) and those aged 85 or over who have respiratory diseases are more vulnerable to the seasonal effect when compared with people aged 65 to 84. Deaths due to circulatory diseases, another major category, are less seasonal, but there is evidence of a strong association with age for men. Epidemiologists have considered a number of possible causes for the excess winter mortality of those in the oldest age category: geographical location, poverty and socioeconomic factors, living alone, home heating and insulation, current health and ongoing illnesses, past health, smoking and alcohol. The MRC trial of the assessment and management of the needs of older people in Britain is perhaps the most authoritative study to date (Fletcher et al, 2002), drawing on a large UK-wide population-based cohort study of people aged 75 years or over. Analysis of the data placed a question over some of the assumptions about the causes

---

of vulnerability. In particular, the researchers concluded that the lack of a socioeconomic gradient had implications for public health policies. In their view, fuel poverty relief alone may be only partially successful in reducing excess mortality (Wilkinson et al, 2004).

Table 3.1: The EWM Index, 2007–08, England and Wales

Sex: Age	Cause of death		
	All causes	**Circulatory diseases**	**Respiratory diseases**
Males:			
0-64	8.7	11.9	41.6
65-74	11.2	13.6	29.2
75-84	13.4	15.1	34.1
85+	21.5	20.6	42.1
Females:			
0-64	8.2	15.3	52.0
65-74	11.4	14.3	44.3
75-84	16.5	17.1	39.5
85+	21.8	17.9	49.2

How then might further research help to explain why EWM among older people is so high in the UK, and to suggest how it might be reduced? We have argued that the diaries collected for the TOG project cast light on questions concerning risk (Bytheway and Bornat, 2010). Our guidance to the 12 TOG recorders (see Chapter One) was that they should think of their diary as an *ordinary* personal diary, in which they kept a record of their contact with the senior and the senior's contact with other family members. In particular, we said, we were interested in events that could be dated (for example anniversaries, visits), life transitions (moving house, illnesses) and the ebb and flow of everyday life. The recorders were supplied with one-month diaries and asked to send them to the project office at the end of each month. Of the 12 diarists, there were nine who provided day-to-day accounts of the lives of their seniors over the course of the 2007–08 winter. Four of these nine seniors were in a state of life transition (illness, house moves), three were fit and active and had frequent family contact, and two were oriented primarily to their own housekeeping routines. The seniors in this third category are Marion Arthur and Alice Watson. Although Marion Arthur and her husband, Adam, are wealthier than Alice Watson, enjoying a more comfortable lifestyle, both households are in hilly villages in the north of England, and their daily lives are centred on house cleaning, shopping and gardening. Of the 12 diaries theirs are the only two that regularly feature the weather.

Both the Arthurs celebrated their 87th birthdays in 2007. Adam was a professional engineer before setting up his own business. Marion trained as a teacher. They have two daughters, whom they see once or twice a year. Marion has poor mobility and, as a result, they rely heavily on their car. The Arthurs are fond of their large garden and Adam keeps records of the weather and visiting birds. There are entries in his diary for every day of the 2007–08 winter and the weather is mentioned in 97 out of the 122 entries. Here are just a few examples. First, an extract from his entry for 21 January:

> As it was pouring with rain, we decided to stay in. There were quite a few birds again. Obviously food being more important than being dry. [...] When the rain eased to a drizzle, I took a letter up the road to the post. The rain restarted when I got in [...] Marion reading most of the day. We changed the bed linen & she put it through the wash.

On many days, the entry begins with Adam describing how they drive into town early, in order to secure a parking place near the market. On days when it is raining, however, as here, they stay in. Note how Adam takes advantage of a break in the rain to post a letter, and how, given the poor weather, he and Marion decide to undertake some indoor domestic chores. Marion normally rests in the afternoon and reads. The following day, he wrote:

> Weather improving – but we had 19mm of rain yesterday, and this puts us over 150mm for the month, making it the wettest January in the last 15 years, and one of the wettest of any month in this period. Made a quick trip into town while Marion did her monthly check of her personal alarm. I spent quite a time on paperwork while she got on with her book. Glad to be warm & comfortable. We had a pleasant lunch out.

It is interesting to note that despite being glad to be warm and comfortable, they still go out for a pub lunch. They do this regularly, sometimes with friends and neighbours. Marion has a personal alarm because if she falls she is unable to get up, even with Adam's assistance: the alarm alerts the neighbours who come and help. Two months previously (according to Adam's diary) they had used the alarm when Marion fell, the day after being discharged from hospital.

On 31 January, Adam wrote:

> We were threatened with bad weather for Friday & Saturday so did some precautionary shopping today. It was very cold. I went for the blood test missed yesterday. [...] In the afternoon it started to sleet which later turned to snow. We soon had a white covering over the garden, though not really thick. We stayed firmly indoors.

Again this illustrates well how their outdoor movements are constrained not just by the weather but also by forecasts. They feel threatened when bad weather is predicted and, as a result, they prepare in advance. On this occasion, they discovered the following day that the forecast was accurate but, despite having done some precautionary shopping, they still felt they needed to drive into town early to catch the market:

> We woke to find a fierce wind blowing. We went as soon as possible to the market, as worse weather is expected. There were very few stall holders, because of problems with the awnings in the wind. We managed to get fruit and vegetables and Rebecca the fish lady was there. We then thankfully returned home to put up the proverbial shutters. The day passed with domestic chores and reading. We watched rain turn to sleet and then snow, which ceased by evening.

Phrases such as 'glad to be warm and comfortable', 'stayed firmly indoors' and 'thankfully returned home to put up the proverbial shutters', are evidence of how they feel safe and secure in their home.

Alice Watson was 83 in 2007. She is widowed and lives alone in a cottage in a hilly village. She has two sons and a daughter, all three live in villages close by. Alice has had a number of part-time jobs working in the health service or care homes but, over the years, she has been primarily occupied in caring for sick and disabled members of her own family. In particular, her husband, an engineer, suffered a serious stroke at the age of 40 and died 12 years ago.

One of her sons, Brian, kept the diary and this includes references to the weather in 82 of the 122 entries for the winter of 2007–08. He writes in a rather more cryptic style than Adam Arthur and, as far as possible, describes the day in his mother's own words. Here are entries for two consecutive days in December:

> Mother reports that it is still very windy. She visited ducks to 'recycle' scraps of bread and pastry [... and the] bakery for loaf and two fruit teacakes to toast. She reports that she

is stocked up in case weather turns bad! Her own welfare and ability to cope with weather continue to preoccupy her thoughts and activities.

Mother reports another duck feeding day 'as I have a big bag of scrap bread and pastry [...] it only needs one frosty night and I am housebound, as my front path never thaws out once frozen over.'

A small river flows through Alice's village and she regularly feeds the ducks. For her, walks in the village to the ducks, the library and the local shop, are part of keeping active and healthy. As evidence of this, Brian sent us a photograph of her feeding the ducks on a nice day in the middle of January. In this, she holds a shopping bag and carries a walking stick.

As with the Arthurs, Alice anticipates bad weather and stocks up 'just in case'. Brian's comment on her preoccupations is evidence of how families talk about the challenges of the weather and how the welfare of older people is a continuing concern. The second entry above confirms her concern to minimise the risk of falling on her front path and that she is aware that, as a result of this, she may become housebound.

At the beginning of January, the weather deteriorated. Alice reports to Brian that:

As snow is forecast for tomorrow I shopped for essentials. I do have adequate food in the fridge and freezer to see me through two weeks.

And the following day:

Bin bag today, I must be up and get it out for 7.30am. The collection wagon is coming to us first now. The snow has come along with a biting wind. I am glad I went out yesterday to get essentials I need. [...] It was late afternoon when Mary, my granddaughter, arrived, the snow has become a soggy dirty mush but she says the roads are quite clear.

Here again is evidence of anticipatory shopping. Note the word 'essentials' and how she knows what she needs for a 'siege' lasting two weeks. Mary's visit is further evidence of how her family maintain contact with her. Later in the month:

The rain is still pouring down. I took a leisurely toilet this a.m. concentrating on oiling the dry skin of my legs and arms. I think it is wearing the woollen tights and jumpers which causes this dry flaking skin. Also I have to minimise my fat intake. But I can think of a worse condition. As I have a hair appointment I prayed that the deluge would stop and it did – just a damp drizzle.

[Rachel], my granddaughter, phoned me in a panic. She had been told [my village] had been cut off to motorists and she [...] did not know if she could get home so I put on my waterproofs and walked down to the main street, and yes there had been a flooding just outside the village where 70 staff had to be rescued from a flooded factory.

This diary entry provides evidence first of how winter clothing can be thought to exacerbate the effects of the weather; second, that hair is so important for Alice that she 'prays' for a break in the deluge; and third, that members of the oldest generation are able to provide support for the youngest faced with wintry conditions. Despite the weather, Alice ventured out in order to supply Rachel with essential travel information.

Finally, at the end of January 2008, the 'real winter weather' arrived. A series of entries read:

And now another month into the New Year gone by. We are now about to experience real winter weather. Gale force winds have blown my garden tubs over. And now there is sleet/rain pouring down.

I shall not venture out. I would probably topple over in the wind. My friend, Margaret, has just experienced just that, falling over and breaking a bone in her shoulder.

I enjoyed my soup from the freezer, enough for two more days and I spent the afternoon cooking veg etc. for a new supply.

Friends and garden tubs alike are toppling over and breaking up. The siege is on. I shall not venture out. I will enjoy making and consuming my vegetable soup.

The following conclusions can be drawn from these two case studies. First, for some older people the weather is a dominant concern in winter. They recognise that, as a result of the weather, they may become housebound for a number of days. A particular anxiety is with food stocks and, as a result, they engage in anticipatory provisioning. Freezers play an important part in this. Second, being confined to the house is seen as an opportunity to engage in indoor household tasks. Third, inter-generational support with neighbours and nearby family works both ways. Overall it is evident that older people face certain risks that are distinctive to the winter, risks that threaten their health and well-being.

This suggests that one explanation for excess winter mortality among older people may be that in winter they are more isolated as a result of the simple fact that everyone, not just older people, is less likely to be out and about. Staying 'firmly' indoors for two or three days at a time with the proverbial shutters put up, and well-provisioned in advance, they may be glad to be 'warm and comfortable', getting on with indoor tasks. But the Arthurs' experience of Marion's fall in November 2007 and the accident of Alice's friend, Margaret, suggest that this is a particularly dangerous time to have an accident or to fall ill. Personal alarms may have more than a symbolic function in reducing risks. More generally these case studies pose interesting questions about the independence and isolation of older people, particularly in rural areas, and how this might vary with the seasons. In particular, it would be surprising if older people in similar situations did not look forward to the renewal of life brought by the returning spring. Conversely, of course, they view the coming winter with some trepidation, having survived the risks posed by the previous one.

Returning

In 1996 I had an unexpected opportunity to discuss later life experiences with a writer approaching her 80th birthday. Margaret Goodchild lived in Cambridge and had written a word-processed document of about 30,000 words, titled *A Mad Woman Walks Alone in the Mountains*. There was no publisher and she herself is not named on the cover page. She had produced copies of it for a local 'sale of work' and the son of a friend had purchased one. Some time later, my friend lent it to me and I subsequently corresponded with Margaret.

The document is an account of a ten-day visit in 1989 to a village in the French Alps. She had last been there in 1938 on a skiing holiday organised for British workers. In addition to a straightforward description of her return, the document includes reflections on her long life and her disenchantment with the contemporary state of the world. In particular, she combined her distant memories of 1938 with a narrative describing her unfolding late life adventure. I wrote a detailed paper based on it, which I sent to her for comment. With her agreement I turned this into an article that was subsequently published (Bytheway, 1996b).

What was of particular interest to me was the way she invoked memory and experiences in thinking through her anxieties about time and age. So, for example, she described how the impulse to return was triggered by something she read and then, as she thought back to the mountains, 'tremendous happiness, once experienced, floods back and demands to be relived'. She found her preparations to be 'incredibly rejuvenating', and as her adventure progressed, she said the years 'seemed to drop off' her. In contrast to this sense of returning to where she had been 50 years previously, she also described a profound sense of finitude. This is evident, for example, in her use of the word 'last'. She described this as her 'last great adventure' and:

> A terrible melancholy line came into my mind: 'Look thy last on all things lovely'. I felt convinced that I would never be able to return to that world of mountains, my beloved village.

In describing her adventure she repeatedly found herself being 'taken back' and recognising 'familiar' sights. What she valued she frequently called 'old'. Here, for example, is how she described the town near the village:

> I soon found myself among the old familiar stone-walled chalet-type of houses with wide arched doorways [...] There were the lovely old fountains, some built of granite stone, crowned or surrounded by bright geraniums ... The focal points of the old quarter were the old church, graced by two beautiful, tall old lime trees, and two magnificent old chestnut trees outside the old Town Hall.

At this point in the adventure, this reassuring familiarity contrasted with the anxieties she felt as she set off for the village:

> How often have people revisited scenes of childhood, or even of the fairly recent past, only to find that devastating changes have taken place? What if I find my village built over; replaced by smart, sophisticated hotels; expensive places for après-ski entertainment; none of the ordinary folk left whom I once knew, nor any of its rural beauty left?

She need not have worried. With her first sight of the village from a bend in the road, 'it seemed unchanged'. She had 'got back' to a place 'where [she] had had such a wonderful way of living'. In the village itself:

> I closed my eyes and saw again [...] the old houses which
> even at close quarters seemed totally unchanged [...] all as
> if I had left the day before. I had the extraordinary feeling
> of permanence of enduring.

It was only individual people who had changed. In particular, she met once again her old sweetheart, then a ski-instructor, now 'an elderly, heavily-built man', disabled after a skiing accident and living 'in a world of his own'. He briefly reacted to their reunion when 'the ghost of a young man' emerged. Unexpectedly, she found herself attracted by the women in his family:

> They all lived in old houses, which did nevertheless have
> modern appliances, yet they clung to old practices.

Margaret's adventure is a good example of how in later life we might return to a place from long ago, and how the experience revives all sorts of emotions. Fearing the worst, she was astonished to discover how little had changed and, as a result, it was not difficult to imagine that she was in reality 'back' where she had been in 1938. And there is of course a 'Shirley Valentine' scenario in prospect: need she return to Cambridge? Why not remain in her idyllic place? Regrettably her resources were limited and she was not well. She felt she had no choice but to return to Cambridge. Her return to the Alps was not a whole new start in life, as it might have been. Rather it was a fleeting visit to a significant place in her past that sustained, for her, a sense of continuity rather than revealing the intolerable changes she had feared.

Her account demonstrates how a return can be interpreted, not only as 'going back' (temporarily as well as spatially), but also as the last time this will happen. She had exhausted her savings and her illness was progressive. This was her 'one last great adventure'. Regarding the relationship between age, time and events, specific types of experience can be interpreted as 'firsts' in what is expected to be, and may become, a series of equivalent events: teeth, spoken words, birthdays, love affairs, jobs or 'great adventures'. As life progresses, the same sequences may begin to generate an awareness of potential 'lasts': as someone is seen to be approaching the end of life, the possibility that a particular experience could be 'the last one' gains added poignancy.

Lastness, however, is not just about finitude. At the end of her document where she reflects back on the women she had met in the village, Margaret anticipated that when 'they have gone, part of the old world, as everywhere, will have vanished with them'.

Questions for discussion

1 Is it absurd to suggest that the tick of the clock is relevant to understanding age?

2 Picture it: a landscape, a family enjoying a picnic, rolling hills in the distance. Can you think of an equivalent timescape?

3 How routine is your daily life? Do you think it is becoming more routine as you grow older?

4 In this chapter you have read about different aspects of the lives of various older people: Daphne Smith, Marie White, Jane Neal, Angela Rammell, Adam and Marion Arthur, Alice Watson and Margaret Goodchild. They have illustrated different aspects of the link between age and time. Which has proved the most revealing for you?

FOUR

Representations of age

> The history of gerontology may accurately be described as
> the history of the social construction of meaningful images
> or metaphors of old age. (Hepworth, 2004, p 11)

While engaging with people in interviews or other participative activities is essential to gerontological research, this in itself is not sufficient. The analysis of language and image and how they are used to represent age in the wider cultural landscape, is just as important. So the issues I address in this chapter relate to roadside billboards, government documents and statistical samples – any attempt, in fact, to 'represent' age.

Representation is a word with many associations (Hall, 1997). I use it here to cover the ways in which words, pictures and diagrams might be used in attempts to convey the realities of age, not only about what age is, but also about how it could be different. These attempts are often described as 'models': what it is to grow older is represented by a model. Essentially, as Mike Hepworth implies in the quote above, such models are metaphors. Each representation produces an image not of age itself but of 'what age is like'.

Words and images underpin models of age. In particular, they create structured understandings of the characteristics of older people: what they might need, how they might behave, where they might live, and how 'we' should relate to 'them'. The idea of 'model' is helpful insofar as it implies mechanisms that explain how circumstances change and people age. A model might be devised, for example, to represent the ageing process. But it is important to appreciate that at best a model represents 'a truth', not the whole truth about age.

Words

From his study of the history of gerontology, Stephen Katz concluded that 'gerontological texts linguistically shaped old age' (1996, p 79). He referred in particular to terms such as 'senile'; to the organisation of textbook chapters and the use of scientific rhetoric; to the production of inventories and cataloguing charts; and to the endorsement of how gerontology might parallel other, more established, areas of research such as paediatrics. What he argues is that textbooks have not only disseminated knowledge, they have also influenced the ways we think.

As explained in Chapter One, for my 1982 project I undertook analyses of a wide range of texts, beginning with the 1972 edition of *Chambers Twentieth Century Dictionary* (Macdonald, 1973). Using eight roots: age, eld-, ger-, old, pension, presby-, retire, and sen-, I identified 17 words that were each at the head of a new entry in the Dictionary (see Table 4.1). Within these 17 entries there were 64 direct derivatives (such as 'aged' and 'older') and 86 compound words or phrases (such as 'old boy' and 'pension off'). In total, these 167 words and phrases were given a total of 280 definitions by the Dictionary. Some were given several; the word 'old' itself for example had as many as 21 definitions. Table 4.1 shows how the headword 'old' and, to a lesser extent, 'age' and 'retire' were dominant.

Table 4.1: Roots, headwords and definitions

Root	Headwords	Number of definitions
Age	age	30
Eld-	eld, elder	21
Ger-	geriatrics, gerontology	8
Old	old	113
Pension	pension	18
Presby-	presbyopia, presbyte, presbyter	27
Retire	retire	35
Sen-	senate, senecio, senescent, senschal, senile, senior	28
Total		280

Using *Roget's Thesaurus* and other dictionaries, I identified 122 other words in *Chambers Dictionary* that included any of the above terms in any of their definitions. For example, 'decrepit' was defined as 'worn out by the infirmities of old age' and 'dotage' as 'childishness of old age'. I found 194 such definitions.

In total, this made 474 definitions that had a direct relationship to age. As such this constitutes a substantial body of literature. I was particularly interested at that time in 'old age'. It was granted only one definition, 'the later part of life', and this, I argued, was little more than a way of registering that the term existed. In contrast 'old age' is found in at least 20 definitions and, in five cases, 'old age' constitutes the complete definition.[1]

'Age' is accorded 16 definitions and 11 derivatives. With regard to human experience, it has three definitions as a noun and four as a verb. In writing this chapter, I decided to visit the online version of the 2010 edition of *Chambers Dictionary*. Table 4.2 indicates how the definitions of 'age' have changed.

Table 4.2: Definitions of 'age' in *Chambers Dictionary*

Age defined as a:	1972 edition	2010 edition
Noun	duration of life	the period of time during which a person, animal, plant or phenomenon has lived or existed
	the time of being old	the fact or time of being old
	mature years	a particular stage in life – old age
		one's developmental equivalent in years compared with the average for one's chronological age
Verb	to develop the characteristics of old age	to show signs of growing old
	to grow old	to grow old
	to mature	to mature
	to make to seem old or to be like the old	to make someone seem older or look old

In 1982, I argued that the second of the noun definitions ('the time of being old') was 'virtually tautological' since one of the 21 definitions of 'old' was 'having the characteristics of age'. This illustrates the extent to which the meanings of 'age' and 'old' are taken for granted and how they are so closely intertwined.

Arguably most of the changes shown in Table 4.2 are stylistic, but it is interesting to note how the definition of age as a noun has become rather more specific. As a verb, despite two definitions remaining unchanged, the switches from 'characteristics' to 'signs', from seeming 'old' to seeming 'older', and from 'being like the old' to 'looking old' all reflect conceptual changes in what 'to age' means. In particular, these definitions no longer make explicit the association of ageing with old age and the characteristics of 'the old'.

Focused as I was in 1982 on the use of the term 'old age' (rather than 'age'), I concluded from these analyses that old age is used widely as a subject heading and standard reference term, that it holds a complex relationship with certain other comparable terms, and that its meaningfulness is taken for granted, both in the definition of obscure terms and in the classification of literature. In revisiting these analyses, it is apparent that these conclusions apply equally to the more general concept of age.

Words are significant not just because of their individual meanings but because grammar plays a part in constructing ideas about age. How pronouns are used, for example, in texts and speeches about age can be extremely revealing. I came to realise this when the government issued a White Paper in 1981 titled *Growing Older* (Department of Health and Social Security, 1981). The first sentence of the Foreword was deliberately inclusive: 'We are all growing older'. In the third paragraph, however, 'we' became 'a trading nation', and then 'we, the government' in the fourth and fifth paragraphs, and finally 'we, the Secretaries of State' in the final paragraph. In the White Paper itself the third person pronouns were more dominant: 'many people [...] as they grow older, find themselves generally slowing down', for example (para 6.1).

Similarly, the choice of nouns that are used to refer to older people also reflects subtle differences of emphasis. Table 4.3 demonstrates how the White Paper associated 'pensioners' with income issues and entering retirement, 'older people' with retirement opportunities, and 'elderly people' with accommodation and care concerns.

Table 4.3: Frequency of the use of words by chapter in *Growing Older*

Chapter titles	Pension/er	Older	Elderly
Income	71	2	14
Entering Retirement	58	2	0
Retirement: A Time of Opportunity	2	13	25
Where to Live	4	1	37
The Need for Support and Care	3	3	25
Community Care Services	0	0	26
Care in Hospitals and Nursing Homes	0	0	41

Tense is another aspect of grammar that can consolidate a sense of age. As argued in Chapter Three, 'What did you do?' is one of those questions which imply that the active life of an older person is over. Conversely, many researchers hesitate to ask older people questions about the future and where they expect to be in a few years time – the kinds of questions that are so common in research with schoolchildren and students.

Words are often used to generate images. Shakespeare's 'sans teeth, sans eyes, sans taste, sans everything' is a classic example of how simple words can be used to invoke an unattractive picture of the older person. The negative use of age words such as 'geriatrics' is now well known. Whether in birthday cards, alternative comedy routines, or simple verbal abuse, there is no need to search out further examples of how words are used to exclude or humiliate older people. But one aspect that is not fully appreciated and which casts some light on the wider use of the age vocabulary is the way in which ordinary words can be combined to create an abusive term: 'silly old cow' for example is made up of three ordinary words that can be used individually in unobjectionable ways. It is often in the linking of a noun to one or two adjectives, perhaps in series, that words can be most powerful in the creation of an abusive verbal image. Nascher (1919), for example, in describing how the aged individual can be differentiated from the rest of the population through the characteristics of their bodies, includes chapters on the following topics: 'thin hair, brittle nails, dry and loose skin, uneven muscle texture, slackened jaws, loss of teeth, and slouching posture' (Katz, 1996, p 85). The images that these words create are echoed in many ageist birthday cards on sale in the 21st century. Similarly, I remember being shocked in 1982 to find that the dictionary definition of 'senile' included reference to the 'imbecility' of old age.

Images

Visual, in contrast to verbal, images often have a power that overshadows the impact of any accompanying text. There is a well-known UK road sign that portrays two pedestrians with bent backs, the one in front leaning on a walking stick, the one behind, shorter and holding on to the arm of the first. One popular view among gerontologists is that this is an ageist image. A contrasting view is that the bent backs and walking stick are unambiguous indicators of poor mobility and, as such, an appropriate way of representing people who, regardless of age, have difficulty in crossing a road. Insofar as the sign is effective and reduces accidents in which vulnerable pedestrians might be injured, then many would argue the warning sign can only be considered 'a good thing'.

A link with age is only made explicit when the sign also includes the words 'Elderly people'.[2] The sign is still intended to warn motorists that pedestrians with mobility problems may be crossing the road ahead, but the addition of the two words can be interpreted to imply that elderly people, all elderly people, have mobility problems, and that people with mobility problems are all elderly. It is not difficult then to see how people might take offence for very different reasons: arguably, it represents a two-way act of stigmatisation.

Captions and accompanying text not only consolidate visual images of what people of different ages look like, they can also create expectations of what it is to be a person of a particular age. In Bytheway and Johnson (2005) we discussed a striking example: a successful British picture library that had 320 photographic images catalogued under the heading 'old age'. Each photograph had a brief caption and of these captions, 280 (87.5%) included the word 'elderly'. The library specialised in social issues and so it was no surprise when a detailed analysis of images and captions revealed an association with the provision of care. We analysed the content of the photographs and concluded:

> Someone who does not have any signs of age such as a lined face, clothing characteristic of older people, spectacles, a walking stick or a carer in attendance, is someone who will look 'far too young' to represent old age. ... To be considered valid, a series representing old age can only include photographs that include some combination of lined face, old-fashioned clothing, walking sticks, care setting, etc. (Bytheway and Johnson, 2005, p 185)

More recently, Rolph et al (2009) offer a subtle analysis of the interplay between image, caption and commentary. In reporting on their revisiting study of residential care homes in the UK, they reproduce a photograph taken by Townsend (1962, illustration 30) captioned 'Apathy in a day-room'. They comment: 'The caption, briefly and economically, does some of the work of analysis and argument; the photograph itself, however, does much of the work of indicating cause (of apathy) as well as effect' (Rolph et al, 2009, p 429).

Cultural gerontologists have been interested in how age figures in the popular media and in advertising (Ylänne et al, 2010). It has often been noted that advertising directed at the population at large rarely uses older people as models (Carrigan and Szmigin, 2000). However, marketing has become a little more sensitive to accusations of ageism. Blaikie (1999, p 126) argued that fashions in advertising practice changed 'quite markedly' in the 1970s, following the publication of Sontag's *Saturday Review* article on the double jeopardy of ageing (Sontag, 1972), coinciding as it nearly did with the publication of the first of her influential essays on photography (Sontag, 1977). More recently the Dove 'Campaign for Real Beauty' has won awards for the use of models who deviate from the beauty stereotype of 'thin, young and blonde'. Nevertheless, it should be noted that the oldest model on the 2010 Dove website is just 59 years of age. Moreover, she is quoted as saying: "I shall be 59 in August, which means, horrifyingly, amazingly, unbelievably and quite ridiculously that I shall become a pensioner next year." (See Chapter Five for further comment on the interpretation of birthdays.)

Older people have always been targets for particular kinds of products, but in recent years this has been extended to include previously unfamiliar markets: cosmetics, holidays and health clubs, for example. Advertising campaigns are regularly aimed at persuading older people that these products will open the door to alternative lifestyles that they can enjoy (Sawchuk, 1995). Typically, as with most marketing, satisfaction is associated with positive attributes such as personal fulfilment. Almost without exception, the message is reinforced by someone's smiling face. This trend has attracted the interest of cultural gerontologists. One early UK example of empirical research in this area is a study of *Retirement Choice* magazine (Featherstone and Hepworth, 1995; Blaikie, 1999, pp 98-102). Over the 20 years since its first issue in 1972, the magazine's target group had shifted towards younger people not yet retired, and the analysis demonstrated how this was reflected in its editorials, features and, in particular, the images on its cover.

Each day, dozens of advertisements for anti-ageing cosmetic treatments are published in women's magazines. The market for treatments that promise to help us regain a lost youth is vast (King and Calasanti, 2006). Consider just one example of an ordinary advert in an ordinary women's magazine.[3] The headline reads:

"I'm 61. But my face is 35."

And it's 'her' face that smiles out at the reader above the simple slogan:

"LOOK GOOD FEEL GOOD".

The next line reads:

"Try my 90 Second Facelift on my 30 day NO RISK TRIAL."

The advert then attempts to engage 'you' in sharing her anxieties:

I'm almost sure that you, and 20 million women like you
– look older than you feel. Our faces grow old faster than

our minds and bodies. Our skin is damaged by sunshine, pollution, makeup, diet, smoking, weight loss, and dry homes and offices.

So, as a result of the environment and modern lifestyles, our faces, it is claimed, may look 61 even though we – our minds and bodies – feel only 35. Note how this implies that chronological age itself is irrelevant.

But this is not just ordinary skincare. The second paragraph begins 'FIGHT AGE AND LOOK YOUNGER. When your face is under attack, you fight back with powerful weapons.' Our skin is damaged, it would seem, not just by the environment but by age as well. Your face is under attack. Take action now and you can save your face! But, despite the military metaphors, this is not just a crude battle: 'Then just like me, YOU can turn back the clock and look many years younger!' The reader might ask: Is it possible? Can you really turn back the clock? Will it really make me look younger?

> I GUARANTEE THAT PERSONALLY. Look very closely at my face in the photo. It's unretouched! That's me. My birth certificate says I'm 61. But my face says I'm 35.

A careful inspection of the photographic evidence suggests she may indeed have lovely blonde hair with lots of body, confident eyes, a generous smile, healthy skin, no wrinkles and only a few smile lines. But we are not told whose face this is, who 'me' is. 'Me' is the unnamed woman in the photograph and in an attempt to create a real identity behind the photograph, the text reads: 'It's unretouched! That's me.' But, in the reality of advertising practice, this 'me' is intended to represent no more (and no less) than a possible 'you': 'just like me, YOU can turn back the clock and look many years younger!'

The text becomes even more dramatic in the next paragraph:

> Every morning I know that in just 90 seconds my mirror will show me some wonderful changes. Wrinkles gone. Crow's feet vanished. Smile lines erased. Just you. But a younger you, with a perfectly natural look.

This is the nub of the message. Shifting from the anonymous 'me' to the 'you' in the mirror, the text also promises a transformation following the 90-second treatment. The image in the advert is, *in effect*, a mirror reflecting a *different* you, a *35-year-old* you, feeling good and looking good.

This message is not peculiar to the advertising industry. Daily newspapers regularly include articles under headlines such as 'Recapture your youth' reading just like the advertisement. Often products will be named, with photographs of models smiling beguilingly, and phrases such as 'turning back the clock' used freely. News agencies are full of these images reflecting cultural values that celebrate youth and deplore age. As we grow older, we participate in a constantly reinforcing cycle of self-deprecation, and the fear of age and ageing that we learn at an early age is continually being reinforced.

The body images conveyed in such advertisements are a denial of age. In a famous attempt to challenge this practice, Age Concern produced a billboard poster. This echoed a well-known advertisement for Wonderbra that had featured the model, Eva Herzigova. In focusing attention on her bosom, Wonderbra had been widely accused of sexism. Age Concern's poster featured another model wearing a bra and its slogan was 'The first thing some people notice is her age'. What do they mean by 'her age'? There's no reference to age on the poster, no word, no number. Possibly we are expected to recognise age in the model's face. Whatever the case, the message is very different to that of the advertisement for the facelift. First, the words are those of Age Concern, not the model. And rather than urging us to apply creams every morning, Age Concern is effectively saying: 'Here she is, posing as if she were advertising this bra. This is her, unretouched. But don't just notice her signs of age. There's more to her than her age.' A newspaper columnist, discussing the advertisement, described it as an 'unsettling sight':

> True, this is an exceptionally attractive and well-preserved
> 56-year-old who could easily shave a decade off her age. But
> she patently lacks the bloom of youth of the stereotypical
> lingerie model, and thus subverts the Herzigova ad – which
> is what Age Concern intended. (Marks, 1998)

As a poster, it certainly stopped me and made me think. Arguably Age Concern demonstrated that an older woman is just as capable of modelling a bra as a younger woman. The assumption that a successful modelling career ends in your 20s was shown to be false, and by implication discrimination against older women is unacceptable. But, to an older generation, the Age Concern model may have appeared comparatively young, someone who retained much of the beauty of her youth. So the question remains: can the body image of an even older generation be similarly changed?

Photographers and portrait painters have long appreciated the power of the image of age. We may stand back and admire the beauty of youth, but it is the older person who raises questions about human life and what it is we value. By being obliged to look the older person in the eye (as on the cover of McDonald and Rich's celebrated book of essays, *Look Me in the Eye*, 1983), perhaps we will face up to our own ageing and realise that it need not be quite as bleak an experience as we have been led to expect. Age has its own kind of beauty.

After Ninety is a collection of 82 black and white photographs, taken by the celebrated American photographer, Imogen Cunningham (1977). The book was first published in 1975, the year before she died at the age of 93, and with only a few exceptions it contained new, recently-taken photographs. In an introductory essay, Margaretta Mitchell reminds us that 'our future' included the prospect of being as old as the people portrayed. She introduces Cunningham and her photographs in this way:

> No words can describe old age as well as the photographs reproduced in *After Ninety*, which is a direct result of Imogen's own confrontation with life after ninety. (Mitchell, 1977, p 9)

Thus the book offers us an 'inside' description of what life is like 'after ninety'. Turning the pages, we are repeatedly presented with images accompanied by Cunningham's cryptic captions; for example: 'John Roeder worked in an oil refinery, but was really an artist'. Although a few captions specify the subject's age ('My father after ninety'), Cunningham's preference is to consolidate a distinctive individual identity: 'He's proudest of his potatoes and he gave me this big one', and a few relate to past achievements: 'She was a famous pianist [...]'. Only three captions quote the words of the subject.

Most of the photographs are of the upper body with the head near the centre of the image. About half are wearing spectacles and six have a walking stick. At least half are seated. Half the subjects are looking directly at the camera and only seven are actively engaged in an activity other than posing for the camera. Only one of these involves vigorous movement. So, broadly speaking, old age is portrayed as a time of contentment, fulfillment and continuing engagement in former activities. There is a pervasive sense of calm and dignity. There are 10 captions that unambiguously celebrate achievements (two use the significant word 'still': 'He's still teaching the history of American films at three universities every year' and two refer to a length of time: 'She was a high school teacher for more than fifty years [...]') but most of the remainder are much more oblique. There are only four photographs that convey struggle or defeat.

In my analysis of the book, I discussed the similarities between Cunningham's method and that of social research in how both attempt to present a systematic coverage of a representative sample of subjects (Bytheway, 2003). Indeed Mitchell reported that social scientists had discussed ageing with Cunningham. She claims that:

> These photographs are a kind of visual research, straightforward studies of the way people are at the end of life, revealed in a face, an expression, a gesture, a posture. (Mitchell, 1977, p 11)

So the photographs, as implied in the book's title, were intended in her view to represent 'the way' we all are 'at the end of life'. Like researchers such as Peter Townsend (1962), Cunningham was unhappy with the situation of many older people:

> When she went to see homes for the aged, she did not like what she saw, and she became progressively aware of the true situation confronting many elderly persons in our culture. So often they had become dependent, as a result of circumstances over which they had lost control, but Imogen sought out individuals whose independent spirits had managed to transcend their problems. (Mitchell, 1977, p 11)

Thus Cunningham decided not to portray the negative side of old age, despite this being the 'true situation' of many. Rather she wanted to illustrate positive ways in which problems had been overcome.

I concluded from my analysis that:

> [she] clearly intended that her subjects should 'represent' a wide variety of people of great age, and that the photographs should generate a general and positive image of old age. In the interplay between herself and her subjects, the mirroring of experience and appearance, and in the selection of photographs for inclusion in the book, she intended that a *particular* understanding of old age should emerge, an image of how late old age *can* be a positive phase in life. (Bytheway, 2003, p 38)

Mitchell interprets the collection as a reflexive 'portrait of old age' and invokes the idea that the photographs are a mirror of Cunningham's own experience of old age:

[her] courage to look through the lens and see herself mirrored in others, always looking with a childlike curiosity, learning from another's reality ways to be strong, active, interesting, and useful. (Mitchell, 1977, p 18)

Nevertheless, Mitchell also comments: 'These are the helpless victims of the stereotyped view that sees ... their ability to contribute to our fast-paced consumer society [to be] a thing of the past' (p 9). So, in addition to mirroring Cunningham's own experience of life after ninety, the collection portrays 'them' as helpless victims of 'our' society. Despite her intention to challenge the stereotyped view, Mitchell's use of pronouns, along with the emotive term 'helpless victims', serves to consolidate the sense of distance that has already been created through Cunningham's focus on the age of 90. There appears to be an underlying assumption that 'we' who view these photographs are concurrently contributing to 'our fast-paced consumer society' and that we have failed to recognise that those people amongst us of great age, far from being helpless, non-contributory victims are actively contributing too. There is no acknowledgement of the possibility that we who view the photographs might be of a great age ourselves.

For the cultural gerontologist, this collection, like many other books and exhibitions, provides fascinating insights into the construction and interpretation of images of old age. Mitchell expresses the popular view that old age is most clearly illustrated ('better than any words') by portraits of older people and that it is the ageing body (gestures, postures and, in particular, the expressions of the ageing face) that is the classic representation.

Representation

In considering how age figures in the world around us, it is important to recognise that words and images are there to guide our thinking. The government, advertisers and photographers are not publishing randomly selected pictures or descriptions: they are all attempting to direct the way we see age. Some may be attempting to document the current reality in a statistically representative way, but others are more interested in alternatives. In Bytheway (2003) I argued that both Cunningham and the advertisers were attempting to persuade us that later life doesn't have to be as it is: it can be better.

As argued above, advertising images are intended to invite identification: you look at the photograph and read the slogan 'This could be you'. The photograph is chosen not to portray a 'typical' customer but rather the kind of person that prospective customers can imagine themselves being or, at least, the kind they can dream about being: dreams rather than reality, but plausible and meaningful dreams. In the business meetings of advertisers, prospective customers are identified as the 'target population' and the market research that is commissioned is based on random samples of this population. In this sense there are similarities in the kinds of representation attempted by commerce and gerontologists. So, how might social research represent the lives of 'ordinary older people'?

Throughout its long history the MO Archive has sought to record the thoughts and experiences of 'ordinary people' living in the UK. Since 1981 it has maintained a panel of writers who are invited to respond to 'directives' issued two or three times a year. Although the size of the panel has varied, it has always been over 100 and often numbers nearer 500. The primary concern of the Archive has been diversity and, to this end, it has from time to time limited the recruitment of new participants to certain groups (for example, in 2009 it prioritised young people, men and people living outside the south-east of England). The aim of this, the Archive sometimes claimed, was to make the panel more representative statistically. In 2004, discussion of the representativeness of the panel was prompted on the Mass Observation JISCMail by the publication of Harrison and McGhee (2003). This is an extract from my contribution to the discussion:

> What makes a panel 'representative'? The scientific ideal is that the panel should be recruited through strict random sampling procedures. A more realistic alternative is that the panel should have a 'proper' balance between the proportions in various basic categories: that they are the same as in the wider population. Either way, tick boxes are needed if the claim that the panel is representative is to be defended.
>
> A third alternative is to ensure that certain basic categories are represented *adequately* rather than in the right proportions. In other words the aim is to represent the diversity of the population, ensuring that there are 'enough' rather than the 'right' numbers in specific categories. For example, I have described the representativeness of those who responded to the Birthdays directive in the following way:
>
> 'Information is available regarding the occupations of the respondents and where they live. This demonstrates

that most are associated with middle class occupations and most live in southern England. That said however, there are many exceptions: a typist, HGV driver, carpenter, cleaner, artist, labourer, florist, waitress, bed and breakfast proprietor and postmistress. And respondents include people living in such places as the Shetland Islands, west Wales, Jersey and Northern Ireland, and even one in Paris and one in Kalgoorlie, Australia.'

In short I was both unembarrassed to concede that there are proportionately more living in southern England than in west Wales (where I live), and pleased to register that there is at least one living in my neck of the woods. And the great thing about this approach is that tick boxes aren't essential. The background information already available, plus the mini-biogs, are more than adequate.

A few years ago the Archive decided to anonymise contributions and, as a consequence, it gave each panel member a code number. This number remains constant, and as a result the researcher is able to collate the contributions of any one writer in response to different directives. The aim of anonymisation is to conceal identities and to protect the guarantees of confidentiality that the Archive issues. There is, however, another consequence that has been overlooked in discussions about anonymisation: that anonymisation consolidates the objective of giving voice to the views and experiences of ordinary people. Contributors are not writing in their own names but rather on behalf of 'ordinary people'. Potentially, they decide to contribute to the Archive specifically in order that 'ordinary people' are well represented in public debates and discussions about contemporary life and the issues of the day.

Anonymisation is an issue that often taxes social researchers. There has been an assumption that people will only 'tell the truth' about their opinions and lives if guaranteed comprehensive confidentiality. Some people of course will claim that they are willing to answer any question put to them, fully and honestly. That may be the case, but on many topics they will be the exception. Most people would be anxious if they fully appreciated that what they said in the privacy of an interview, might be saved and filed away and some day, just possibly, used against them. It may indeed be the case, for example, that many people would refuse to reveal their age if there was no promise of confidentiality. So the offer of anonymity is intended to increase the ability of research to represent *all* views and circumstances of the wider populations from which samples may be drawn.

In conclusion, all representations of age are intended to convey ideas that make us reflect on our own opinions and experience of age, perhaps changing the way we 'see' or think about age. In this objective, 'we' are populations of people unknown to the person who produces the representation. The latter, whether a writer, photographer, advertiser or social researcher, is seeking to represent age, setting criteria that define its boundaries, and forwarding a message that conveys a novel or challenging image of age.

Questions for discussion

1   What words spring to mind, when you think about age?

2   Who would you pick if you needed a photograph of someone who represents older people? And what would you like the photograph to show?

3   Are you persuaded when reading an anonymous letter in the newspaper that begins 'Writing as an older person myself ...'

FIVE

Growing older in an ageing body

We are all growing older and our bodies, slowly but surely, are constantly ageing. So we all have some first-hand experience of what this entails. But only up to a point: our understanding of what it is like to be older than we are currently is, necessarily, only second-hand knowledge gained through observing and listening to our elders. And what older people tell us about being the age they are is, of course, loaded with all sorts of emotions. 'When you're my age, then you'll understand ...' is a classic put-down that reasserts the authority of personal experience.

In Chapter Six I consider relative ages and the significance of age differences. In this chapter I first consider the significance of lived experience in understanding how people account for age, and then I move on to the business of living in an ageing body. In the second half of the chapter I contrast how the annual routines of life such as birthdays signify the ageing of the self, before finally considering evidence of the impact of transforming experiences on the course of life.

It is important to recognise how, both at the cultural and individual levels, growing older is something that is paradoxically both resisted and accepted as inevitable. It follows that there is always a tension surrounding debates and discussions about 'the reality' of age.

Experience

Experience is a concept that should be fundamental in gerontology. In Bytheway (1996a) I sought to make a clear distinction between experience of the ways of the world and the lived experience of growing older, arguing that this distinction should be incorporated into social theories of ageing. On the one hand we gain experience by observing and learning from others; and on the other we ourselves experience and survive a wide range of challenges and life transitions. In the inter-generational conflicts that often characterise work relations, it is the experience of the older worker that is challenged by the up-to-date expertise of the newly trained; tried and tested methods set against innovations and new resources. In the broader historical picture, the older worker loses, of course, and traditional methods are adapted or abandoned. The sense of being locked in a losing battle is well illustrated by the following comment of Simone de Beauvoir on the ways in which the older worker is 'tossed into an outdated past':

> I have learnt a great deal since I was twenty, but year by year I become relatively more ignorant because there are more and more discoveries; the sciences grow richer, and in spite of my efforts to keep abreast at least in some fields, the number of things I do not know increases. (1977, p 425)

But experience is more than just an accumulation of knowledge and skills. As examples of the lived experience of ageing, the classic 'embodied' accounts of 'being old' (such as Elder, 1977; Newton, 1980) bring out 'the long and continuing experience of loss, threat and personal survival' (Bytheway, 1996a, p 620). Experience is the stuff of survival.

In 1979, Pat Moore famously attempted to experience later life through prosthetic alteration. At the age of 26 she transformed her body into that of a 'woman of more than 80 years of age':

> Hidden prosthetics blurred my vision, reduced my natural level of hearing and altered my posture and range of motion, for the portrayal of a variety of levels of health and personal ability. With the use of canes, walkers and a wheelchair, I was able to approximate reduced mobility and confront physical and emotional inaccessibility. (Moore, 2005)

As this older woman, she visited more than 100 cities in North America. She experienced kindness but she also described being mugged and left for dead. She claimed that 'When I reemerged, as a woman of 30 years, I was forever changed, both as a person and a professional' (Moore, 2005). Her pioneering use of prosthetics was followed in many training courses; for example, the use of gloves and ear-plugs to simulate 'being old' became a feature of Reality Orientation programmes in the 1980s (Holden and Woods, 1988).

But how effective can such simulation be in capturing the lived reality? In the following extract from a 1986 short story about Jean Serjeant, a centenarian, Julian Barnes directly challenges gerontology over the problem of representing the lived experience, how to convey what it is to grow older. It is quite possible that he had heard Moore being interviewed on the radio:

> Jean had often wondered what it would be like to grow old. When she had been in her fifties, and still feeling in

her thirties, she heard a talk on the radio by a gerontologist. 'Put cotton wool in your ears,' he had said, 'and pebbles in your shoes. Pull on rubber gloves. Smear Vaseline over your glasses, and there you have it: instant ageing.'

It was a good test, but it naturally contained a flaw. You never did age instantly; you never did have a sharp memory for comparison. Nor, when she looked back over the last forty of her hundred years, did it seem to be initially, or even mainly, a matter of sensory deprivation. You grew old first not in your own eyes, but in other people's eyes; then, slowly, you agreed with their opinion of you. It wasn't that you couldn't walk as far as you used to, it was that other people didn't expect you to; and if they didn't, then it needed vain obstinacy to persist.

At sixty she had still felt like a young woman; at eighty, she felt like a middle-aged woman who had something a bit wrong with her; at nearly a hundred she no longer bothered to think whether or not she felt younger than she was – there didn't seem any point. She was relieved not to be bedbound, as she might have been in earlier times; but mostly she took the medical advances of her lifetime for granted. She lived increasingly inside her head, and was content to be there. Memories, there were far too many memories; they raced across her sky like Irish weather. Her feet, with each succeeding year, seemed a little farther away from her hands; she dropped things, stumbled a little, was fearful; but mostly what she noticed was the smirking paradox of old age: how everything seemed to take longer than it used to, but how, despite this, time seemed to go faster. (Barnes, 1986, pp 139-40)

Barnes uses his literary skills here to align his readers with Jean, first in her 50s, then at ages 60 and 80 and finally as she approaches her 100th birthday, all the time relating her experience to that of others and to what she had previously expected. Over a lifetime of wondering, looking back, listening to others and experiencing age, she had acquired a rich understanding of what it is to grow older. Through Jean, Barnes spells out something of the complex relationship between chronology, time and age.

The sight of the body

The mask of ageing is a powerful metaphor that has resonated with the experience of many students of social gerontology. It was first articulated by Featherstone and Hepworth (1989), drawing on Gubrium's analysis of the history of how the concept of senility had underpinned the campaign in the US for increased investment in the treatment and management of Alzheimer's Disease (Gubrium, 1986). They also used the testimony of the English author J.B. Priestley to illustrate how the appearance of age or senility might mask the 'real' person. This is how Priestley described his reaction when catching sight of himself in a shop window:

> It is as though, walking down Shaftesbury Avenue as a fairly young man, I was suddenly kidnapped, rushed into a theatre and made to don the grey hair, the wrinkles and the other attributes of age, then wheeled on stage. Behind the appearance of age I am the same person, with the same thoughts, as when I was younger. (Featherstone and Hepworth, 1989, p 148)

Expressed like this, age is an affliction, as if from an acute attack of an external virus, one that masks (literally, as in the use of masks in the theatre) the victim's body. The claim to be 'the same person as when younger', echoes the title of Sharon Kaufman's influential book, also published in the 1980s, *The Ageless Self* (1986). Note how Priestley identified his older self not with the young boy he was as a child but with 'a fairly young man': the same ageless person he had always been.

Currently *The Saturday Guardian* magazine runs a column called 'What I see in the mirror'. Of the first 36 contributions published in 2010 only three ignored age. Of the other 33, 24 revealed the individual's chronological age. Most were fairly negative. Alison Steadman, the actress, for example, wrote: 'I don't like looking at myself in the mirror now. I still want to be 25 and slinking around. It's silly because we've all got to age' (*The Guardian*, 28 August 2010). And, reflecting the thoughts of Mr Bergstein and Anssi quoted in Chapter Two, Jeremy Hardy, the comedian, wrote: 'I see someone who is much older than I was expecting. The image of my face I hold in my mind is always about 10 years out of date. I am aware that I am 48, but think of that as being quite young, which it isn't' (*The Guardian*, 20 March 2010). Barbara Hulanicki's description was extreme:

The first thing I ask is, 'Who is that person in the mirror?' I'm not pleased with the way I look, it's horrible. I try to use mirrors for a quick glance at my silhouette. I particularly avoid mirrored elevators with all that lighting. I usually inspect my haircut to give myself something to focus on. I'm 73 and I don't lie about my age, although I lie about my son's – he's 43, but I say he's 39, which somehow makes it sound better. There's a stage in your life when people stop asking how old you are. What annoys me is when they find out and say, 'But why are you still working?' (*The Guardian*, 24 July 2010)

What these extracts (and many others in the series) demonstrate is that people interpret what they see in the mirror in terms of age, and that, like Mr Bergstein, they compare this with standards of how they imagine people of different ages look and 'should' look. Confirming the importance of age, their commentaries tend to drift away from what they see in the mirror, and they feel obliged to acknowledge their failure to accept that 'we've all got to age' and that 48, for example, is no longer 'quite young'. Diana Athill, at 93, was the oldest of the 36 contributors. Reflecting the thoughts of Priestley, she wrote:

However old one is, one still feels inside like the person one used to be. It's a foolish mistake to try too hard to look like that person, but it would be a bit sad to look very much like something else. (*The Guardian*, 26 June 2010)

As an example of a more negative, and less public, reaction, Martha Gellhorn, at the age of 84, wrote to Victoria Glendinning:

I have become ugly. You may be surprised that at my age this both horrifies me and startles me. My idea of the bad part of old age was just that; getting ugly. I never thought at all about the inevitable decay of the body and what that could mean, I only thought about my face. Now it's plain hideous. The left operated eye, which is far from a miracle job, is so much smaller that I have a Picasso touch and all around my eyes is soggy and dreadful. I have to wear dark glasses to save my own feelings. The rest isn't much cop either. I am sure that vanity (physical) never dies in either men or women; all that happens is you feel unacceptable because there is nothing left to have vanity about. (Moorehead, 2006, p 494)

Although Gellhorn says she had not anticipated the decay of age, it is the sight of her face in the mirror that horrifies and startles her. As Hockey and James explain in discussing the work of Turner (1995) on the somatisation of the self:

> Though we might not directly experience the bodily process of ageing as it occurs in time, nonetheless, the body does provide ample evidence for us that ageing is taking place. (Hockey and James, 2003, p 50)

Many celebrated novelists have described how people use mirrors to look for signs of ageing (Hepworth, 2000, p 44). Here is Iris Chase, the protagonist in Margaret Attwood's novel, *The Blind Assassin*:

> When I look in the mirror I see an old woman; or not old, because nobody is allowed to be *old* any more. *Older*, then. Sometimes I see an older woman who might look like the grandmother I never knew, or like my own mother, if she'd managed to reach this age. But sometimes I see instead the young girl's face I once spent so much time rearranging and deploring, drowned and floating just beneath my present face, which seems – especially in the afternoons, with the light on a slant – so loose and transparent I could peel it off like a stocking. (Attwood, 2001, p 53)

This is a telling account of how mirrors are used. It ends with an allusion to the mask that is the older face, 'so loose and transparent'. Were it to be peeled away, the young girl's face, Iris believes, would be revealed 'just beneath'. And here is Alix in Linda Grant's novel *Still Here*, describing how a belief in a precise link between chronological age and the quality of one's skin is passed down from generation to generation, constraining her choices as a young girl:

> Mamma's mother had put her on the train with six jars of *Violette Schimmer* in a separate suitcase, wrapped securely in brown paper, and instructions that under no circumstances was she to begin its use until her sixteenth birthday. ("Not a day before, not a day later." "*Why?*" "Because now you have the skin of a child and the process of ageing has not begun. But the *moment* it starts ... Until then, only soap and water.") On the morning of my own sixteenth birthday Mamma took me into the bathroom, dim under overcast October skies, filled the basin, holding her little finger under the tap to test the temperature, and at once the walls' blue tiles

swimming with red and turquoise fish misted with steam. She handed me the jar. "Darling," she said, "dip your hand in and spread a little over your face." (Grant, 2002, p 124)

So the face in the bathroom mirror is a constant preoccupation, a surface which can be treated with *Violette Schimmer* or whatever, but one which is doomed to age. For many, such as Gellhorn, this change is thought to lead to eventual ugliness, often as a result of surgical interference.

Hepworth, adopting a social interactionist approach, has contributed much to our understanding of how we manage the appearance of our ageing bodies. He describes how looking into a mirror, is 'an act of self-comparison and classification' (2004, p 10), comparison with culturally prescribed visual and verbal images (for example, as by Jeremy Hardy, quoted earlier). He suggests that 'the looking glass is not a glass we look into to see ourselves but a glass through which we look to gain an impression of ourselves through other people's eyes' (p 10). While this may be true, it is important to recognise there are two 'we's in this interpretation. What Hepworth is suggesting is that 'we 1', looking in the mirror, becomes a critic of 'we 2', there in the mirror, and of how we 2 has composed and presents we 2's body. We 1's concern is to assess what other people might think about what they see when looking at we 2.

How, in this context, does age complicate the assessment? Hepworth's argument is that we 2, the self in the mirror, protests: "Please don't think that I am as old as the body you see! I am as old as I feel, and the age I feel is something much younger. What you see is no more than a mask, a mask that I have not chosen to wear but a mask I am unable to remove." The mask is an image that, according to Hepworth, enables older people to reject the imputations of old age.

What makes the concept of mask all the more interesting is the extent to which some of us, as we age, attempt to mask our faces and bodies through the use of cosmetics and what we perceive to be fashionable clothing. Our aim is to present an image to others that is compatible with our continuing sense of who we are, that is, the 'same person as when younger'. The reality though is that in using cosmetics we are applying a further mask to the masked self. Given the huge growth in the market for anti-ageing products and interventions, the issues raised by the idea that the self can be unmasked rather than masked yet further, are extremely significant (Vincent, 2007). Julia Twigg sees the choice of clothing as a potential form of age resistance:

> We can see some of the ways in which these tensions are played out in clothing choices. Age-resistance can mean rejecting the cultural denigration implicit in the processes that assign to older women drab, frumpy, shapeless and concealing garments – clothing that endorses the cultural norm of invisibility and that acts to entrench the sidelined status of the old. (Twigg, 2007, p 299)

This is not easy, however, because the body changes as it ages and adjustments have to be made:

> Styles that once fitted or 'suited' – the category is, of course, cultural – may no longer do so as the body ages. (Twigg, 2007, p 290)

So the older person who wishes to resist the appearance of age ends up with a compromise: the image of someone who believes they look younger than they are but still not as young as they feel. Throughout the struggle, the accusation of 'mutton dressed as lamb' hangs in the air, as evident in this comment from Vera Griffiths, a contributor to the RoAD project:

> "I don't look in shops for older people. If I do, my daughters whizz me past but I still have this notion of 'mutton dressed as lamb'. I think this idea is instilled into us. Now if I try something on that I like and I can see my mother in it, I change my mind. I don't want to look like that."

Echoing such inter-generational judgements, Fairhurst (1998, p 263), in contrasting 'mutton dressed as lamb' with 'growing old gracefully', notes the role of adult children in advising their mothers on their appearance. Might there come a point when the older person abandons resistance? Hair is a key element in our appearance and there is a substantial industry surrounding the ways in which it is managed and dressed. Biologically, hair changes as we age, not just in colour and quantity but also in texture. This raises important issues for the industry and how it provides an appropriate and satisfactory service to older people. As part of the RoAD project we commissioned a case study of a salon in South Wales (see Symonds and Holland, 2008). Here is what Freda Jones, one of the customers, said:

> "I always come here. I come every Friday unless I'm going away on holiday, then I come another day. I've only been to Susan's for years. I wouldn't be happy going anywhere

else. Susan's very accommodating, she knows exactly the way I want it done.

"I like having my hair done. It's important because when you get older you can't do it yourself, at least I can't now because I have arthritis. I only used to go to the hairdressers to have a perm; I set it myself, unless I was going somewhere special – but I don't do it now.

"I'm having a cut today, then I'll have a perm at the end of March so that it's right for Easter. I like to have my hair set on rollers, but I'm leaving my hair go grey gently and naturally. I don't mind grey hair. The worst thing about getting old is that your bones get older. I like to have it set because it will last until next Friday. If I had a blow dry it wouldn't last. It lasts for a week with a set."

For Freda, the consequences of an ageing body are inevitable – her hair going grey and her arthritic bones aching. At the same time she lives a life that is stable and well ordered. She values the routine of visiting Susan's and the fuss that is made of her hair. In contrast, Connie Watkins, another customer, was concerned about the appearance of age: she claimed that "grey hair ages you", and she was the only customer who claimed to have chosen a hairstyle that made her 'look younger':

"I like to have it blow dried, I don't like my hair too tight. A blow dry makes you look younger. I always have the same blow dry but I like it a bit curly. That's how my husband used to like it. He's been dead for 27 years now, but I keep it the same. I like to have a rinse every two months, it makes me look and feel younger. I won't go grey unless the time comes when I can't be bothered."

Like Freda, the other customers, all older women, stuck to two claims: that they had kept the same style for many years, and that they left it to Susan to choose a style she considered appropriate. So in part their hair was how it had 'always' looked and in part how the hairdresser thought the hair of older women should look. All except Connie had abandoned resistance; they appeared unconcerned that Susan might be making them 'look old' (Ward and Holland, 2011).

In recent years, there has been a growing interest in gerontology in the significance of the body (Bytheway and Johnson, 1998; Woodward, 1999; Faircloth, 2003; Twigg, 2006, 2011). Much of this has focused on how the older person is portrayed in magazines and other popular media. As argued in Chapter Two, such documents are important to gerontology, not least because promotional literature is intended to encourage us to buy clothes and cosmetics. Insofar as the prominent visual images in advertisements serve as a guide, we find ourselves checking the mirror before making a purchase. Nevertheless, there is a strong element of fantasy in such imagery and, as we found in South Wales, the lived experience can be very different.

Consider what is involved in living with 'an ageing body'. The face in the mirror after all is no more than a two-dimensional visual representation of a small part of the body's surface. Turn your eyes away from the mirror and downwards and you can see your hands, and as you climb into the bath you are able to consider the sight of other parts of this object, your body. The visible surface may include tattoos or the scars of past injuries or operations – features that you think of as unique to yourself – and you may be concerned to check on the state of current blemishes such as bruises or bunions. As indicators of age, apart from the state of your hair, there may be 'flab' or 'loose flesh'. Whatever the detail, the sight of your body is very familiar to you, and most likely, as you look down, you will not spot any discernible changes since the last time you bathed: you follow your simple routines for washing your body before drying and dressing, and returning to the world outside the privacy of the bathroom.

During the course of each and every day, there are occasions when your body absorbs and discharges material. You have to manage each such occasion; typically your hands are put to work, ensuring that food and drink are consumed and that 'waste products' appropriately expelled. Social expectations about such routine practices are powerful, ensuring that certain tasks are undertaken competently in private, that a degree of hygiene is assured, and that the social pleasures associated with meals, for example, are not spoilt by unseemly behaviour. Indeed, expectations are so powerful, that much body maintenance is undertaken without thought. Each visit to the lavatory is a fleeting opportunity to have a moment to yourself; to think about other 'things' or to have a brief read of the newspaper, while your body gets on 'mindlessly' with its familiar tasks. Many of these tasks require degrees of dexterity, agility, mobility and strength that are commonly thought to decline with age (as recognised by Freda Jones and by Julian Barnes' character, Jean Serjeant, discussed earlier). Incontinence is often cited as a key indicator of this decline, and Joan Barfoot provides a telling account of this on the very first page of her novel, *Duet for Three* (1985). Aggie wakens with the impression that something is different and not nice. She recognises that it's a smell in the room:

Usually it would smell of dusting powder, and floor wax,
and years of accumulated this and that. This, she sniffs, is
acrid, piercing, sharp in the nose, and nasty. (p 2)

She then realises that there is a further unpleasantness: part of her is
chilly and uncomfortable. Her nightie is cold and wet. In her thoughts,
she asks could she have 'peed the bed'? If so, then:

she has crossed some boundary she hasn't taken into account;
no minor lapse, like forgetting how much sugar should be
combined with rhubarb for a pie. (p 3)

And at this point Aggie begins to worry about what her daughter
will say when she finds her in this state. Thus, as we grow older, body
maintenance is not just about keeping fit and preventing illness: it also
entails ways of monitoring and managing the state of the body, not
just the sight but also its smells, sounds, aches and pains.

Birthdays

In planning the Birthdays project and, in particular, in drafting the
directive issued by the Mass Observation (MO) Archive in 2002, I
wanted to test the idea that birthdays are an explicit marking of the
ageing of the individual. Just as the sight of our bodies might provide
non-negotiable biological indicators that we are growing older, the
'celebration' of our birthdays may be the sociological equivalent. In
2003, while I was analysing responses to the MO directive, I gave a
lecture titled 'Living by numbers: the significance of birthdays'. The
following is an edited version of the script.

First, why be interested in birthdays? Consider how birthdays feature
in the *Faber Book of Diaries* (Brett, 1987). It includes approximately
1,400 extracts taken from 108 published diaries and, in total, 24 of the
entries were for the diarists' birthdays. What is perhaps most striking is
that in all but three of these, the diarists specify their chronological age.

Often the entry starts with particularly short sentences. For example,
the following are the first sentences of five of these entries:

To-day is my birthday. I am to-day fourteen years old! How
very old!! (Queen Victoria)

Today it is my 18th birthday! (Queen Victoria)

To-day was my 21st birthday. (Vera Brittain)

My 35th birthday. ('Chips' Channon)

My 39th birthday. (Evelyn Waugh)

Starting a diary entry with a short declaratory sentence may reflect the urge to give the day a 'name', to make it 'special' and more than just a date. It is not insignificant that three of these opening sentences end with exclamation marks. And by adding the number, a unique identifier is created for the day, in much the same way as the actual date does. So the above are registering not just 'another birthday', but the fact that it's their 18th/21st/35th/39th birthday. In subsequent years they can refer back (possibly drawing on their diaries) to the events of that particular day. But the number also locates the birthday in a sequence of birthdays. Life is full of sequences and many events are numbered: the 40th annual conference, the fifth test match, etc. Potentially, every such event can be enumerated and documented in diaries and, as a result, events can be compared: this one with the last one, and so on.

In contrast to these opening sentences that pronounce the day to be a birthday, there were two entries in the collection, equally brief, that refer just to age:

Forty-six today; fifty in sight. (Peter Hall)

I reach the age of sixty. (Harold Nicolson)

These two diarists simply register a change in age. Peter Hall effectively declares 'I'm 46'. Only by implication is this his birthday and that he was just 45 the previous day and, like Harold Nicolson, a milestone, his 50th, is 'in sight'. He continues, in writing this entry, to relate his age to plans for the future and the further development of his career:

Forty-six today; fifty in sight. The good thing I suppose is that I have reached a point most people reach in their fifties rather than their forties, so I reckon I can sit out the swing of fashion against me.

Similarly, Chips Channon, in reaching his 35th birthday, sets age in a broader timescape. Very succinctly, he makes the contradictory claims of not knowing his age, looking younger and feeling even younger. The full entry reads:

My 35th birthday. Actually I have lied so much about my age that I forget how old I really am. I think I look 28, and know I feel 19.

This is a classic illustration of the paradox of age identified by Nikander (2002, p 214): it is so inconsequential that we can forget it, but at the same time we must remain alert as to how old we look and, if necessary, we have to lie.

The Faber anthology is a selection of the writings of the famous and published. What I wanted in planning the Birthdays project, as discussed in Chapter Four, was a rather more representative source of accounts of how 'ordinary' people experience birthdays. I wanted to test how they relate this, if at all, to a sense of growing older. So I turned to the MO Archive.

The panel in 2002 numbered around 350. For the June directive, panellists were invited to write about birthdays and, in particular, to 'explore' six areas:

- your previous birthday
- people who remember your birthday
- people whose birthdays you like to remember
- your most memorable birthday
- the significance of birthdays
- what you record in a seven-day diary.

My paper in Oxford drew upon an analysis of responses to the fifth of these. The full guidance that I offered in the directive read:

> Looking over what you have already written, what do you think is the significance of birthdays for you, your family and friends? What for you are the ingredients of 'a good birthday'? How have they changed over the years: attitudes, celebrations, experiences, cards and their messages? How do you think growing older changes the meaning of birthdays?

The intention here was to encourage panellists to reflect upon what they had already written about previous and memorable birthdays and to comment on the significance of these experiences. I was particularly interested in the comments that they might make in response to the prompt about 'growing older'.

Not surprisingly, some of the panellists were able to draw on the source of their personal diaries to detail their previous birthday. One man transcribed his diary entries verbatim:

> 2001: It wasn't until lunchtime when [my wife] realised it was my 62nd birthday today.

> 2002: Well, it's my 63rd birthday today. How many more birthdays? (L2604)

Note how both entries number the birthday, and note the short declaratory sentence that starts the second. For some respondents their coming birthday marked a substantial change in circumstances. One man wrote:

> I'll be retiring on my sixtieth which in its way will be a memorable occasion after thirty five years of shift work including twelve hour nights. The alarm clock will be tossed in the bin. (W2174)

There is here a poetic conjunction of 35 years of shift work and 12-hour nights. The symbolic act of discarding his clock echoes the comment of a GP who told me of how he had celebrated retiring on his 60th birthday by burying his stethoscope in the garden.

Birthdays may coincide with life transformations and the coincidence makes both events all the more significant. For example, the 10th birthday of the journalist, Decca Aitkenhead, was transformed by her mother's terminal illness:

> I can remember the night she died. It was a week before I was going to be 10, and she was lying in her dressing gown, leaning against a pillow. [...] "I hope you don't die on my birthday", I said. It seems such an incredible thing to have said that sometimes I think I must have invented it. But I can hear the sound of my voice – so brittle and breezy – and I know it is true. I think she smiled, and agreed it would be terrible timing. (Aitkenhead, 2005)

Similarly, an MO contributor wrote to contrast her experience of two consecutive birthdays:

> It was in December 2001 and was my 51st birthday. It was memorable because that was the day I received the news that I had the bones of a 65 year old woman, with more than a 50% chance of being in a wheelchair in 10–15 years time unless we tried to prevent that happening! A sharp contrast to the previous year, when on my 50th birthday, among the presents and cards was a box full of presents, fifty in all, ranging from the sublime to the ridiculous. (K798)

For this woman her birthday in 2001 coincided with a key life event: the news that her bones were effectively 14 years older than the rest of her body. Not only that, but in 10 to 15 years' time (when, by implication, they will be the bones of a 75- to 80-year-old woman) she will be 'in a wheelchair' unless they succeed in preventing that happening. Finally, note the way in which her 50th birthday in 2000 was celebrated by a variation on the candles theme. The two birthday accounts provide contrasting evidence of how some people mathematise age.

There are two ways of keeping track of your age as you grow older. One is to check your date of birth and undertake a simple arithmetic calculation. A 69-year-old MO panellist said she always has to work out her age in this way as she didn't believe that she's 'really as old as that' (B2154). Similarly, a 56-year-old woman found the arithmetic hard to believe:

> Nowadays I try hard not to subtract the year I was born from the year I'm living in, as the number is growing far quicker than the years are passing. Time is doing more of its variable speed thing. (A1706)

The alternative way of knowing your age is to make sure, come the birthday, that you remember to add one to the total. Here's a 76-year-old man describing the typical course of later life, starting with retirement:

> The pensionable age arrives, no more commuting, no more decent suits for work are required, every day is a Saturday, if you like, and then the birthdays become significant again, will I make seventy? Or seventy five? Other problems arise but still the anniversary is celebrated and an extra digit added to the toll. (L1504)

Some MO writers commented on the relationship between chronological age and a sense of ageing, and many implicitly acknowledge finitude. One, for example, implied that length of life is pre-determined:

> I prefer not to believe that growing older changes the meaning of birthdays – the idea that the number is finite and I've had 50 of them does not cheer me up. (G2640)

I concluded the lecture with two extracts from the MO Archive. The first comments on the significance of the day, then on special birthdays and, finally, on the significance that is given to these events:

> It is a day on which we become a year older. I'm 76 today. On 25 August I shall be 77. Not a lot of change at my age but when you are young a year makes a big difference. Especially

the birthday which marks the beginning of a new decade: 30 – 40 – 70, 80, 90! It is only the significance that we give to these figures, of course, but tradition is very strong. A friend once argued that we should not mark chronological age at all, that it only encouraged stereotyping, and I think that he had a point. (P2546)

Finally, ending on a positive note, I offered a striking example of how significance is placed on birthdays, how they can be seen as marking a transition in the course of life. Note the references to youth, times, the future and a new beginning:

It wasn't so much the presents or the party, though. It was the delight at turning 30 – leaving my 20s behind and finally feeling grown up. I was very miserable in my early 20s, suicidal at times, and by the time I met Paul at 26 I learned how to be happy but didn't really believe in my right to be happy. To me 30 was a very positive milestone – saying goodbye to those bits of my youth that had caused my misery, while still retaining enough youth and energy to leap forward and embrace the future. It was a sloughing off and a new beginning. (P2957)

I ended the Oxford lecture by discussing the question: what does it mean to be so many years of age? Some people insist that it means nothing. That chronological age is 'just a number'. What gerontologists ought to be studying, they argue (like Jan Baars: see Chapter Three), are the processes that make us grow old. Implicit in this is the aim of 'doing something about it': finding ways of avoiding growing old, or making it less difficult or depressing. Well, I argued, there's a lot of exciting biological research under way that I don't doubt will transform the ageing landscape. But even so, individuals will still live with an accumulating biography, full of dates, and a constant sense of being 'of an age', an age that is constantly increasing regardless of what does or doesn't come with it. To a much larger extent than most people realise, our lives are regulated according to chronological age. It's not just travel passes and insurance. Most of the current NHS targets are age specific and this has important consequences for the ways in which medical treatments are made available. As Michael Young has commented:

Every parent who organizes a birthday party is an unwitting agent of the state, even if its power is masked by tying every birthday to the annual 'life cycle' of the sun. The state and the sun make a powerful alliance. (Young, 1988, p 108)

In the course of undertaking the Birthdays project, I analysed the audio-diaries of Tony Benn. I wanted to see how one person commented on birthdays over the course of several decades of diary-keeping. Will he provide evidence of how our experience of this annual event changes as we grow older? Here, in 1949, is his first diary description of a birthday:

My twenty-third birthday. Today the world is heading straight for war. I wonder whether these words will ever be read by anyone who survives. [...] On this 23rd birthday of mine I am faced with the problem of what to do with my life. In a year's time I shall have left Oxford behind and shall be working for a living.

Note how this entry is oriented towards the future: of the world, the diary and his own life. Here, 20 years later, is how a birthday has to be fitted into a day dominated by work:

My forty-third birthday and the children came in with their presents in the morning, which was very sweet of them. But it was an awful day for a birthday because I had to go in very early and I was extremely tired, having been to bed so late.

Similarly, the following entry illustrates how birthdays might be celebrated at work, providing a release from interpersonal tensions.

At one stage Denis leaned over and said, "You're being very helpful. Why are you so cheerful?" I said it was my birthday in half an hour, so, as midnight struck, Denis announced, "It's Tony's birthday", and Jim started singing, and then everyone joined in: "Happy birthday to you, happy birthday to you. Happy birthday, dear Tony, happy birthday to you." I said thank you very much and that I wished I had my tape on to record it! The whole evening was a funny mixture of table-banging, shouting at each other and slightly nostalgic sentimentality. There was a lot of conning and overawing going on. [...] To bed at 3.45am and Caroline, bless her heart, wished me happy birthday, my fifty-fourth.

Tony Benn's account of his 60th birthday introduces his fear of the well-meaning but patronising ageism of younger people:

I have had five invitations to go on chat shows, because it's my sixtieth birthday on Wednesday. I suppose when you reach sixty the journalists think they can rehabilitate you as an eccentric, lovable old character. These shows would be entirely personal, nothing to do with politics, and I would be presented as an attractive person if I was prepared to go along with it on their terms. But people at home who know me as a fighter would say, 'God, he's sold out.'

In contrast, his 70th birthday was an occasion he thoroughly enjoyed, surrounded by good friends and entertaining celebrations:

My seventieth birthday and there were masses of cards and telephone calls. I really think I'm going on to the Internet – move into the high-tech age – because when I was fifty-eight in 1983 I was ready to move onto BBC computers and they really have been such a success. [...]

I went to the House of Commons by taxi for the birthday party that Ruth, Sheila, Tony Banks and Chris Mullin had organised. I don't know how to begin to describe it – it was beautiful and lovely. There must have been sixty or seventy people there. [...] The cake was a large model of the Houses of Parliament, which Ruth had had commissioned, with Big Ben at five to three: the moment that I was born.

We all went down to the Crypt, where Tony Banks made a speech by the broom cupboard and presented me with a beautiful plaque. It says, 'This historical broom cupboard is dedicated to Tony Benn, MP, on the occasion of his 70th birthday in recognition of his lifelong work for Parliament and the people, Monday 3rd April 1995.' Well, as the Speaker has removed the other plaques, I don't really know what to make of this, but I made a little speech and we went upstairs again. There were more speeches and a cutting of the cake – just lovely. I'm overwhelmed by it.

Five years later, his birthday was overlooked in the House except for another moment of patronising prejudice:

My seventy-fifth birthday. [...] I went to the House of Commons. I had put a note in to the Speaker saying that I'd like to ask a question about pensions during Social Security questions, and obligingly she called me. I made a strong point about linking pensions to earnings, and in reply

Alistair Darling, the Social Security Secretary, wished me a happy birthday and said that he was sure I was looking forward to my free television licence – which really was an insulting response.

One year later, five weeks before he finally retired from the House, he records a touching moment when, for once, work and family were joined:

There was a vote at 10.45 and I went into the Tea Room where Tommy McAvoy [a government whip] was sitting, and I said, "Tommy, it's my birthday today, so will you let me go home?"

"Yes", he said, "there is a handful of Members very bored with having to stay."

And I asked, "Can I take my boy home?"

So they all said, "Aaah", and sang "Happy Birthday". I took Hilary home and I got back at midnight.

These diary entries illustrate some of the different ways in which birthdays become significant. There is a shift from the future orientation of the earliest entries to the reminiscences associated with the latest. But through much of middle life, everyday domesticity and work dominate the course of the day. The gift-giving, cakes and singing are routine rituals that are squeezed in, reaffirming relationships in the context of relentlessly busy lives.

Transformations

Mike Bury (1982) introduced the idea that the onset of chronic illness constitutes a 'biographical disruption'. He described how rheumatoid arthritis, in particular, involved 'a recognition of the worlds of pain and suffering, possibly even of death, which are normally only seen as distant possibilities or the plight of others'. Routines and the 'normal' rules of reciprocity and mutual support involving individuals, families, and wider social networks are disrupted. The plans that individuals may hold for the future have to be re-examined (Bury, 1982, p 169). The account in the MO Archive, quoted earlier, of the news of ageing bones and the prospect of using a wheelchair is a good example of such a disruption, one that perversely coincided with a birthday.

The diagnosis of chronic illness is just one example of how individuals can encounter turning points in their lives. Over the last 50 years, gerontology has debated the question of whether retirement and entry into old age is a similarly transformative experience. There is much evidence that the idea that there is a threshold that sets old age apart has dominated the thinking of many cultures. It is linked, of course, to the tendency to categorise: a threshold justifies categorisation and makes the crossing of the threshold easier to implement. But it is also linked to prejudice and the tendency for people to distance themselves from those who appear different, particularly if stigmatised by stereotyping beliefs. In this context, 'the old' are simply one of many groups that are viewed negatively by those in the mainstream.

Pat Thane has considered the history of how old age has been defined:

> But it has long been recognized – and commented upon by classical and early modern writers, as well as by British observers in the nineteenth century and in the 1980s and 1990s – that old age is not simply definable by birthday and there is great individual variety in the pace and timing of human ageing. (Thane, 2000, p 4)

Despite this reservation regarding the significance of birthdays, chronological age has been used in government policy throughout the 20th century to mark the onset of old age. As a result, Thane acknowledges its relevance but questions its 'accuracy':

> It is statistically convenient to describe the proportions of people aged 65 and over through the twentieth century and projected for the twenty-first, but it is questionable whether 65, which was an accurate enough marker of the onset of old age for most people in 1925, when it became the state pensionable age, remains so in 2000 or will be in 2050. (Thane, 2000, p 14)

Is there a threshold in the lives of individuals that marks the onset of old age? State pensionable age, of course, is something that changes, if not transforms, the financial basis of everyday life. Is it accompanied by any kind of ceremony? In my experience, the link between the receipt of pensions and retirement from employment is becoming more complex, entailing a number of decisions and events and potentially straddling a number of years. Arguably deca-birthdays, the 'big ones', have increasingly been seen to mark thresholds rather than the bureaucratically determined pensionable age. But does old age begin with the 60th or the 70th birthday, or indeed the 50th or the 75th? Sometime in the early 1970s, I tore out the following short story from a local newspaper:

GEORGE BOWS OUT WITH SUPER PARTY

Stafford pensioner Mr George Hillman saw the truth in the song: 'Enjoy yourself, it's later than you think'. He was not going to be caught with money in the bank. After all, "you can't take it with you when you go". So George, aged 70, of Marston Road, drew out his life savings – several hundred pounds – to hold one memorable party with more than 100 relatives and friends. No expense was spared on food and drink and there was a present for every guest.

George, who held the party in St John's Church Hall, said: "I thought it was a much better idea than leaving the money in my will. Everybody enjoyed themselves, including me, and you cannot enjoy your own funeral, however grand it is."

George, who is a 'lollipop' man is now down to his last few pounds, but he is happy and contented – especially as his spending spree had the full approval of his wife, Hilda.

Of many such cuttings, this is one that has subsequently remained in my mind. There is something charmingly positive and cavalier about George's decision, not unlike Margaret Goodchild's decision to sink her savings in one last trip to the French Alps. All sorts of questions are left begging however: not least, whether some of his guests might have preferred to receive help with their own 'cost of living' rather than receive an invitation to one big party. But what caught my attention was the stark contrast between 'his life savings', which he drew out of the bank, and 'his last few pounds' that he was left with. For him, the party was a bridge-burning, once-in-a-lifetime occasion, never to be repeated.

The decision was prompted by his recognition of finitude; not only that you 'can't take it with you' and you 'can't enjoy your funeral' but, most significantly, that 'it's later than you think'. Whereas some gerontologists would urge him to recognise that he might still live a further 10, 20 or even 30 years, he could just as legitimately claim that in reality there may be no more than five or even two years remaining. Were he to postpone his 'one last party' for five years, say, he might not have lived to enjoy it, and then Hilda would have been left widowed and adjusting to a new life without George.

Cumming and Henry (1961), in developing disengagement theory, drew upon the argument that widowhood for women is equivalent to retirement from work for men. Setting aside the implicit sexism and structural determinism, it is interesting that they overlooked the fact that retirement is a transition that is managed and usually scheduled in advance, whereas becoming widowed is an experience that can happen at any age without forewarning. Tony Benn wrote movingly about his 'immeasurably sad' experience of becoming widowed (Benn, 2003, pp 637–41). Similarly, Caroline Moorehead described how, from the age of 62, Martha Gellhorn mourned the death of her mother 'for the rest of her life' (2006, p 3):

> She [Martha] was dazed by grief and, talking to no one, crept into bed and spent a week sleeping, trying to adjust herself to a loss she had spent her entire life fearing. 'Since she was the only person who ever possessed me,' she told a friend, 'life is unlivable without her.' (Moorehead, 2006, p 372)

Daniel Cole, one of the TOG recorders, provided a similarly moving account of the death of his mother, Rebecca. On 9 December, Daniel emailed us to bring us up to date on his mother's failing health:

> The overall prognosis remains limited however; the aim of all current treatment is palliative only but within that if Mum's mind can properly get round being in a wheelchair and partially incontinent (signs are she's making the very best of it) then the quality of whatever time she has left can remain good. The doctors are talking 'some months' but notably not weeks or anything like 'maybe a year'.

Over the following eight weeks Rebecca remained in hospital. Daniel was constantly surprised by her ups and downs but then, on 5 February, he wrote:

> I go to nursing home to make final arrangements for admission. [It] is a nice place which Mum had expressed a strong liking for. In the evening Mum develops very severe, unbearable pain which (in my view) the hospice people should have had controlled by now. 3 hours wait for doctor and nurses to arrive. Very distressing for Mum, and of course me. Eventually after a team of people call to get Mum free of pain she falls asleep. Marie Curie nurse fronts up at 10.00pm.

Rebecca died at 5.50am the following morning. The day after her funeral Daniel wrote a moving message to her in his diary. With her death, his was now the oldest generation in his family. The following week he took his grandson on the long journey to visit the house where Rebecca had been born and brought up, the house where Daniel himself had been raised. Various mementoes were left and collected and, for Daniel, the experience 'brought a lump to my throat and tears to my eyes'. Returning home he slept 'the clock round', waking up feeling 'oddly revived and revitalised, emotionally and mentally': a turning point in the course of his own life.

Frances Partridge's diary (1990) similarly includes a powerful account of the death of her husband, Ralph. He died on 1 December 1960 at Ham Spray, their home. She stayed with Janetta, her friend, in London over the following two weeks and then joined two other friends, Julia and Lawrence Gowing, in the south of France. There she occupied her time helping them sort out the paintings and books of a friend, also recently deceased: the painter, Simon Bussy. She wrote her first diary entry after Ralph's death on 17 December. It begins:

> I cannot write about these last seventeen days – not *now*, anyway. Nor can I see that I shall ever want to remember them. It's been all I could do to live them. (Partridge, 1990, p 9)

There followed expressions of grief punctuating the details of more mundane activities:

> Writing letters sitting up in bed before my breakfast tray arrived, an agonizing process, drawing tears and blood. I can only do a few at a time. (18 December, p 11)
>
> When ten o'clock came round I toppled into bed and despairing desolation. Can I possibly go on? The word NEVER echoed horribly through my brain and I lay flat and passive under the repetitive pain of it. But I said I wouldn't write of it and what is the use? I'll only *en passant* note that the life-instinct makes it impossible for me to think either backwards or forwards, and I live uneasily on a tiny island of the dreadful present. (19 December, p 12)

She wrote to a friend, Gerald Brenan, about suicide:

> It seems to me so much more logical and dignified and altogether respectable than continuing to struggle as I seem to be doing. [...] but the fact remains I am fighting

desperately to keep my worthless life going. (Chisholm, 2009, p 258)

On 20 December her son Burgo arrived to join them, and Frances started to work on a translation. She confided in her diary:

I notice no-one ever mentions Ralph's name to me, though I often do to them. I find this horribly unearthly. [...] Letters 'of sympathy' still arrive and I toil painfully through the answers. [...] I long to hear from friends [...] but naturally no-one wants to think about me, though they wish me well. Only my own efforts can make me otherwise than a black spot to be avoided, and I have no strength to make efforts. (22 December; Partridge, 1990, p 13)

So the days pass. A sort of routine takes shape and I'm getting better at dealing with the surface of things. Rather to my surprise I find I want to be alone quite a lot in my room. When my thoughts grow unbearable I either translate (in the day-time) or take to dope at night. (28 December, p 14)

I see it is vital to keep a tight grip on my reins; any loosening of them, any momentary wondering what to do next, is fatal. I simply *must* make the decision, however arbitrary, to do *something* – it hardly matters what. (31 December, p 15)

She was visited by relatives of Simon Bussy and described her conversations with them in her diary, before writing:

This is all pretty dull, but it has been the only intrusion from the outside world, so it was a relief to have to think of it. The first day of 1961 was dripping and foggy, cold, dank and pitch dark. Feeling as I do, on the rack all the time, these outward misfortunes make no difference. I'm in a Japanese concentration camp anyway and expect nothing more than survival. But for what? Heaven knows. (2 January, p 18)

I somehow do manage to work and I clutch at it like a drowning man. I have to – I'd sink otherwise, not that I do it effectively or well. (3 January, p 19)

On 5 January, she wrote:

It looks anyway as if Julia and I have another week here. I think of it as 'doing time' and try to avoid remembering that nothing lies beyond but more time. (p 19)

She remained in the hotel until 12 January, when the Gowings returned to England and she moved to join friends in Menton. On 17 January she was ill in bed ('I longed to be dead', p 22). She recovered but, following her first venture outside the hotel, wrote:

> Left my prison and found it was still with me. The whole world is a prison to me and I seem to have adopted the humble, crushed attitude of a person in a concentration camp, expecting nothing – certainly not happiness – glad to have the attention of a prison mouse or spider, futilely grateful to be alive. (20 January, p 23)

Two days later she again wrote about the mice, spiders and concentration camp. But she also talked to a friend about 'my future'. Chisholm says she 'tried to peer into the future' (2009, p 260). At the beginning of February, Frances wrote:

> These pitiful scribblings are like scratches on the vast monolith of my desolation, and I only go on having recourse to them because they are in some way an outlet. Alas, I can't tell Ralph what a desert my life is without him, describe the extraordinary wooden unreality of it. [...] Yet I *can't* get down to the deeper areas of my misery – because it's a region so painful that the scalpel (being held in my own hand) recoils instinctively from the exposed nerve. (1 February; Partridge, 1990, p 29)

She moved to another hotel, resisting a decision to return to England. She wrote to various friends discussing where she might live in the future, and then she confides in her diary:

> Suddenly, this French episode, like the last phase of the eclipse, is rushing to its conclusion. My hands are already tightening a little (as I foretold) around my prison bars. The shadow of the world to come was thrown on my page by two letters from Craig [her solicitor], in answer to a vague one asking him how much money he thought I would have and whether he agreed I must sell Ham Spray. (25 February, p 37)

This entry marks a turning point as she returns to oversee the sale of Ham Spray and the purchase of a flat in London. It is clear from her diaries and from Chisholm's biography that this response to her bereavement was a transformation, a point at which she reconstituted herself and her relations with her family and friends by turning her back on a life based in Ham Spray.

As the first anniversary of Ralph's death approached, her friends were 'anxious and watchful' (Chisholm, 2009, p 266). On 1 December 1961, her diary entry began: 'Yesterday's anniversary is over'. She had thought she would be 'immune' but realised she preferred not to be alone and went to the cinema with a friend. On 4 December she received a letter from Gerald, which read: 'This is the saddest of anniversaries and I thought I'd write you a letter to say – but what is there to say? Only that I haven't forgotten it.' In the days that followed she found that she was still finding it hard to control her tears.

Another year later, at the end of 1962, she was now mourning the loss of her son, and she wrote: 'I've thought a lot lately, with more detachment and even pleasure than I've been able to before, about my life with Ralph' (Partridge, 1990, p 140). And so her 'new life' proceeded.

These various examples demonstrate how life can be transformed by experiences that become increasingly common as we grow older. Some transformations can be interpreted as rejuvenating, 'a fresh start', a new anniversary to celebrate, while others leave a person feeling devastated and uncertain about their ability to survive. Typically these changes radically upset all sorts of continuing routines: life is put on hold and then revived. It is only when the transformation is complete that routines are re-established, possibly unchanged but possibly, as in the case of Frances Partridge, completely different as life is started afresh in a new home.

Questions for discussion

1 Which do you value most highly: experience or expertise?

2 Have you seen yourself on video recently, or heard your recorded voice? When did you last look in the mirror and think about age?

3 Is it possible to celebrate a birthday 'agelessly', totally ignoring the number and not giving it a moment's thought?

4 In how their hair is dressed, Freda and Connie have a different view. Do you like your appearance to be age appropriate or age defying? Or have you never thought about it?

5 Apart from illness, bereavement and retirement, what other later life events might be life transforming?

SIX

Being older

Age is a relative phenomenon as well as an absolute one. What does it mean to say that A is older than B? What is the significance of age for the relationship between two people? If A is chronologically older than B, can B be older than A in other ways? Well, regarding that last question, I remember at the age of 21 being the proud owner of a second-hand Austin A30 and being taught to drive by my younger brother who, unlike me, had passed his driving test first time: an example of how the teacher-pupil relationship does not necessarily reflect differences based on chronology.

Parents and children

The parent–child relationship, possibly more than anything else, socialises us as children into a social order that incorporates age. It is probably fair to say that relative age first impinges upon our consciousness when we absorb as fact that our parents are not just taller, heavier and stronger, but also older than us. They're 'grown up', adults; we're just 'kids'. The distinction could hardly be starker.

Birthdays are numbered and when we learn to count, perhaps around our third birthday, we realise that thirty-something (or however old our parents might be) is an awful lot older than three. Moreover, our fourth birthday seems a long way off, never mind our 34th. So we quickly learn that interpersonal age differences can be indicated by number and by generation.

Childhood birthdays are complicated events. The fact that on that day you are a 'special person' creates various tensions and anxieties, and some of these may survive well into later life. Here is how one Mass Observation (MO) writer described her childhood birthdays:

> Looking back at my childhood my parents always made a great fuss of my birthday – there was a big party, lots of presents & a 'rainbow' cake.
>
> However I can remember lots of the birthdays somehow went wrong by the end of the day & 'ended in tears' usually because I got what they called 'over-excited'. Looking back I think my parents expected so much from my

birthday – I always had a new frock made by my mother – usually something frilly & decorative. So one of their disappointments was that I was a very plain child who actually did not live up to the dress. Then the party always involved all the usual children's party games: 'Postman's Knock', 'I Sent a Letter to My Love', 'The Farmer's in his Den', 'Nuts in May', 'Blind Man's Buff', etc. etc. – the games were more competitive as we got older. I was a bad sport & didn't like losing or looking a fool so often came out of these events rather badly. They 'ended in tears' as threatened.

Parents often complain about children being 'overexcited' – I still hear parents say this as though it's something the CHILD creates. Usually it is the parents who have wound the child up with promises & by the parents' own anticipations – however the parent knows when they want to call a halt to the excitement – the child spirals up & up (often ending in a smack or other disgrace).

Partly triggered by your survey I had a discussion with colleagues about childhood celebrations & parties. Most could remember the kind of anti-climax I spoke of – the feeling of having actually been naughty, etc.

The other thing I remember is being ashamed of my parents making idiots of themselves. My Mum & Dad were amateur dramatics enthusiasts. Dad would always do a comic song at my parties dressed up as 'Varmer Giles' or as a Mad Professor, etc. All the other children would be shrieking with laughter. I nearly died of shame. My mother would sing at the piano 'There are fairies at the bottom of our garden' or 'Mary Virginia Ursula Ella had for her birthday a lovely umbrella'. I couldn't bear her singing in public as it always made me want to cry. She is now nearly 90 & it is only in the last 5 or 6 years I've been able to bear hearing her sing. (N1592)

This account reveals the power of parents to dictate the ways in which childhood birthdays are celebrated, and the constant risk of humiliation and embarrassment for the child. The final sentence confirms the way in which a lifelong relationship can be interpreted in terms of changing attitudes to particular forms of behaviour.

Children face a further complication in that some have birthdays at a difficult time in the school year, some at a good time and some when they are always on holiday. Here is what another MO writer wrote:

Reflecting on birthdays & considering why they are special & why I always want to celebrate, I keep thinking back to being at junior school. Being the youngest in the year, my birthday right at the end of our academic year, I still had to drink milk when the other children didn't have to. There were four of us who had to be held in at playtime to drink that warm milk through the pink straw! Birthday parties were a flop because people didn't remember after the long six week holiday – or being Bank Holiday had gone away. When I went on to secondary school & met closer friends & when I met my first boyfriend having a birthday in the summer holidays was great. No school. (W 2959)

Tensions can complicate teenage birthdays. In her novel *Unless*, Carol Shields offers the following exchange between Reta Winters and her daughter, Christine:

"Thank you for releasing me from your loins," my middle daughter, Christine, said to me today, October twelfth, which happens to be her seventeenth birthday.

Loins. Where had she got a word like loins? "It's from Tom Wolfe's novel," she explained. "It means uterus. Or else womb."

She was standing in the kitchen and eating a breakfast of leftover pizza and washing it down with a mug of apple juice.

"You're welcome," I said, and then, to keep the rhythm of our conversation going, I added, "It was a pleasure."

"You don't mean that," she said. She had exactly two minutes to put on her jacket and run down to the road for the school bus. "Giving birth cannot be filed under one of life's pleasures."

"Well," I said, working for a noncommittal tone, "now how do you know that, Chris? How exactly?" I glanced at the clock over the stove and she watched me glance at the clock and I watched her watching me. Her mouth was stretched with half-chewed pizza crust, her strong, healthy teeth going at it. Not a pretty sight, though I adore this slightly chunky daughter of ours and attempt every day of my life to keep her affectionate and close to us.

"Well, really," she said, exasperated, "I did watch that video on home birth. And so did you. And so did your husband." (Shields, 2003, pp 153-4)

The awkwardness of adolescence and the ways in which it complicates the parent-child relationship can subsequently become the object of shared reminiscences. Here is the novelist Jean Rhys, writing to her daughter:

> Do you remember the time I bought you a hand bag from Paris – for one of your birthdays? I thought it lovely – but you were not pleased because it was a *little girl's* bag you said and you were at least fourteen or fifteen – I forget. "*Can't* you understand that I am grown up" you said very indignantly. Well do you know I still don't – quite. It is my private and particular belief that very few people change after well say seven or seventeen. Not really. They get *more* this or *more* that and of course look a bit different. But inside they are the same. (6.3.1955; Rhys, 1985, p 122)

These examples illustrate ways in which the parent-child relationship changes over the years. The initial power of the parents is replaced by more complex beliefs and practices.

The parent-child relationship is sometimes invoked in comments on changes and differences. Calculations about interpersonal age differences become complicated when comparisons are made between 'our age' now, 'their age' then, and what their age would be now. Here's one of the more exotic examples from MO:

> One of the reasons I am so good at remembering birthdays is that I have a little book 'The Floral Birthday Book'. Each day has a bit of verse and a coloured painting of a flower. My grandfather gave it to his sister on her 14th birthday – she died soon after, many years later he gave it to me because she had the same birthday as I have – I have treasured it ever since he gave it to me. On the 16th August this year I will be 79, the book will be 124 years old, and if his sister were still alive she would be 138 years old! Fancy living to that age – that's a really horrid idea, and unlikely, very unlikely. (D1697)

Most MO writers offer more prosaic, but just as telling, comparisons:

> I was 56 years old in May – quite an achievement, my mother only lived to 39 yrs and my father to 59 yrs. So by their score, I've had a good innings. (F218)

Comparisons are often made with those who have died:

Every so often, my mother will say 'Your father would have been – years old next week.' He died in a road accident when I was 3 years old. (H1745)

The idea that, eventually, roles reverse and old age is a second childhood is widely accepted and deployed in everyday exchanges (Hockey and James, 1993, p 17). It reflects the circular view of life: the rise and fall of the journey from cradle to grave. Conflicting expectations surrounding this idea colour the unfolding history of many parent-child relationships. Sometimes, after a phase of resistance, the parent begins to defer to the views of their now-adult children. The parent might anticipate the switch in power and responsibilities with a degree of resignation. Here is an example, an extract from a letter received by the actor Tom Courtenay from his mother (Courtenay, 2000, pp 204-6):

28th May 1959

Dear Tom

[…] I hope I arent talking queer and people will remark on it. Then I'll get put in an institution and you and your father looking weary will have to come and get me out. When you was home you said people are stupid when they are old. Maybe that is what is happening to me. Hell! […]

Love Mam Dad and Ann

At that time, Tom was at the Royal Academy of Dramatic Art, and his mother was 45, living in Hull with his father and Tom's sister, Ann. Three years later, at the beginning of 1962, she was in hospital being treated for cancer and, while there, she fell and broke her leg. Tom was busy filming *The Loneliness of the Long-Distance Runner* and she was visited by his father and Ann:

She was moved to the broken limb department of the Hull Royal Infirmary. Pointlessly, as it turned out, for there was no way her leg would ever mend; but at least it was easier for Ann and Dad to get to see her. I wrote to her, and she wrote to me. I think these last four letters are heroic – she even managed a title. Perhaps the act of writing made her feel better. Or was it simply that she wanted to keep the worst from me? Ann and Dad were not so spared. She didn't shield them from her rage and her bitterness. (Courtenay, 2000, p 361)

Tom was there when she died:

> I had missed the previous weekend's visit, when, Dad told
> me, she had been childlike and as lively as anything. (p 370)

There are many similar autobiographical accounts of the later life,
dependency and eventual death of a parent, and it is often the case that
the final image is described as 'childlike'.

The age at which we become parents depends on fertility and on
social norms, including those associated with marriage. Women are
fertile for a limited period in their lives, essentially the period between
menarche and menopause. The biological details of fertility underpin
a complex array of cultural expectations and the overall result is that
relatively few women in the UK become mothers either before the
age of 15 or after 45. Given this, it is important to note that those who
have daughters at the age of 20 may well become grandmothers at the
age of 40, and so it is possible, and broadly acceptable, for mother and
daughter to become pregnant and give birth at the same time. The
result of this is that the association between chronological age and
intra-family generational identity is not necessarily straightforward
and some confusion can easily arise.

The availability of treatment for infertility means that there is
bureaucratic regulation that constrains age and pregnancy. The
guidelines of the National Institute for Health and Clinical Excellence
specify that treatment should be available for women aged 23 to 39,
and in vitro fertilisation is not recommended for women over the age
of 42 'because the chances of a successful conception are thought to
be too low to justify the treatment'. The success rates in 2006 were
29% for women under 35, 11% for those aged 40 to 42, 5% for those
aged 43 or 44 and less than 1% over that age.[1]

Despite this guidance, there is a growing demand from older women,
particularly following the success of Adriana Iliescu to give birth to
twins in 2005 at the age of 66. Following this news story, the medical
director of a clinic specialising in providing in vitro fertilisation for
older women was quoted as saying:

> We believe in giving them [older women] a chance.
> Certainly the age limit might be pushed. Women are living
> longer and healthier lives. At the turn of the century women
> were dying before the menopause, when now they survive
> into their eighties. So there has been a massive increase in
> life expectancy in one century. I don't believe in an upper
> age limit. It depends on the circumstances. We would not

treat anyone of the Romanian woman's age. It is against the interest of any unborn child to have a mother of this age. A doctor who provides this treatment is not thinking about his patients, the mother or baby.

It does smack of double standards that men can father children at any age. But women still assume the role of carers in society, whether that is fair or not. If I were faced with a 52-year-old woman with a younger husband I might consider [treating them]. But it might be different with a 49-year-old woman with a 70-year-old husband. (Laurance, 2005)

It was not explained why it would be against the interests of the child to be born to a mother of 66. However, comments posted on the internet indicate that many people disapproved on the grounds that the mother might well die before the child becomes an adult: 'it is going to be the child who ends up suffering, losing a mother way ahead of time'. However, another comment suggested that 'a nearly 70-year-old woman obviously does not have the energy and the health to take care of a newborn and be running around after the infant'.[2] These comments illustrate well the confidence that people have in the universal assumptions they make about age.

Siblings

Age differences matter, even when slight. The question of 'who is the older' is typically resolved by recourse to chronological age. In September 2010 the BBC issued the following report on the new leader of the Labour Party:

To some extent, Ed Miliband has spent much of the first 40 years of his life in the shadow of his older, better-known brother David, the former foreign secretary. He did the same course – Philosophy, Politics and Economics – at Oxford University, at the same college, and followed David into a similar backroom role in the Labour Party, albeit on different sides of the Tony Blair/Gordon Brown divide. The two even lived in neighbouring flats in the same building for a while. They both sat in Gordon Brown's cabinet, with Ed filling the less high profile role of climate change and energy secretary. Ed used to introduce himself at meetings as 'the other Miliband'.

His stunning victory in the Labour leadership contest may mean David will soon have to start using that line. We can only speculate about what effect this sudden upheaval in the fraternal pecking order will have on their relationship, which they never tired of telling us during the leadership election is 'close'. (Wheeler, 2010)

In this account, Ed's age (40 years) is immediately followed by David's relative age (older) which is then associated with various differences ('better-known', 'different sides', 'less high profile role'). At the same time the report emphasises their sameness (course, college, etc.). Until now, the younger sibling ('the other one') has been overshadowed, but now the 'pecking order' has been overturned. This is a vivid example of the attention given to relative age in the discussion of political relations.

In 2008, two Timescapes projects, *Siblings and Friends* and *The Oldest Generation* (TOG), collaborated in a study of siblings (Bytheway et al, 2008). The aim was to engage the general public in all parts of the UK in exploring the significance of sibling relations throughout life, but particularly in childhood and later life. We invited people to send us postcards, either virtual postcards through a website or real postcards available at mounted displays in locations such as Regional Offices of the Open University. The postcard requested basic information (age and sex) on each sibling with a linked space for a brief, optional description or comment.

The following is an extract from the response of Muriel Pawson, born in 1949:

My sister is a year and ten months older than me and will forever remain my 'big sis', though I'm not sure she's entirely happy with what she thinks I imply by this – i.e. issues of power and status – while I struggle how to explain the feeling of being a second-born without reference to how first-borns, for some time at least and albeit unwittingly, 'lead the way'. My sister and I lived together with our parents for 16 years, until my sister left home to go to university.

Note how Muriel translates relative age into a distinction between first-born and second-born, and how she sees the former as having the advantage of 'leading the way' (if only for 'some time at least'). Here is another lengthier response, from Olive Jamieson, born in 1954:

I was the youngest in a family of four, 3 girls and 1 boy. We were very spread out in ages. My two sisters [Alice and

Beryl] had the same father; my mother divorced him after
it was discovered he was sexually abusing my eldest sister.
We called mother 'mam'. She had another relationship
with a man who would not marry her and as that was in
the 1940s there was probably quite a lot of stigma attached.
She went to work for my father as a housekeeper and then
ended up marrying him. My mother was 39 when I was
born and my father was 49, so they always seemed old to
me – especially my dad. My parents separated when I was
2 and I used to hate having to go and see my dad once a
week – I felt ashamed to be seen with such an old man. It
was a very matriarchal family. Influenced by Granny and
Aunties. I loved my sisters even though they were much
older. My eldest sister already had a daughter when I was
born and had moved away from home. As my mother
was often ill my eldest sister, Alice, often acted as another
mother to me. It was really when we were older that I really
thought of her as a sister.

Alice (born 1936)

She was such a warm-hearted person who would take you
under her wing. [...] It was only when Alice was in her 50s
that she confided in me what had happened to her. [...]

Beryl (born 1942)

As a child I thought she was so glamorous and sophisticated.
I remember watching her spit on a little block of black
mascara and do her eyes. [...] I loved my sister's boyfriend
she had when I was little [Denis ...] I remember going into
town with them and Beryl saying you can have whatever
you want. Denis was trying to impress big sis by getting
something for little sis. I chose a manicure set with a
ballerina on the front. [...] I love Beryl dearly but we tend
to stay in touch by occasional phone calls.

Fred (born 1947)

Fred was the closest sibling in age to me and so we used to
rough and tumble. I got used to mixing with the 'big boys'
via my brother. If anyone threatened me – e.g. they were
going to steal my marbles – I would tell them I was going
to get my big brother onto them, then they would leave

me alone. [...] My brother helped me when I was very ill in my early 20s, for which I am very grateful, but sadly we had a falling out and I have had hardly any contact with him in more than 20 years. Fred is the only other sibling to have any higher educational qualifications. After being told that he was 'slow' and lazy at school, he later studied and attained two degrees.

Our request for separate details on each sibling generated many detailed accounts of early family life such as this. Each description spells out an age distinction that, although related to chronological time ('very spread out in ages') and many chronological ages (39, 49, 2, 50s, early 20s all feature in Olive's response), is essentially relative, as indicated by terms such as 'big sis', 'little sis' and 'closest sibling'.

Couples

Over the last few decades, marriage has become a rather looser institution than it used to be. The Office for National Statistics (ONS) has recently reported that the provisional 2008 marriage rates for England and Wales are the lowest since rates were first calculated in 1862 (ONS, 2010c). Moreover, an increase in second (and further) marriages has led to an increase in the average ages at marriage: over the past decade, the mean age at marriage for men has increased by nearly five and a half years and for women by just over four and a half years, to 36.5 and 33.8 years respectively in 2008.

Despite this loosening of the institution, the fact remains that most adults are married, and marriage remains a common experience and another anniversary to celebrate thereafter. The total number of marriages in England and Wales in 2008 was over 230,000. What can we learn from marriage statistics about age and age differences?

In 1974, using national data on the ages of all those who married in 1971 in England and Wales, I presented a paper addressing these questions to the annual conference of the British Sociological Association. I began by expressing the view that there is more to be learnt from such data than the conclusions published in official reviews. I commented on the notable fact that in four out of five marriages, the woman is younger than the man. The relevant table for 1971 (Table J, Registrar General of England and Wales, 1973) also confirmed that most people married in their early 20s to someone in the same five-year age category. Was there anything more to be learnt, I asked, from what appeared to be a standard two-dimensional bell-like statistical distribution? I went on to calculate the statistics presented in Table 6.1. This confirms the fact that for all age combinations, the woman is most likely to be the younger partner, and that this is most likely in marriages with large age differences. So, whereas the woman is the elder in more than one in three marriages when both partners are in their 40s, the equivalent proportion is less than one in 10 when there is a 20-year age difference. In so far as one is old enough to be the parent of the other, then this is largely characteristic of men: a man marrying a woman young enough to be his daughter.

Table 6.1: Percentage of marriages in which the woman is the elder, by age combinations of the elder and younger partner. All marriages, England and Wales, 1971

Age of the older	Age of the younger											
	-20	20-	25-	30-	35-	40-	45-	50-	55-	60-	65-	70-
20-	8											
25-	3	19										
30-	4	14	30									
35-	2	11	19	34								
40-	3	9	13	24	37							
45-	-	7	9	17	26	38						
50-	-	4	5	11	19	27	35					
55-	-	-	-	7	10	14	21	29				
60-	-	-	-	-	6	9	14	16	32			
65-	-	-	-	-	-	5	8	8	16	28		
70-	-	-	-	-	-	-	-	6	8	15	31	
75-	-	-	-	-	-	-	-	-	5	9	16	26
80-	-	-	-	-	-	-	-	-	-	-	-	16

I then calculated the same percentages for each age category for women and then for men (Table 6.2).

What this reveals is that the chance of the woman being the elder is nearly 50% when she is aged 25-29 years: she is nearly as likely to marry a man under 25 as one aged 30 or more. Moreover, it is notable that a man aged 45-49 is more likely to marry someone older than himself than is a man aged 30-34. This seemed to reflect the entry into 'the marriage market' of women who had previously been married people and, in particular, the re-entry of widows, a consequence in part of the tendency of younger women to marry older men.

What I was keen to develop in 1974 was a way of using these demographic statistics to uncover ways in which changes in the age-specific characteristics of the population might affect the individual life course. It still seems appropriate to consider how marriage statistics might reflect wider patterns relating to cohabitation and other forms of social networking. The opportunities that we have to form lasting one-to-one relations, it would seem, are limited by age and age differences. This is due not just to the norms imposed by the family, the law and other social institutions, but also to changes in the characteristics of the population of 'available and willing partners'. What this argument implies for research methodology is the need to shift the focus from the individual to the network, and to questions such as: how do changes in networks over time reflect and affect changes in the individual life course?

Table 6.2: Percentage of marriages in which the woman is the elder, by age. All marriages, England and Wales, 1971

Age	Male	Female
16-	40	7
20-	24	22
25-	20	46
30-	19	45
35-	21	42
40-	26	38
45-	27	37
50-	24	35
55-	22	35
60-	21	38
65-	19	42
70-	14	52
75-	9	62
80-	5	73
85-	3	87

Networks

It has long been argued that social networks are critical for support in later life (Thomése et al, 2005). Through the help of friends, relatives and neighbours, it is argued, older people can remain living in their own homes for far longer than might otherwise be the case. 'Close-knit' communities are popularly seen as providing such support, and the implication here is that the needs of older residents will be observed, and appropriate action taken as a result of the frequent contacts implied by the term 'close-knit'. The term 'convoy' has been used in studies of how networks are sustained over time, particularly in the face of attrition and changing relationships (Antonucci et al, 2009).

Some relationships in later life are lifelong while others are more recent, including those developed in response to need. In researching ageing in the context of whole lives, it is important to take account of the length of time each relationship has existed. The part played in a person's life by an 80-year-old neighbour can, potentially, be taken on by a new neighbour, but nothing can make up for the loss of an 80-year-old sibling. Indeed, relationships may exist for no more than a few minutes between the people queuing at a bus stop. These may be defined as 'weak links' but, arguably, they may be critical in resolving an immediate crisis and may in time become much more significant (Granovetter, 1983). However, in maintaining a secure and continuing sense of self, there can be little doubt that most people need a well-established set of close relationships. The importance of such networks for sustaining this sense of ontological security is evident in the following comments from MO writers about the importance of birthday cards:

> I like to get cards, presents are very nice but, to me, as long as I'm sent a card I know I have been remembered. (D156)

> The most important thing is to be remembered with a card. I always say it doesn't matter about presents but cards are a must. (B1771)

> I always send cards to family members and some friends. I list all the birthdays in my address book and try not to forget any. (S2581)

Reliance on such contact, however, has long-term risks, as is evident in the following rather wild generalisation:

> For some older people it is just another day – nothing special happens, they get less and less cards and presents as their friends and relations die. (J1890)

The size of networks is something that has concerned those researchers who have been developing the convoy model, and there is evidence that a decline in size is statistically associated with both age and poor health (Litwin and Shiovitz-Ezra, 2006). Most of this research, however, has been cross-sectional and, in this context, age is treated as just one of a number of key variables. Thomése and colleagues have reported that research has not revealed a general decline in total network size with age: 'networks only get smaller at very old age, mainly due to health changes' (Thomése et al, 2005, p 464), but they also note that the effects of specific role changes have not been adequately researched longitudinally.

Chisholm's biography of Frances Partridge is particularly detailed in documenting her wide social network (Chisholm, 2009). A total of 187 people are named in the biography. Of these, 32 were born between 1890 and 1910, within 10 years of Frances' own birth: they were her age peers. Within this group of 32, four friends died in the

1930s, including Dora Carrington, who committed suicide, and Julian Bell, who died in the Spanish Civil War. In 1940, 10 days after Frances had reached the age of 40, her sister, Ray, died of cancer. Although they were close, the death caused some tension between Frances and Ralph at the time: 'Frances had to deal with her grief for Ray while feeling at odds with her husband' (Chisholm, 2009, p 183).

There then followed 20 years before the next age peer died, Ralph himself (see Chapter Five). Possibly his death was particularly distressing for Frances, then aged 60, because he was the first of her age peers to have died of seemingly 'natural causes'. In contrast, during the course of that same year another of her age peers was asphyxiated by a faulty gas heater (Chisholm, 2009, p 254). Her son, Burgo, died three years later in 1963, and Chisholm offers some telling comment about the impact of these deaths on Frances:

> It was during the mid-1960s, as the double bereavement [of husband and son] that had altered her life changed, as all such losses do in time, from being an open wound to a dull, familiar ache, that Frances began to contemplate her own mortality. [...] With Eddie Sackville-West's death that summer, another friend of her youth was gone; 'Life', she wrote sadly, 'suddenly seems a mere antechamber to the tomb.' (2009, p 285)

At this point, Frances would have been astonished had anyone suggested she might live another 40 years. Chisholm records that seven age peers, all old friends, died in the years 1970 to 1974, and that the period from 1979 to 1981 was particularly hard with the deaths of another sister ('Frances noted the event without emotion', p 327), an old friend ('almost the last great friend who stood between me and the end', p 329), her widowed brother-in-law and her own brother ('she was surprised by how upset she felt when he died', p 332). Her old friend, Julia, 'the strongest link of all' with her childhood, also died in 1979. Although Frances had been expecting this, Julia's life being 'so wretched as to be not worth living' (p 328), she was surprised to be so upset:

> Why, she asked herself, had she been moved to tears? Perhaps because 'early friends become a part of one, like the yolk of an egg inside one's shell, so that I am not just me but made up of bits of Ralph, Julia, Burgo, Janetta.' (p 328)

Further deaths of friends occurred regularly through the 1980s, her sole surviving sibling dying in 1989. Meantime, her younger friends and relatives were growing older; five died during the 1980s and another five during the 1990s, all people who were more than 10 years younger than Frances:

> Inevitably, she continued to lose close friends. Lawrence Gowing died that year [1991], and Frances spoke at a memorial event at the Slade. An even greater blow fell when Eardley Knollys was found dead of a heart attack in his flat above hers. Since living in the same building they had become increasingly companionable, and she would miss him badly. She mourned the loss of 'the last bastion before complete isolation closes me in its prison'. (Chisholm, 2009, p 347)

Several of those who died in the last five years of her life were the children of her age peers. When she herself died in 2004, Janetta, her 'adopted' daughter, aged 82, and Sophie, her granddaughter, aged 41, arranged her funeral.

What this history documents is the disintegration of a substantial network over a comparatively brief period of time. In her network, Frances Partridge was exceptional only in that she lived so long. It is not difficult to imagine her attending parties in the 1950s in which she and her age peers, all in their 50s or 60s, swopped notes on their experience of age, speculating perhaps on who might live the longest. What her biography shows is that, at that time, her own personal experience of mortality was limited to the loss of her parents and their generation, and a few tragic losses such as Dora Carrington and Julian Bell. The death of Ralph not only cast her into widowhood and a solitary domestic life, but also a phase in life when her own generation would be steadily decimated. Although her social world contracted, not only through death but also through her own reduced mobility, she actively cultivated relations with younger people. Opportunities for this increased as a result of her publishing successes and public celebrations of her great age. Many times over the 40 years following the loss of Ralph she anticipated her own demise. Through work on her diaries she spent much time reliving her early adult life and defending the reputation of Ralph and others. Despite this engagement with, and commitment to, the past, she remained actively interested in contemporary events (for example, writing in her diary a telling comment about the attack on the Twin Towers in 2001), and she resisted death until the very end.

Succession

In her early adult life, Frances Partridge was a member of the 'Bloomsbury group'. She worked in the bookshop that initially gave the group its identity. She loved 'their passion for talk and ideas' (Chisholm, 2009, p 43) and, when Ralph inherited Ham Spray after Lytton Strachey's death in 1932, she became a central figure in the group's social activities. The Second World War disrupted these and by the late 1940s the group was 'past its peak' (Chisholm, 2009, p 190). Critiques were published during the 1950s and then, in the 1960s, interest in the group was revived following publication of a number of biographies. She felt that some of these were unfair, and it was this that spurred her into developing her own publishing career. In this way she 'inherited' the challenge of defending reputations and sustaining the group's values. In 1920 the group set up 'The Memoir Club' and this met intermittently until the 1960s. In the late 1940s Frances had been 'elected' as a member and she 'took up her duties again' in 1962 (Chisholm, 2009, p 268). Arguably the Club ran out of steam because it was overwhelmed by the popularity of the biographies of the older generation. But it could have survived as an increasingly well-established institution.

I recognised the importance of the concept of succession for social research when interviewing the Port Talbot steelworkers in 1984 (Bytheway, 1986). The view was expressed at the Trades Union Congress at that time that, with over one million young people without jobs, older workers should 'make way' for them. It was also widely believed among the public that older workers should accept early retirement in order to free up jobs for younger workers (McGoldrick and Cooper, 1980). Alan Walker's was a lone voice arguing, in contrast, that 'unemployment should be shared equally amongst people' and he protested that the idea of making way had been actively encouraged by the government (Walker, 1982).

The British Steel Corporation's redundancy programme was launched in 1980 as a 12-week strike in the industry came to an end. The agreement that had been reached with the union included the reduction of the workforce in Port Talbot by about 5,000. This would be achieved by the closure of some departments and by the unions calling for volunteers from other departments. The agreed package made a clear distinction between age groups. Younger redundant workers, those under 55, were to be assisted in finding work, not only through grants to cover the costs of retraining, travelling and resettlement, but also in wage supplements known as 'make-up money'. Receipt of this was conditional upon them finding alternative employment. It was a policy intended to minimise unemployment among younger workers, and to maintain continuity in the younger worker's income. In effect younger workers were expected to adjust to redundancy from the steelworks by being actively involved in the labour market, leading to work with another employer. Local firms were not slow to appreciate the implications of this: that the steel company would in effect cover some of their own employment costs.

In contrast, older workers, those who had passed their 55th birthdays, were offered (a) an immediate single payment dependent upon years of service, (b) the immediate receipt of their occupational pension, and (c) make-up money bringing their income in the first year up to 90% of their previous wages and then 80% over the following 12 months. It followed that they had little to gain, at least in the first year or so, from further employment, since this would generate little extra income. In effect the older workers were being encouraged to leave the labour market and to treat their redundancy as a form of early retirement. The cut-off age of 55 years was rigidly applied – to the extent that one man told me that when the offer was made he was still some weeks short and, in order that he should remain employed until his birthday, the union negotiated his appointment as an advisor, employed on the redundancy programme itself.

It is important to appreciate that there were other factors that the older workers took into account in accepting redundancy. For example, after 12 weeks on strike they knew that they were not as fit as they had been. Many had used the time when on strike to get on with other things in life: visiting family or repairing their homes. They knew that, when the strike was over, the workforce would be reduced in number, and it was popularly believed that those who remained would be expected to work even harder. In addition, they suspected that much of their hard-earned specialist skills and knowledge would be set aside.

When I interviewed 108 of these older workers, four years after their redundancy, I found that just over half (57 of the 108) agreed with the idea of 'making way' for the younger generation, and only one in 10 (11 in number) disagreed. A total of 15 reported that they knew the man who had taken over their job. One commented: "He's still doing my job as a matter of fact", and another, Pete Allen, offered a detailed account of his successor's circumstances:

"Did you feel you were making way for a younger man?"

"Well, I did. My job was open. The man who took my job now, I see him now and again, Jim. Well, he was 38 and he had asthma ..."

"Do you feel better about it, knowing that he's got that job?!"

"Oh, yes."

"Would he have got one if you hadn't, do you think , or ..."

"Well, put it this way, he wouldn't have gone out but they would have put him in part of the mill where the poor chap would be [panting] and then what would have happened? He'd have had a medical and they'd say 'Well, I'm awfully sorry –'. It could have been."

Many felt that the older generation had collectively made way for younger men and they did not object to this: "With me going, somebody could come and take my job, from another department. I was happy with that", said one.

Some of the interviewees had sons, nephews or neighbours working in the steelworks and described the conditions under which they were working: the longer shifts, the varied work and the pressures this was placing on the men and their families. They themselves felt relieved not to be working there any longer. They recognised that it was arduous work that younger men were physically more able to handle.

This project was a case study of how one large employer used chronological age in managing its workforce, and how this had major consequences for the employees. But at the level of individual decision-making, it was relative age rather than chronological age that was taken into account: what was important for Pete Allen was not that Jim was 38 but that he was *younger,* a man who would have struggled to remain in work had Pete not accepted the redundancy deal.

There are many other areas of life where an older person is expected to make way for 'the younger generation', allowing a younger person to step into 'the shoes' of the person who is 'retiring'. As I complete this chapter, for example, I've just heard the news that Ryan Sidebottom, the England fast bowler, is retiring from international cricket:"It is time to hand over the ball to those a little younger", he said. In reporting his decision, however, *The Guardian* (20 September 2010) commented: 'But at 32 he has been usurped by younger, sharper bowlers'.

Associated with the idea and practices of succession are those of inheritance. As you leave and younger people take your place, what do you leave behind, and what do they know about what they have inherited? I have thought about these questions with regard to the origins of the British Society of Gerontology. A meeting to set up a 'learned society' for psychologists and sociologists interested in age had been called in 1971 by Denis Bromley, Arthur Bigot and Sheila Chown, all prominent psychologists. Reflecting the aim of forging a coalition of disciplines, it was initially named the British Society of Social and Behavioural Gerontology. The following few years were not easy: seminars or one-day conferences were organised in different parts of the country but, rather than attracting researchers, members were recruited from various non-academic sources, notably voluntary organisations and local authorities. While this led to fruitful discussions and debates with some sociologists, the psychologists tended to drift away. In recent years, as various anniversaries have been celebrated, there has been growing interest in the Society's history and, in 2008, a number of us were elected 'Founding Fellows'. This was an opportunity for the older generation to indulge in some reminiscence. I was the only one who had been at the initial meeting in 1971 and I was disappointed that there was no mention of Denis, Arthur and Sheila, or of how it was a group of psychologists who initially saw the need.

So the social significance of age differences is closely tied to generational identities. To return to the family, these differences are often derived from parallels with the age difference that is typical of parents and their children. The power of these differences and how they turn on generational identity and the question of age is well illustrated by the following extract from a short story by Julian Barnes. Gregory is having his hair cut by Kelly, who has just told him that she has applied for a job in Miami. In response, Gregory asks:

> "How old are you?"
>
> "Twenty-*seven*", says Kelly, as if at the ultimate extremity of youth. Without immediate action her life would be compromised for ever; a couple more weeks would turn her into that old biddy in rollers on the other side of the salon.
>
> "I've a daughter almost your age. Well, she's twenty-five. I mean, we've another one as well. There's two of them." He didn't seem to be saying it right.
>
> "So how long you been married then?" Kelly asked in quasi-mathematical astonishment.

Gregory looked up at her in the mirror. "Twenty-eight years." She gave a larky smile at the idea that anyone could have been married for the enormous length of time that she herself had been alive.

"The elder one's left home, of course", he said. "But we've still got Jenny with us."

"Nice", said Kelly, but he could see she was bored now. Bored with him, specifically. Just another ageing geezer with thinning hair he'd soon have to comb more carefully. Give me Miami; and soon. (Barnes, 2004, pp 20-1)

This exchange begins with Kelly's age: 27. Her emphasis on the word 'seven' seems to indicate disbelief that she could be so old. To counter this, Gregory invokes his daughter's age, thereby indicating something about his own age. This prompts Kelly's reaction, not about his age but about the length of time he'd been married. He amplifies this in a statement about family transitions, distancing himself still further, to such an extent that Kelly then, seemingly, dismisses him with her own ageist defences. Rather than his middle-aged lifestyle, she preferred the prospect of life in Miami.

What I have attempted to uncover in this chapter is evidence of the social significance of age differences rather than age itself. It is often the case that, like Gregory, we are reminded of age when faced with the contrasting timescape of a different generation. When this is expressed in the context of a lifelong, continuing relationship, such as that between a parent and child, then the meanings attached to the contrast can change with time and, eventually, become the stuff of reminiscence, as Jean Rhys and her daughter found.

Questions for discussion

1   How stratified by age was your first school? Were all your friends in the same 'year'? Were you bullied by older pupils?

2   Can you think of someone of a different generation whom you think of as 'one of my best friends'? If so, can you honestly claim that the age difference is of no consequence?

3   Olive Jamieson's is a family that has a complex muddling of the generations. In such situations, do age differences help sort out family relationships? How might the significance of these differences have changed as she has grown older?

SEVEN

A great age

While I was drafting this chapter, *The Guardian* published an interview with Deborah Cavendish, the Dowager Duchess of Devonshire (Moss, 2010). When asked about the postnatal deaths of her three children she commented:

> When you are very old, you accept what has happened. You cry over some things, but not a lot. It's too distant. It's as if part of you gets nearer to it yourself, and then you think the churchyard here is very handy ...

It is not often that people describe themselves as 'very old', but when they do it is often, as here, in the course of claiming some kind of temporal distance along with acknowledging the proximity of the end.

The ebb and flow of debate over the definition of old age and the homogenising effect of any such categorisation have generated periodic interest in the idea that there is a category beyond 'ordinary' old age. This is rather different to proposals to divide the category of old people into 'the young old' and 'the old old' and, similarly, different to the more radical re-categorisation of the stages of life that launched the concept of the third age. To quote Mike Hepworth (2003, p 93):

> If we live long enough there comes a time when we really are 'in' old age and there's no escape and biological embodiment claims us at the last.

What does he mean by the idea of 'really being in old age'? In analysing documents for my 1982 study of the uses of the concept of old age, my attention was caught by some of the ways in which the word 'very' was used, and how being 'very old' was linked to 'frailty'. For example, the Secretaries of State, in their Foreword to the White Paper *Growing Older* (Department of Health and Social Security, 1981), claimed that they had in mind the needs of 'the growing numbers of elderly people – particularly the very old and frail'. Later the White Paper referred to the same group when expressing concern over the quality of life of 'elderly people, especially the very old and frail' (para 1.5). For the same project, I analysed the content of 15 editions of a well-known nursing journal and found claims such as 'Staff attitudes must change dramatically if the acute sector is to care successfully for the growing numbers of the very old.'

This association between 'very old' and frailty raises the issue of what constitutes the latter. Grenier (2007) has demonstrated how frailty is used by care providers to justify ways of categorising clients. When she interviewed older people, what she found was that they wanted a label that captured age-related vulnerability, using phrases such as 'worn out' and 'so ill' in association with frailty. Consider the following response from Martha, one of Grenier's interviewees:

> "If you are ill, you're frail. [...] If, if you can't walk on your own, you're frail; if you can't eat by yourself, you're frail; that to me is frail. I don't think it's anything to do with age, I would say that most frail people are older people, your body is worn out: you're frail. My mother died, she was 101; she was frail when she died. She was small. I'm short too, but I'm chubby and when you're thin and, and you can't move, you can't do things: you're frail. That to me is, is being frail." (Grenier, 2007, p 434)

Age is invoked by Martha when she cites her mother as an example of someone who is frail: she implies that frailty is characteristic of people aged 101, who cannot eat unaided, who cannot move and who are on the point of dying.

In part, these attempts are intended to refocus the attention of gerontologists on those older people for whom age, ill-health and physical condition combine to make them heavily dependent on others. As a category, they are increasing in number and this has direct implications for the resourcing of health services. But, setting to one side ill-health and incapacity, age itself can in time generate a sense of distance, difference and possible detachment, as Deborah Cavendish implies.

On occasions, when I have wanted to refer to 'very old' people without implying that they constitute a special category, I have used the term 'indisputably old'. The attraction of this is that 'indisputably' implies that Deborah Cavendish, is still 'old' but, in addition, has been for a long time. Similarly, in seeking to draw attention to the situation of very old people, I have used a different phrase in advocating a renewed focus in gerontology on 'extreme age' (Bytheway, 2003, p 74).

A centenarian

In Chapter Two, I discussed the history of Frances Partridge's diary-keeping practices, in Chapter Five her experience of bereavement and then, in Chapter Six, how her social network changed as her generation grew older. She was born in 1900 and lived to the age of 104, and here I consider what life was like for her when of a great age. As indicated in Chapter Two, Frances continued to keep her diary until some time close to her hundredth birthday and, as a result, her biographer, Anne Chisholm, was able to provide considerable detail about her later life.

You may remember from earlier chapters that a key person for Frances was Janetta. In 1990, when Frances reached the age of 90, Janetta and her husband, Jaime, had a house in Spain. Here is how Chisholm described the birthday in London:

> Her ninetieth birthday saw a cascade of flowers and cards, and Janetta gave a supper party for about thirty of Frances' nearest and dearest before taking her back to Spain four days later. It had been, Frances recorded, 'a fabulous day, a day whose significance it's impossible to understand [...] Looking back at its steamroller approach I really believe I had equated it with death, for how could anyone be so old and still alive?' (Chisholm, 2009, p 344)

That year, 1990, Frances' diaries from the years immediately following Ralph's death were published (Partridge, 1990), and there was a massive response to her description of bereavement: 'letters poured in, many of them from the bereaved, especially widows, who found Frances' account of her struggles with grief and despair in the wake of Ralph's death both moving and inspirational' (Chisholm, 2009, p 345). Frances was thrilled by the impact that her diaries were having and, according to Chisholm, it brought 'excitement and attention' in her old age (p 346), although she disliked being labelled 'wonderful for her age'. Frances' stamina did not fail her, even though she needed stronger glasses and increasingly preferred small gatherings to large parties. The continuing loss of friends was balanced by the success of her publications. But, by 1992,

> some of her friends were starting to worry about her living alone except for a daily help two or three times a week, and to panic if she did not answer the telephone when they rang. There was talk of her wearing an alarm call button, or accepting daily visits from the social services to help

with her morning bath or to put her to bed; when she got wind of this, she was not pleased, and when it turned out that there had been great hesitation about telling her that Sophie [Burgo's daughter] and Wenzel's marriage was in difficulty in case the news gave her a heart attack, she was furious. She felt quite capable of looking after herself and she found her friends' concern insulting. 'They seem to harp on my age in a way that has only one conclusion – an old folks' home, and I find it intolerable,' she wrote. 'Fuming over my cornflakes I mutter to myself crossly: "You can all fuck off and leave me to die in my own way!"' Frances' independence of spirit grew fiercer as she grew older. (Chisholm, 2009, pp 347-8)

While Chisholm may have had some sympathy with the friends' concern, it is important to note that in this extract she ends up quoting from Frances's diary. Because of this, the above is a good example of the well-worn cliché about older people being 'fiercely independent' and Chisholm is able to use the diary quote as confirmatory evidence of this.

Frances celebrated 'the day I never thought to see, my 95th birthday' in Spain with Janetta (Chisholm, 2009, p 354). It coincided with news that her diaries would be appearing in paperback. According to Chisholm, she felt rejuvenated: 'Few people in their mid-nineties can ever have been as busy and sought-after as Frances, still comparatively unaffected by her great age' (p 354). She was, however, increasingly aware of finitude:

Every now and then, in her later nineties, Frances used her diary to face another truth: that her death could not now be far away. 'That is something I think about more and more, and more. What a bore,' she wrote. 'But how, when driven relentlessly towards this tunnel, can one help it? However there is a change. It has become more "how" than "when", and sometimes my thoughts verge on panic about not dying soon enough [...] I fear living too long in a decrepit or deranged state, and almost welcome signs of increasing physical feebleness.' Under pressure from her friends, she had finally agreed to have an alarm call button, but refused to wear it, keeping it in a bowl by her bed. (Chisholm, 2009, p 355)

The idea of 'not dying soon enough' implies that surviving to a great age is failing to die at 'a more appropriate' age. When she was told of a rumour that she had already died, Frances wrote: 'of course I realise that everyone must expect me to be the next death. I do myself' (Chisholm, 2009, p 356). Despite this, everyday life still gave her much pleasure:

> Yes, it's true – even at my age one can still say to oneself 'I'm happy!' At what? Because the birds all over London have been singing these last few days [...] All little humdrum things but there has been blue in the sky, and yes, I've been happy and busy. (Chisholm, 2009, p 356)

Chisholm provides an account of Frances' daily routine in 1995, something that 'more than ever' she needed. She woke 'around 6.30 or seven', read or wrote, had a bath at 8am, and listened to Radio 4 over breakfast. Her housekeeper arrived around 10am. Frances liked to walk every day and to rest in the afternoon. If out in the evening, she would arrange for the taxi driver to help her open her front door. Otherwise she prepared her own supper, 'always preceded by a whisky or two'.

Her friends remained concerned about her welfare, particularly after she was burgled in 1996. Her eyes were 'bothering' her and she began to feel unsteady on her feet. A neurologist was consulted but he found nothing wrong and said she was 'fantastic for her age'. However, according to Chisholm, it seemed likely that she suffered a small stroke and Frances wrote: 'slow recovery after a peep into the abyss' (p 357). Her sight problems were due to macular degeneration but she never gave up trying to understand and overcome her condition, and was determined to read and write for as long as she possibly could.

However she fell again and 'was shaken by these depressing reminders of her frailty'. Her comment in her diary was: 'Back to childhood must be swallowed. I have caused quite enough trouble and worry by not facing facts' (Chisholm, 2009, p 357). So, at the age of 96, she began to accede to the wishes of her friends. Another fall after being blown over by the wind resulted in a black eye and bleeding nose and an unsatisfactory visit from the doctor. This led to a change to a doctor who was interested in 'helping her continue to be as independent as possible' and whose advice she followed.

On her 97th birthday, she said she 'felt happier and better than she had for some time' even though she was now using a walking stick. She was 'thrilled' by the result of the general election, took another burglary 'in her stride' and prepared her 1970-72 diaries for publication. Chisholm, however, offers a detailed account of the strains that were being placed on Frances' friends during 1997, and on Janetta in particular: 'What Frances could not see was that her determination to live alone with minimal help was increasingly unnerving for those who loved her' (p 360).

In January 1998, Frances wrote: 'I find I desperately need some little form of endeavour and if possible success, so as to counter the endless dégringolade, the "downhill all the way" effect of old age' (p 360). But, after another wind-blown fall, she began to anticipate the possible need for a wheelchair and wrote about 'the old folks' home waiting to scoop me up' (p 360). Before the end of 1998, plans were in hand for a new edition of all her books to be published in time for her 100th birthday. Her eyesight and steadiness were worsening and, despite visits and occasional trips away, some weekends in London were spent feeling lonely. Also, she was the victim of a sympathetic conman who stole some of her books and letters.

It was as her 100th birthday approached that she agreed to Anne Chisholm working on the biography and visiting her regularly. This enabled Chisholm to provide a revealing account of how her 100th birthday was celebrated:

> The approach of her hundredth birthday was regarded by Frances with mixed feelings. She wondered if she could rise to the various occasions confronting her, particularly the big party being arranged by Janetta and other old friends at the Savile Club. In the end, she managed it all with striking composure, and found herself soon afterwards recording a series of triumphs and a sense of renewed energy. On 3 April 2000 she wrote in her diary, 'I am dug into my 101st year – surely a good time for fresh starts!' and then summed up the year so far. 'I have passed the following ordeals,' she wrote, and listed the CBE ceremony, a 'state' or courtesy visit from her landlord, the Duke of Westminster, a lunch on 15 March for twelve close friends by Janetta and Jaime, and the next day the 'Grand Birthday Party for about 150 people' at the Savile Club. A week later there was dinner at the Ivy [...] All this, she added, had left her feeling 'unjustified hope for the future'. No-one who saw her during the celebrations could doubt that she found life still very much worth living. Although she felt exhausted by all the excitement for some weeks afterwards, and her diary petered out again, she was able to say, on 10 April, her handwriting quavery, the lines straggling down the page:'Strange as it may be "crossing the bar", in other words become 100 plus, seems to make me feel more my old self.' (Chisholm, 2009, pp 362-3)

Throughout this account there are indications of how the event marked a moment of revival: 'renewed energy', 'fresh starts', 'hope for the future' and feeling 'more my old self'.

Three months later, Frances enjoyed another visit to Spain and, later that year, received an honorary degree from London University. The following spring she tried to revive her diary but failed. She despaired when she heard of the attack on the Twin Towers in March 2001:

> I've felt ever since the Second World War and the dropping of the bomb that we would do ourselves in. The world will end and it will be our own fault. (Chisholm, 2009, p 367)

She made another attempt to write in her diary because it struck her that 'I should keep writing for myself alone – just to keep alive' (p 367). But her last entry, written on her 102nd birthday, was illegible. Six months later, in October 2002, she fell and broke her hip. Even so, she left hospital and returned home, and expected Chisholm to maintain her visits. The latter's reactions reflect those of many researchers who have been witness to the final demise of people of great age:

> Everyone around her knew that this was the beginning of the end of Frances' life, and part of me felt that no biographer should be hovering at such a time, observing and recording the approach of death. On the other hand it would be worse should Frances think that my withdrawal meant that I was no longer interested in her or that her death was imminent. (Chisholm, 2009, pp 367-8)

'I want to die' said Frances, 'to get out of the world, but I am not sure how to do it. I also can't stop wanting to get well. One has a life instinct, which struggles' (p 368). She managed to blow out three candles on her 103rd birthday. Remarkably, perhaps, Frances survived for 11 more months, dying on 6 February 2004.

Approaching a 100th birthday

Frances Partridge's diary entries provide some insight into the contradictory scenarios associated with frailty and the approach of the centenary of one's birth. She had wondered if she could 'rise' to the occasion and 'in the end' she had managed it. But what followed? Only a temporary respite from the continuing doomed struggle.

The period 2000 to 2004 is covered in just seven of Chisholm's 370-page biography, and so the day-to-day issues associated with great age are somewhat glossed over. There is little indication, for example, of the extent to which her friends might have feared possible complications with the planned 100th birthday parties and what alternative arrangements may have been made should there have been a crisis in the days immediately preceding the birthday. It is not difficult to imagine her close friends having lengthy discussions about how her care needs might best be met, but these are not recorded in Chisholm's biography. However, through the TOG project we have obtained an account of the 12 months leading up to a 100th birthday, an account that offers many insights into what is involved.

May Nilewska was born in Edinburgh on 3 July 1908 to a Scottish family. She married in 1947; her husband was Polish and they both worked in her father's drapery business in the city centre. They had no children and Mr Nilewska died in the late 1960s. In 2003, at the age of 95, May moved to live in a care home. The following is a narrative, recounting and interpreting the way in which her 100th birthday was anticipated and planned, and how events unfolded.

The story begins early in 2007, some time before May's 99th birthday. It is January and Joanna Bornat and I are planning the TOG project (see Chapter One). We issue our invitation to participate and on 9 February, Daniel Cole volunteers. He mentions his mother and her siblings as possible seniors. He also mentions May, his wife's 98-year-old aunt. We are keen to include a resident of a care home and so, in reply, we ask if Viv Mackie, his wife, would agree to act as a TOG recorder and whether it would be possible for her aunt to be interviewed as the senior. In reply Daniel writes:

> She married after the war but her (Polish) husband died many years ago and they never had children. Yes, prima facie, Viv would be willing to act as Recorder, though she asks me to point out something which we imagine you already know, and that is that, however hale and hearty, any 98-year old fatigues very quickly and so any recording would need to be done in time-limited bite-size bits.

During March Joanna and I meet to begin the selection of a sample of 12 from the volunteers. On 4 May, we inform both Daniel and Viv that we wish to accept their offer with regard to both his mother and her aunt. Three months later, on 14 August, I meet Daniel and Viv to explain what we are hoping to obtain through the diaries they have agreed to keep and the photographs they might take. A week later I write a report and, regarding May, I note: 'The prospect of May's death looms large. Daniel and Viv are uncertain as to whether she will make it to her 100th next July'.

In Viv's view, May's mind is 'beginning to slip' and she is anxious that 'too much is being made of the prospective birthday'. Nevertheless both Daniel and Viv are thinking ahead to the birthday celebration, still 11 months away. We realise that documenting the build up, and recording the way in which it is celebrated, will fit in exactly with our aim of studying how later life is experienced and how life transitions work out in practice.

In July, Viv sends us seven photographs of May's 99th birthday celebration on the third of that month. One has May cutting into a small chocolate birthday cake with four candles. Viv starts her TOG diary on 11 August following a visit to May, and her first entry refers back to this event:

> I took photos of my aunt's 99th birthday party (on 3 July 2007). My aunt was delighted and showed me other photos from Mr Tosh [an old church friend] of the party.

On 18 September, Joanna interviews May. Viv is present too. There is no mention of the forthcoming birthday or of how it might be celebrated. Here, however, is how Joanna raises May's date of birth and her age:

> "Can we go back to the beginning, and can you tell me about when you were born, what year were you born …"

> "On the third of July 1908."

> "So that makes you …"

> "Ninety-nine."

> "Ninety-nine, yes, and er …"

> "And a lot more." [laughter]

Later in the interview, in discussing the cost of her care, May declares that "I don't expect to live much beyond a hundred."

In contrast to Joanna's interview with May, the prospective birthday figures rather more prominently in Viv's diary. Her visits to see May are coordinated with those of Henry Tosh and Ellen Day, a former neighbour of May's. The routine varies but Viv tends to see May every fortnight. After each visit she enters a comparatively lengthy account in her diary, summarising the visit, May's current state, and their various concerns. The first mention of the forthcoming birthday is an entry Viv makes in October. May's recent behaviour has caused difficulties with the care home staff but, in discussing this with Jo, a staff nurse in the home, Viv feels that:

> she had definitely turned the corner and, although it may well take some time, I thought she would make a reasonable recovery. We both laughed and said we thought she would see her 100th birthday yet!

The word 'yet' implies that previously they have had doubts about May's ability to survive so long. The fact that they laugh indicates that they both now view the prospect rather more positively. A few weeks later, Viv speculates:

> going by the current strength of my aunt, I think her 100th birthday on 3 July next year is definitely a possibility!

Over the course of the winter, Daniel's mother, Viv's mother-in-law, becomes increasingly ill and she dies on 6 February. Daniel's diary includes a moving account of his mother's final weeks (see Chapter Five). It is a difficult time for them both, but planning for the forthcoming birthday begins in earnest when May herself raises the subject on 25 February:

> My aunt was wondering what might be being planned for her birthday in July. I asked her if she had ever imagined in her life that she would celebrate her 100th birthday and she said she never, ever had, but now that she was so close it was obvious that she was beginning to get quite excited. She said what had happened for her 99th had been absolutely fine (afternoon tea was laid on for immediate friends and family), but she thought 'they' might do a little bit more for this one.

May is hoping for rather more than her 99th birthday tea party, and is reassured when Viv agrees to consult Mr Tosh. Viv's first concern is to find out about the Queen's message and what needs to be done. She consults Jo, who already knows the procedure since another 100th birthday party is being planned in the home. Viv agrees to talk to Mr Tosh and to 'get some plans in place'. A fortnight later, Viv makes some progress by ordering a duplicate birth certificate from Register House in Edinburgh. Mr Tosh, however, is getting ready to go to the US early in March to visit his daughter.

While Mr Tosh is in America, May remains concerned about arrangements. In particular, when Viv visits her on 17 March, she makes it clear that she considers Mr Tosh's involvement to be essential:

Mr Tosh had been in to see her with the dates of his trip to America, so she told me that 'her committee' would have to wait until his return on 9 April before they could meet to discuss the forthcoming birthday. She was relieved that I had spoken to Mr Tosh and that we had made just that arrangement.

The rising excitement – and anxiety – surrounding the prospective party is evident in an email we receive from Daniel on 10 April:

> Viv and her aunt are, I'm pleased to say, both well. I understand that tentative plans for the big birthday in July are being quietly made, quietly partly because no one wishes to tempt fate, which at 99 going on 100 it is easy to do.

With Mr Tosh's return, planning turns to the question of invitations. May has her own views and sees Viv, rather than Mr Tosh, as the person responsible for posting them. Viv in turn is concerned to avoid causing offence in issuing invitations. In the following long entry for 14 April, she describes these worries, as well as visits from distant relations. She is particularly pleased that her own sister, Liz, is prepared to join the organising group:

> Today I went to see my aunt with the main purpose of attempting to get some kind of idea who she would like invited to her birthday party. Easier said than done! My aunt doesn't want to have an invitation list, she wants an open invitation so that people won't feel left out. I explained that this would make catering just a little bit difficult, but she has such confidence in my abilities she dismissed that with a 'but you'll cope, you always do!' The one person she said that she definitely wanted there was Dorothy Waite. This is the lady from the Lifeboats whom my aunt has known for many, many years in a fundraising capacity. I have only met her once, at my aunt's 90th birthday party, but I do know that she holds my aunt in high regard because of the dedication she has shown over the years to the 'cause'. But I am not to be the one to get in touch with her – my aunt will do that herself. So, I will definitely have to put my thinking cap on and recruit some help. Hopefully Mr Tosh can suggest how to make this 'open invitation' known to the church congregation and friends, and I will do a round robin-type letter to our family and see what results that

brings. In conversation it turns out that Raymond Sheen, from Ipswich (May's cousin), turned up to visit last week. Although he is not well enough to drive any longer, he and his wife had taken the opportunity to come to Scotland on a bus tour and took their own detour [...] so that he could visit his cousin. It's a shame I missed him and I doubt he will want to come back up [...] in July so soon after this visit, but I do have his address and I will write to him.

Today I rang my big sister Liz and said I needed her help with arranging this party and she, thankfully, said that she will be delighted to do so. That makes me feel a lot better and Liz is really, really good with old people. I haven't yet made contact with Mr Tosh but I will do so by the end of this month if he hasn't contacted me. I'm sure it will all work out fine but at the moment it all feels a little tricky as my aunt is so dogged about what I am <u>not</u> to do. Let's see what next Monday brings.

On 31 May, Viv reports further progress and provides a telling account of how ages are checked before the Queen's congratulatory messages are sent. May's health has become a cause for concern again and it is worth noting that it is her age rather than any specific health condition that concerns the nurses. The success of the birthday is now hanging in the balance:

As I said, my aunt's health is deteriorating. Although nothing major has happened she is becoming extremely frail, quite confused, and very, very tired. The nursing home are keeping a close eye on her and are constantly checking blood pressure and urine as required, but they are satisfied that there is nothing lurking under the surface and that it is simply her age; she is wearing out.

Meanwhile, in the background we are moving on with the plans for the big birthday with fingers and toes crossed that we will make it. I have ordered the tele-message – now that was an interesting story. You may already know this, but I hadn't had to organise one of these before. I was told by the nursing home, as well as following instructions on the website the Palace has for these anniversaries that I was required to have either my aunt's original birth certificate, or a copy, which I was then to send along with the completed application form, 21 days before the birthday, to Buckingham Palace.

Because I was hoping to keep this as a surprise I did not ask my aunt for her original birth certificate and phoned Register House in Edinburgh to order a copy. When I told them why I wanted it, they transferred me to the Anniversaries Officer. He was a charming man and extremely helpful. The first thing he told me was that I didn't need the duplicate birth certificate, so that got cancelled. He then explained that it is an automatic process nowadays which the Department of Work and Pensions oversee. Where anybody of that age is still claiming benefits they automatically check (a) if the person is still bona fide i.e. alive! and (b) whether they want to receive the congratulatory message. He told me that when he got his copy of the list for July he would check that my aunt's name was on it and, if for any reason, it was missing he would contact the Work and Pensions Office and make sure it hadn't been missed out. But then I got an email from my aunt's lawyer's office saying that they had been contacted by the Department of Work and Pensions asking what we wanted to do about my aunt's congratulatory message. The lawyer said I was dealing with it and asked me to phone them to let them know where I had got to.

Eventually I managed to get hold of them and, to cut a very long story short, confirmed everything they needed. They wanted to go and visit my aunt to verify the details they had but I asked them not to (a) because she wouldn't like a stranger asking such personal questions, and (b) because I was trying to keep everything a surprise. They were very good about it and said that between me and the lawyer they would be able to verify everything they needed to know.

Gosh, I thought filling in the form and sending a duplicate birth certificate would have been much more straightforward – but who am I to stand in the way of progress!! But hopefully all this will mean that at some time before 1pm on 3rd July, a Congratulatory Message, signed by HRH, will arrive for the attention of my aunt and she will be completely made up as a result and think that the last 100 years have been completely worthwhile just to get that piece of paper! She is such a strong Royalist I am sure that I am not exaggerating this response!

Regarding the celebrations, Viv hopes that the Queen's message can be kept as 'a surprise' for May. This is odd given that May, 'such a strong Royalist', is so alert to the significance of the birthday. Viv then turns, in the same diary entry, to the setting for the party and matters of provisions:

> ... The rest of the arrangements for the big day are proceeding behind the scenes. The nursing home is allowing us the use of one of their sitting rooms (although I am hoping on the day that we might get to use the brand new conservatory, which is just lovely), and they are providing the cake. We (or the 'committee' as my aunt prefers to call us) will provide some champagne for the inevitable toasts, along with sandwiches and strawberry tarts for afternoon tea. My sister and Mrs Tosh (the minister's wife) will help with the baking, and my brother will help anyone who needs transport on the day. I have written a short invitation card which I am going to send out to family members this week, and Mr Tosh was putting a notice in the Duthie Street Baptist Church Bulletin informing the congregation that there is a celebration planned for the 3 July and that anyone wanting to come along should do so, and let me know in advance (purely for catering purposes). So, at the moment we're not sure of numbers but I hope it will be around 25–30, because any more than that will be too many for her and less than that may make it a bit of a damp squib.
>
> It is only 4 weeks away now and I switch between being really excited and really nervous. I think it is an amazing achievement to reach that age but what a responsibility organising the celebration. Next month's diary should be interesting!

The clause about the use of a sitting room reveals something of the awkward relationship between nursing homes and the families of residents. Viv spells out who has agreed to provide what, and this demonstrates the importance of the event being seen to be a collective effort with all those involved making a contribution. Regarding the invitations, it is interesting to note that they have been issued to May's family through Viv, and to church friends through Mr Tosh. What this tells us is that much hangs upon organisers being well integrated into relevant networks.

Viv's next diary entry, on 30 June, starts with a further expression of concern over May's health and evidence that this is not just due to age. This detailed account indicates that May is well aware of the issues and that she has decided that, rather than hospital, she would much prefer to be in the home so that she can be present at the party. She expects the home to do everything possible to support her in this:

> This has been a very scary month. My aunt is 99 years and eleven months old and in apparent poor health. As I said in last month's diary her health has been deteriorating steadily over the past few weeks. It turned out from blood and other tests that she was actually dehydrated. She refused to go into hospital to be re-hydrated because they couldn't guarantee that she would be out for her birthday. She insisted that they keep her in the nursing home and do what they could for her there. The nursing staff asked her how much interference she wanted if she did take seriously ill and the instruction was that up to and including 3 July she was to be resuscitated and that they were to have the conversation with her again on the 4 July! They were to do everything they possibly could to keep her alive until her birthday and if at all possible keep her out of hospital!

Viv then goes on to describe May's reaction to news that a friend has died at the age of 99:

> On top of this her very good friend Kathleen, who [...] was 99, died. Kathleen's son, Roger, had written to my aunt to let her know and I was expecting her to be very sad and I was ready with my words of consolation. However, possibly because she was not feeling very strong herself, she seemed to just let it pass without much comment. I had expected her to express some sadness or feelings of loss but it was explained away simply as 'I thought there was something wrong there'!

There is no indication in this of how close in time Kathleen was to her own 100th birthday, but the news echoes the concerns of Viv and Jo, expressed a few months previously, that May herself might have succumbed in similar fashion. May's apparently casual acceptance of this news suggests that she has got used to this kind of news and that she fully recognises how mortality is steadily reducing her network of friends.

At this point in the diary entry, Viv returns to the prospect of the big celebration, now only a few days away. All concerned have become increasingly excited and May, in particular, appears to have benefited from rising expectations. In particular, she continues to check with Viv on replies to the invitation:

> ...Well I am writing this diary on the last day of June, only 4 days away from her 100th birthday and I am delighted to say that she is not only alive and well, but excited and looking forward very much to her celebration on Thursday. She has picked up over the past two weeks and has gradually got stronger and stronger. She has involved herself in the invitations to her party and her only topic of conversation is to ask me who I have heard from and whether they are coming.

Viv is pleased that the event will be used to mark not just the birthday, but also May's family-based attachment to the Orkney Islands and her life-long support of the Royal National Lifeboat Institution:

> ...I have had several conversations about the birthday party arrangements with Ena Seaton in [the Orkneys]. She is friendly with [...] the Lord Lt of Orkney and has asked him to write a letter of commendation for my aunt on the occasion of her birthday as a token of gratitude for the work that she has done over many years in raising funds for the RNLI. This has always been my aunt's chosen charity as a result of her lifelong connections with Orkney and their fishermen and the tragedies that have been experienced in the past. Her first visit to Orkney was when she was only 3 years old on a visit with her mother. It was a love affair from that moment on and she still has very strong connections there with relatives, such as Ena and her sisters, who still live on the Islands. The commendation is going to be read out at the party and will be a total surprise for my aunt. Sadly Ena cannot be present but her sister Molly will be there.

Regarding arrangements, Viv's primary concern is with the location of the party:

> ...So the arrangements for the day are now in place. I have managed to persuade Sister to allow us the use of the new

conservatory (which the residents use as a dining room) for the party, which I am thrilled about. Apart from it being a beautiful room there is plenty of space and light and it will be the perfect setting for the gathering. We have a total of 34 guests expected ranging from church friends to family and residents of the nursing home who are particularly friendly with my aunt. We will have sandwiches and cakes and fizzy wine to go with the toasts.

There will be balloons and banners and birthday cake and, assuming all my planning worked, the message from the Queen!

Henry Tosh, my aunt's old minister and now Welfare Power of Attorney, has been wonderful helping me with the arrangements. We split the task of inviting people so that he could contact the church people and I would contact the family. His wife Brenda has offered to do some baking and my sister is bringing along the puds! So all in all with the sandwiches I'm bringing along together with the sausage rolls and fizzy wine whatever else happens on Thursday we won't go short of food or drink.

It is just such a relief that my aunt has rallied and we are all so excited and looking forward to the day.

Watch this space ... !

Viv provides a detailed account of 3 July, the big day. It starts in May's own room, where there is a meeting with Viv and family. Viv, Ellen (May's former neighbour) and Liz (Viv's sister) take May down to the party:

What a very special day today is. Aunt May is 100 today and all the plans are in place for her birthday celebration. We are expecting over 30 people to come to the nursing home at 2pm to celebrate this wonderful occasion.

Everything is perfect. The sun is shining and we are able to use the lovely conservatory where there is plenty of space and light. The atmosphere was wonderful and everybody really enjoyed themselves. There was plenty of food; prepared jointly by myself, my sister Liz and Betty Tosh (wife of my aunt's ex-minister). We also provided sparkling wine for the guests along with soft drinks, teas and coffees. The nursing home provided the cake, balloons and banners.

They also gave her a lovely gift of a silver frame to put The Telegram in.

We arrived at the nursing home about 1.15 in time to set the room up before the visitors arrived. I took my son Alistair and his Polish girlfriend, Katia, up to my aunt's room to introduce them. She had been keen to meet Katia because of her Polish connections. Katia had brought gifts from Poland and written a special message in Polish on a card which she gave to my aunt. It was a very touching scene and set the tone for the afternoon.

My aunt was so excited and when she was brought down to the party at 2pm by my sister and Ellen she was just amazed to see so many people and so many flowers. I lost count of how many floral tributes were sent – there were dozens.

Rather than attempt to describe in detail how the party unfolds, Viv allows the photographs to tell the story:

... As you will see from the photographs her eyes are wide open. She is agog with delight. When I gave her the telegram from the Queen her comment was that she thought there might be one of them! She had no idea about the commendation from the Lord Lt of Orkney [...] and I'm sure she will enjoy reading his delightful words over again in the days and weeks to come. It was just a wonderful, wonderful occasion. Everybody enjoyed themselves so much.

It is possible to deduce the identity of 23 participants from Viv's diary entries and captions to the 19 photographs. They include May's great-niece with her husband and their baby. The photographs also provide a record of the party's timing. The first two are taken before the party starts and the next two at its very beginning. Half an hour passes before four more are taken, centred on the cutting of the cake. Another 15 minutes pass, and then seven more are taken between 2.00pm and 2.15pm, when the attention of the party focuses on May reading the Queen's message. Then a church friend reads for May the commendation from the Lord Lieutenant.

Viv's diary entry for 3 July ends:

... I phoned the nursing home the morning after to check she was OK because when we left at 4pm she was thoroughly exhausted and just wanted to go to bed. I was a bit worried that it would be too much for her. Apparently not! She was her old self demanding coffee with her morning tray and declining offers of help to open her many cards and letters.

Ellen is going in today (Saturday) and I will go in on Monday so we'll see how she's coping.

Daniel emails us the following day:

I feel sure that Viv will be writing up full details, with photos, but a quick note meantime to let you know that everything went off superbly well at yesterday's birthday bash. The Guest of Honour was in fine form and everyone who attended deemed it a great success. So big had been the build-up to this important day there was a palpable sense of relief here last night ... because you don't get a 2nd go at these things!

More from Viv in due course, I'm sure.

As promised, Viv visits May again on 7 July. She describes how she is disappointed with May's recollections of the party and subsequent actions:

I was really looking forward to this visit. I thought my aunt would be eager to tell me how wonderful the party had been and how much she enjoyed seeing everybody. I didn't really expect her to thank me for all the hard work of getting everybody together and making it such a memorable day. Well it turns out that she has completely re-written the events of 3 July. She was telling me who was there and who she had got cards from. Some of which was just not true. She definitely had not received a telegram from the Lord Provost! for example; and to prove it I went through every card and message she had received – but she was still having nothing of it. As far as she was concerned she had had that telegram! The only cards that were on display were the one from the Queen, of course; one from the nursing home and one from Mr and Mrs Tosh. All the others – about 40 – were consigned to a tin box at the side of her chair. The staff had asked her what she wanted done with the big helium-filled balloon which had pride of place beside her bed. She told them that she was done with it and it didn't matter what happened to it now – just to take it away.

The lovely, thoughtful gifts that Katia had brought from Poland had been sent to the kitchen to be distributed amongst the Eastern European staff there and not a word about her kindness. I was saddened by this insensitivity I must say.

So, I'm not sure whether this was simply an exhausted reaction to the build up of events last week or whether she feels invincible again and is back to her old self of laying down the law. I certainly took it badly. I was still on a high because of how well everything had gone. I was still getting phone calls and messages from guests and family members saying how much they had enjoyed it and it was just a bit disappointing not to have it recognised in some small way by the guest of honour. However, that is what she is like and to be honest she was looking better today than she has done in weeks. So perhaps I'm doing her an injustice and that it had, after all, been too much for her to take in. Perhaps when I visit this week things will be back on a more even keel.

Clearly Viv herself is moved by the experience and by the generosity and thoughtfulness of the participants and, as a consequence, she is distressed by May's seemingly cavalier comments in looking back on the event. Viv seems to imply that this is typical of May as a person ('back to her old self'), rather than as a person of great age.

Two weeks later, Viv's diary entry ends:

The visits are a bit strange at the moment because for so many weeks we had the excitement of the planning of the party. At the moment there is nothing to be planning for, although by the looks of my aunt today – we could well be organising birthday parties for her for some years to come.

Viv tries to be generous and positive about May but, following the success of the party, she now finds herself feeling deflated. Does she face a never-ending routine of fortnightly visits and annual birthday celebrations?

Joanna and I meet Viv and Daniel and they confirm that the party was 'a big event' but, seemingly, May has had few visitors since that date. A month later Viv writes:

Paid flying visit to Aunt May. Gave her some blown-up photos of her 100th birthday – showed no interest in them.

At the end of the year (31 December), Viv emails us to report:

There was another pleasant surprise for her just last week: Ena from Orkney dropped by. She had to be 'south' for a friend's memorial service in the borders so planned her visit so that she could stop by […] and visit Aunt May. She had not come for the birthday party in July and this was the first visit since about May. Although my aunt was very pleased indeed to see Ena she was critical that her stay […] was so short. 'These people from Orkney will not stay away from the Island. As soon as they arrive here they are planning their journey back. Why can't they stay here for a little while, just for a change!'

On 2 June 2009, a month before May's 101st birthday, Joanna re-interviews May. Viv also takes part. Joanna begins by recalling the previous interview when May had been "still only ninety-nine". When asked about her 100th, she answers with impressive demographic precision:

"One lady who has been a hundred and one for a while, she's becoming a hundred and two. I don't think there's anybody less than eighty in this house. Only twenty eight residents here."

The interview proceeds to discuss the Queen's message ("a letter, it's a very nice picture", says May), before turning to the party:

"So what was it like to be the centre of attention that day?"

"We had a lovely party, it was absolutely wonderful. I can't say anymore than that. There were fifty at it".

About the guests, and in particular her family, May answers again with numerical detail:

"Viv managed to dig out my relatives and close friends, there were thirty four of them. But then some of the ladies from this house were at the party. And of course some of the members of staff, so it went up to fifty. Wonderful, it was a wonderful party."

After some thoughts on drinks and, in particular, how May was toasted, Joanna asks her if there was "anyone very important there". Viv reminds May of the lady from the RNLI and this prompts May to comment that she must remember to phone her. Next Joanna asks about surprises and May refers to the presence of the solicitor, before being reminded by Viv of the letter from the Lord Lieutenant. At this point, Joanna reads this out (amid interruptions from May). It includes various references to family connections and, at this point, Viv and May take over the conversation to discuss surnames and the history of the family, before the interview moves on to subsequent events and the life of the home. When the prospect of her 101st birthday is raised, May simply says "Just let them get on with it. I fit in." The interview moves on to reasons for her longevity and here she returns once again to her interest in numbers:

> "Well a place like this, they're all in for much the same. Lady who has been a hundred and one is going to be a hundred and two, and of course I'm looking forward to a hundred and one. And as I say there's nobody less than eighty."

Upon completing the interview, Joanna makes the following notes in her report:

> She's obviously very proud to be 100 and looking forward to being 101 though she's not the oldest in the home. There's someone already 101 ahead of her.

> I was shown three new photographs by Viv, apart from the display on the wall of photos from last year's birthday. One was produced during the interview. It's the framed card from the Queen taking pride of place on the top of her bookcase.

> Talking about the 100th birthday, Viv said that this was tremendously important to May but that the letter from Orkney (which I read out for the audio) was what seemed to please her most. Very important to her.

Ever since May agreed to participate in the TOG project, her 100th birthday had been an exciting prospect. It is not often that gerontological research has the opportunity to interview centenarians, still less follow events in their continuing lives. Although we were not at the party ourselves, we were excited when we received Daniel's email on 4 July reporting on its success. We had been all too aware of the possibility that May might not have made it or that there might have been a different tale to tell.

On 29 October, less than five months after Joanna's second interview with May, Daniel sent us an email headed 'Sad News':

> Vivienne has asked me to e-mail you with the sad news that May passed away peacefully at lunchtime today. Even cats only have nine lives and May had long since achieved double figures on that count. But true to form she was 'with it' up to and including yesterday though for the past week or ten days her body had been showing distinct signs of gradually and irreversibly closing down. Vivienne was there at the end along with May's minister Henry Tosh and his wife and various of the nursing staff at the home for whom she was their very favourite inmate.

May was exceptional in the TOG study, not just because of her great age, but also because she was the only senior who was resident in a care home and the only one who had no children of her own. We are delighted that she agreed to participate, and are greatly indebted to Viv too for the part she has played. Without their contribution, TOG would have been a much more limited project.

It is difficult to know how to comment on the question of whether May's birthday was 'typical' and whether she is an 'average' centenarian. All centenarians are – of course – exceptional (despite the demographic trend towards increasing numbers). My own personal experience of 100th birthday parties is not extensive: I have attended one and heard accounts of two others. Nevertheless, there are features of May's celebration that remind me of them: the timing (early afternoon), the setting (the lounge of a care home), the self-consciousness of the participants, everyone's delight in the Queen's message and the arrival of the birthday cake. Perhaps the question of whether it was 'typical' is not as important, however, as the fact that, as with the parties for Frances Partridge, all the participants appear to have done their bit in ensuring that the celebrations were 'a success'. With the evidence of May Nilewska's birthday, we can consider in some detail the ways in which great age is experienced and celebrated.

The first conclusion we draw concerns the centenarian's involvement in the planning of the celebration. Despite her obvious physical frailty and delicate health, May was well aware of the significance of the event. She saw it as a notable achievement and was concerned from the outset that her birthday should be celebrated satisfactorily. No doubt the Queen's contribution was an important motivation. However,

May recognised that celebrations need to be organised and that help is needed. Such perception of course is not always possible for people of great age, but it may be, given its very personal significance, that some rise to the challenge: that their 'faculties' and interest in life are revived as a consequence.

Second, it is clear that networks are critical. May had a clear idea of who should be invited and through her 'committee' she appears to have been successful in achieving a satisfactory attendance, thereby reviving many social contacts. With the exception of Raymond Sheen and Ena Seaton, all those she would have liked to be there were there and this reflected well on the networking abilities and resources of Viv and Mr Tosh. There is a real possibility that some networks in deep old age will become so attenuated that links are lost and, as a result, other survivors overlooked when invitations are being issued. That said, in some situations, it may be that networks are revived at the time of 90th or 99th birthdays and the resulting lists mobilised again for the 100th. Indeed, it may also be that centenarians, in previous years, have supported older acquaintances who have reached the same milestone (in much the same way as Viv has supported May). Indeed some may have considerable experience of such parties. Conversely some older participants, such as May's fellow residents, may reflect on the event and develop opinions as to how they would like to see their own 100th birthdays celebrated. It is also possible that the staff of nursing homes, through a close alliance with family and friends, play an important part in sustaining and reviving former networks and, in this way, that such celebrations play an increasingly important part in sustaining supportive networks in later life.

Third, regarding the passage of time, there are two dynamics that, on the basis of Viv and May's experience, seem to be important in understanding the significance of the 100th birthday. The first is that for May the birthday became a target that she was intent on achieving. She wanted to be there, participating in the celebrations. It is not too speculative to suggest that the challenge had a positive impact upon her health. The second is that once passed, it is evident from Viv's diary entries that May's memories of the party almost immediately paled, not into insignificance, but in a way that left them feeling that the everyday life of her immediate future was dull and inconsequential in comparison. May did not appear interested in the photographs nor, when interviewed by Joanna, in 'reliving' the day. But she was proud to have received the Queen's message and to be one of the UK's centenarians. This implies that much social and personal capital is invested in the day itself, and this poses important questions for the subsequent morale and well-being of the centenarian and their supporters.

Lastly, it is evident that a 100th birthday party places a substantial emotional strain on those involved in organising it. Set in the contexts of a continuing routine of visiting and support, of signs of the older person's declining strength (and possibly of more specific health concerns), and of other family matters (as in Viv's experience of the death of her mother-in-law), it is hardly surprising if the lengthy build-up to what is a big, one-off celebration should drain people of much of their emotional energy. And beyond the party itself, the continuing survival of the celebrant raises all sorts of questions along the lines of 'When and how is it ever going to end?' Long-serving supporters, like Viv and Mr Tosh, are themselves growing older and they may see their continuing commitment as depriving themselves of opportunities that they think are their due.

Questions for discussion

1 What similarities were there in the accounts of the lead up to the 100th birthdays of Frances Partridge and May Nilewska, and what were the key differences? To what extent do you think you can generalise from two such case studies?

2 Is there a need for health and care services specifically tailored to the needs of the 'very old and frail'?

3 Do you have experience of organising or participating in a 100th birthday party and, if so, what advice would you offer to others?

EIGHT

The ageing population

The popular media often expresses its concern about 'the ageing population'. How is the population ageing? To answer this basic question, it is necessary to consider first the concept of population and how demographers have studied it.

Although demography, defined as the statistical study of human populations, has developed the tools for analysing any collection of people, much of its literature focuses on nation states and their constituent populations. This is driven by the politics of nationhood. It is in this context, for example, that universal suffrage has been promoted, and it follows directly from this that democracy depends upon there being the political will to identify and register a nation's population. Moreover, policies regarding 'public health' can only be effective if the health of the public (that is, the population) is systematically monitored. These and other national concerns require the compilation of statistics based (a) on periodic censuses that count and locate the national population, and (b) on systems for monitoring the 'flow' of people entering the population (the newborn and immigrants) and leaving it (the deceased and emigrants).

A census can produce the age distribution of the population by recording the chronological age of each person counted. The overall population is then described as ageing if between two censuses the average age rises. Throughout most of the past few centuries, the average age of most national populations has indeed been rising and it is often assumed that this implies greater numbers of old people. It may, however, be due to a falling birth rate just as much as a falling death rate and it does not necessarily follow that there are more old people. The average age of the population will increase if there is a falling birth rate while death rates remain the same. That said, the evidence is that, in the first decade of the 21st century, life expectancy is increasing in many countries and this, not surprisingly, concerns those with responsibilities for the costs of pensions, healthcare and various other forms of welfare arising from the needs of older people. This concern generates political debate and it is here that panic often takes over. This response has a long history:

Alarmist demography and gerontological knowledge came together in the social surveys of the late nineteenth and early twentieth centuries that decried the growth rate and poverty of the elderly population as an economic and moral crisis. (Katz, 1996, p 69)

This, Katz argues, is how 'the elderly' came to be constructed as a 'population-subject'. Possibly he exaggerates a little when he claims that 'the bulk of academic gerontological research is in fact consumed with knowing the elderly population's growth, size, movements, profiles and needs' (p 49), but there can be little doubt that it is the wider moral panic that has driven the funding of much research on ageing: what can we do, governments ask gerontologists, about the 'rising tide' of elderly people (Health Advisory Service, 1982)?

In this chapter I link the idea of 'an ageing population' not just with policies relating to the needs and characteristics of whole populations, but also with some of the more individual experiences and concerns raised in earlier chapters.

Age groups and generations

The crisis over the ageing population is often discussed with reference to the concept of 'inter-generational equity'. This is interesting in that this debate explicitly links age and generation: is the economy in the early years of the 21st century bearing the burden of an *age group* that is increasing in size or of an exceptionally large *generation*, the baby boomers? There are important issues of equity at stake here, and so it is important to be clear about which divisions in society are involved.

The definition of the 'baby boom generation' is unclear. This is hardly surprising since what is essentially a term devised to represent the rise in fertility rates immediately following the end of the Second World War has often been used by students of culture to represent all those who, regardless of age, rejected traditional values in the 1960s. A sense of panic is immediately provoked by the word 'boom', suggesting some kind of explosion. However, it is also the term used by economists, much more generally, to discuss broad historical cycles. Cheung (2007, p 9), for example, writes:

Since Baby Boomers are born before each bout of inflation, near the trough of the long-wave, by the time the next trough is reached 50 to 60 years later, the Baby Boomers will have aged considerably and are ready for retirement. Thus the long-wave is a reflection of this alternation between a generally young society and a generally old society.

This ebb and flow model stands in stark contrast with that of the rising tide of dependent older people assumed to be the consequence of life-sustaining medical interventions. Which model is used depends upon how historical demographic trends are to be modelled and interpreted.

Tomassini (2005) summarises the age structure of the UK population, based on an analysis of age pyramids for the years 1951 and 2001, and the pyramid projected for 2031. The latter is based on the assumption that fertility patterns will remain the same as in 2003, but that 'there will continue to be improvements in survival at older ages'. Note that such assumptions promise an inevitable increase in the average age of the population. She identifies two 'baby-boom' cohorts, those born in the late 1940s and those born in the 1960s. Tomassini comments that the impact of the two baby-boom generations:

> can be traced in the 2001 pyramid where the 50–54 age group is still pronounced (post-Second World War baby boomers), as too are the generations of the 1960s baby boom (those aged around 30–39).

This is a good example of how, in the context of simple chronology, the concepts of age group and generation at one point in time can be merged: how the 1946–50 cohort is deemed equivalent in 2001 to the 50 to 54 age group and likewise the 1960s generation to those aged 'around 30 to 39'.

In the next few decades, the greatest impact on the age distribution of the population will come from the dramatic reduction in fertility that has occurred since the 1970s. Should there be a rise back to the level of more than 600,000 births per annum characteristic of each and every year between 1942 and 1973, then it is likely that the average age of the population will begin to decline whatever increases there may be in longevity. The implication of the assumptions that fertility will remain as in 2003 whilst longevity continues to increase is evident in Tomassini's commentary on the projected 2031 figures. Here she first notes that the baby boom generations will now be aged 80 to 84 and 60 to 69 respectively, and then comments:

> These generations of baby boomers have significantly increased the number and the proportions of older people.

The tendency to interpret demographic trends in terms of age categories rather than birth cohorts (that is, generations) reflects the way national policies tends to conceptualise the population as a static phenomenon: what is of primary concern is the population here and now. One consequence of this is to view age as one of a number of basic background variables.

Age as a variable

Over the years, much social research has focused on the multiple relationships between variables. What are the differences between men and women? What is the effect of social class? What factors are associated with high achievement? Does age cause social isolation?

Multivariate analyses begin with a sample drawn from 'the population' and the selection of various 'dependent' variables that are hypothesised to 'depend' on (that is, to be caused by) various selected 'independent' ones. So, for example, social isolation might be hypothesised to depend on age. An analysis that takes account of the effect of other independent variables may conclude that 'age causes social isolation'. This would imply that as one grows older, one becomes more isolated. This may indeed be the case, but there is an alternative explanation: that older people, at the time of the study, were of a generation that, for whatever reason, was more prone to isolation than the younger participants in the study: greater isolation in the older age categories is not necessarily the result of people growing older.

A multivariate analysis is intended to evaluate systematically the complex set of statistical relationships between the selected variables. This works best when the hypotheses are essentially confined to the individual: psychological or health issues for example. Insofar as a variable selected for a multivariate analysis may reflect *relationships* between people it is through the relationship being cast as a characteristic of the individual. So, for example, a common question is 'How many children do you have?', thereby overlooking the potential complexity of the network of parent-child relationships in which the individual is a parent. More generally, any measure of a social network is conceptualised for such analyses as a characteristic of the individual rather than the network and, as a result, our understanding of how social networks 'work' in later life remains very 'egocentric'.

For much multivariate research age is considered 'a nuisance variable'. This is because the selected dependent variables are known to be correlated with age, but the hypotheses being tested refer to other independent variables. The researchers are aware of the significance of age but the objective of the analysis is to focus on rather more subtle statistical associations. So, for example, everyone knows that the likelihood of most medical conditions varies by age; what researchers want to uncover are less well-known differences. This is done by 'controlling for age': for example, by calculating the age-specific rates of a condition separately for men and women, and then comparing these rates. That way, the impact of sex can be assessed, knowing that age has been 'controlled for'. The fact that the risk of the condition varies with age is taken for granted; what the research is intended to reveal are other differences that might prompt changes in medical practice or health service provision.

Here is a case study, one of many that could have been chosen. There is much interest in how cancer rates vary between different sections of the population and how these rates are changing over time. The Office of National Statistics (ONS) published statistics on cancer in England in 2007 (ONS, 2010a) and made the comment (2010b):

> The overall age-standardised rate of cancer registrations in England remained the same between 2006 and 2007. However for males the age-standardised rate has decreased whilst the female age-standardised rate has increased, both by less than 1 per cent to 403 (males) and 352 (females) per 100,000 population.

Thus proportionately more men than women are registered as having cancer but the difference is slowly reducing. This appears to imply that men are at greater risk, but note that the comment refers to registrations and it may be that there are subtle sex differences in how various cancers are identified and then registered. Whatever the case, researchers are able to analyse the complex relationships between sex and cancer, free from any anxiety that differences may be 'spurious', the consequence of differences due to age rather than sex.

Research based on the statistical analysis of the associations within a set of variables has been enormously productive, but at a price. This is that it implicitly conceptualises 'society' and the individual person as static, unchanging objects, seemingly patiently awaiting the attention of the researcher, and age is seen as no more than one of many variables, invariably operationalised as chronological age. All too often it is either standardised 'out' of the analysis (as in the above example), or it is used as the criterion for specifying one particular section of the population for more detailed research. Nikander has commented that 'age is still often treated as an unproblematic and independent background variable that exerts its influence on the individual' (2002, p 12). It is considered unproblematic because any statistical correlation with age can be explained in terms of age: 'what else do you expect at that age?' Apart from biologists keen to study the ageing processes of the body, there is little scientific interest in explaining how this nuisance variable comes to be so influential.

Chronological age and mortality

In 1969, I decided to embark on postgraduate research into social networks among older people. As a statistician working in a medical sociology research unit, I had turned my attention from fertility to mortality data. In particular, I was interested in clarifying assumptions and expectations about 'life expectation'. I thought this an odd term, since it was obviously determined by expectations of death. The statistical distribution of 'age at death' in most western nations reveals a mean of about 80 and a standard deviation as little as 10 or 15 years. This represents some progress on the biblical 'three-score years and ten', and it fitted in with my own experience of older acquaintances in the world around me.

In planning my postgraduate research I had undertaken a fairly thorough review of the existing literature on later life. Much of this centred on the debate that pitted activity theory against disengagement theory, and there appeared to be little interest in clarifying the basic concepts of gerontology. What do we mean by 'old age'? How do we define it? What do we mean by 'elderly'? Why do we call it 'retirement'? What constitutes the ageing process? It seemed to me, naively perhaps, that gerontology was essentially about the approach of the end of life and, given this, that age-specific mortality rates were central to understanding the truth about age. It was obvious, for example, that if our life expectation were to be 200 years, say, then old age would not be associated with our 65th birthdays in the way it was in the UK around 1970. It is because mortality in the western world is associated with a narrow age range that we can expect to live to celebrate our 65th birthdays but that death becomes an increasingly likely prospect thereafter. Not only that, I argued, but should we survive to that age, then we can expect to lose increasing numbers of age peers, people of our own generation, in the years that follow.

In order to substantiate this view, I devised various simple stochastic models of how social networks change and then applied age-specific mortality rates to them (drawn from the 1966 Annual Report of the Registrar General for Scotland). This was the basis of my first contribution to gerontology (Bytheway, 1970). The paper began with claims that social gerontology had neglected (a) the definition of old age, and (b) the impact of mortality upon social networks of older people. With regard to the latter, I offered the following analogy:

> If a football match is played and each player is allowed to stop playing and go home when he feels tired, then the character of the game will change with time not only as a result of the players becoming tired, but also due to the decreasing number of players. Social gerontologists have studied in some detail whether the players mind getting tired, how they adjust to their tiredness, and how to postpone as long as possible their decision to leave the field. They have not studied directly the effect of depletion upon the remaining players and the characteristics of their game. (1970, pp 337-8)

In formulating this analogy I was attempting to focus attention on the network (that is, the game) rather than the individual. I applied the age-specific male mortality rates to the models I had devised and then, referring to the ubiquitous 'A', concluded that:

> ... with the perception that some of his peer acquaintances have died not as the result of tragic accidents but, as it were, of their own accord (as a result of reaching the 'natural' end of their lives), A makes a number of crucial adjustments. He begins to see death as normative behaviour for his age group. The deceased are no longer parties to deviant acts. The deceased have behaved appropriate for their age. Deaths of his friends may have a certain poignancy. He attends their funerals, but they are anticipated (if random) events which become part of his regulated life, like visits from his adult children, and wins on the horses. (p 339)

Setting aside a certain youthful irony in this commentary, there is perhaps an unwarranted confidence that the analysis had uncovered 'the truth' that this perception of a disintegrating network was a universal experience. I went on to pose the question: at what age might this occur? My analysis led to the following cautious conclusion:

> ... if this ageing man suddenly perceives death to be possible for his age group in non-accidental circumstances, by inference from either a perceived increased frequency of peer bereavements, or on the occurrence of more than one death within a short period of time, then this can be

expected to occur during his fifties, and almost certainly
before he retires at the age of 65. If he then goes on to see
this as an indicator of old age, and in so far as people 'enter
old age', then the final conclusion from these results is that
it seems reasonably likely that a considerable proportion of
people will be in the throes of entering old age well before
they retire at the age of 65. (p 341)

When this paper was published, I remember Raymond Illsley, then in
his 50s, jokingly expressing some disquiet at this conclusion. Some time
later, in 1999, I commented at the annual conference of the British
Society of Gerontology (BSG) that three well-respected members of
the Society, Anne Gilmore, Tom Kitwood and Margot Jeffreys had
died in the past year and, even allowing for some variation in age,
this tended to confirm my 1970 conclusion: that when three or more
age peers die within a relatively short space of time this marks the
approach of old age.

Setting this early analysis in the context of this chapter, what it
illustrates is the relevance of a more sociological perspective on the
experience of ageing in later life. Between the individual ageing process
and mass inter-generational relations, there are many social worlds
(for me, the BSG is a good example) within which interpersonal
networks and a shared sense of generation develop. How these worlds
are sustained and, if necessary, regenerated and how these efforts might
colour the later lives of participants, are questions that have been
neglected by gerontologists.

Demographic statistics

In February 2009 I posted the following somewhat intemperate letter
to *The Guardian*. It was published on its Letters page:

Dependency time-bomb?
Major demographic trends have resulted from the successes
of public health policies: as a population we are indeed
living longer. But George Magnus reacts with outdated
apocalyptic rhetoric (Dependency time-bomb, 4 February).
The idea that as we pass our 65th birthday we become
'dependent' on those still of 'working age' is as absurd as
the idea that we cease to be dependent the morning after
our 16th birthday. The 'time-bomb' will be defused the day
the government makes age discrimination in employment

illegal (including the mandatory retirement practices of some employers), and economists develop less hysterical and better informed analyses of population trends.

My interest in how demographic statistics are used by writers such as Magnus dates back to the 1970s, when I was struck by the ways in which pre-retirement manuals used demographic statistics to portray later life as a time of both opportunity and risk (Bytheway, 1981). It was not just the ways in which statistics were used to inform retirees, but also how the form – large numbers, small percentages and phrases such as 'at least' and 'many more' – served to dramatise the presentation of the data. More recently, I had discussed how the use of chronological age to define age groups can, paradoxically, expose evidence of age discrimination while at the same time consolidating ageist prejudice (Bytheway, 2005), In particular, I criticised the widespread use of open-ended upper age categories and how this practice homogenises all who are included.

Here is an example of such use (discussed in more detail in Bytheway and Johnson, 2009). The discussion document *Preparing for our Ageing Society*, published by the Department of Work and Pensions (2008), begins:

> Within 20 years half of the adult UK population will be over 50. One in four children born today will live beyond 100. These are dramatic shifts that have far-reaching consequences for us all, and our ageing population will change our society in many ways.

Note in particular the use of open-ended upper age categories: 'over 50' and 'beyond 100'. Note too the personalisation implicit in the unqualified claim that one child (in four) born 'today' will live to reach 100, and how this success overlooks the fate of the other three children.

This example illustrates how demographic statistics are used to gain the attention and concern of the wider public: 'dramatic shifts' in 'our society'. The potential influence of statistics on popular opinion is evident when we consider the impact of the news release that the ONS issued on 21 August 2008. This related to the same statistics that the Department of Work and Pensions drew upon, but the ONS demographers were primarily concerned to feature overall population growth: a rise of 0.6 per cent over the previous 12 months, not exactly headline material. Only on the third page did the news release address age, under the heading 'Other key points':

For the first time ever, there are more people of state pensionable age than under-16s. This reflects a decline in the number of under-16s, which fell to 18.9 per cent of the population, compared with rising numbers of men aged 65+ and women aged 60+, who accounted for 19.0 per cent of the population at mid-2007.(ONS, 2008)

These were the statistics that grabbed the attention of the press. Perhaps it was the opening phrase, the claim that this was 'the first time ever', which appealed to journalists. The news release went on to describe those aged 80 and over as 'the fastest growing' age group, another somewhat dramatic phrase.

Some press reactions were striking:

Britain is now home to more pensioners than children for the first time in the country's history, official population figures have disclosed

[...] The data re-ignited the debate over whether the Government is sufficiently prepared to deal with the long-term effects of an ageing population.

Ministers are grappling with the problem of how to fund the growing costs of social and nursing home care for the elderly. The NHS is also restricting access to drugs that could benefit sufferers of Alzheimer's and other conditions amid fears that the costs could cripple the health service. [...] (*Daily Telegraph*, 22 August 2008)

Ancient Britain: For the first time in history, there are more OAPs than children

[...] The astonishing milestone follows years of steadily rising life expectancy and a significant fall in the number of children and young teenagers.

Experts described the watershed moment as a 'wake-up call', warning of grave implications for many aspects of national life including the Health Service, social care for the elderly, pensions and housing. [...] (*Daily Mail*, 22 August 2008)

Grey Britain has more pensioners than children

[...] The long-term implications [...] will affect housing, health and education in the years to come. As soon as the preliminary figures emerged, officials of the ONS were

called in by ministers to discuss the policy implications. [...]
(*The Times*, 22 August 2008)

So what, we might ask, if there are now more people over 60/65 than under 16? Is this not simply evidence that the population is ageing? What's new about that? It is clear from the above extracts that the statistics were not the story, rather the press used them to remind the government that an ageing population implies increased costs in providing care, treatment, pensions and housing.

As was evident in George Magnus's article in *The Guardian* (referred to earlier), the age of 16 and pensionable age (currently 60 for women, 65 for men) have been used by welfare economists and government statisticians over many years to mark the boundaries of 'working age'. Setting the number of people of working age against the number under 16 plus the number of pensionable age is the basis for calculating the 'dependency ratio' that has been used extensively in this area of research. The ratio itself is nothing more than a rather odd arithmetic indicator of the ageing of the population, based largely on chronological age. It is the word 'dependency' that gives it some political charge. What the ONS new release implied, thereby exciting the press, was that 'for the first time in recorded history' there were more old people than children 'depending' on people of working age. In real life of course, the reverse is often true: people of working age depend on the unpaid domestic and caring work undertaken by pensioners and children. But that is beside the point: the image of officials being 'called in' and ministers 'grappling with the problem' as soon as 'the preliminary figures emerged', reflects the kind of moral panic in which ageism flourishes and the lives and well-being of older people are put at risk (Thane, 2000).

Living alone

One reason for concern over an ageing population is the implication that the costs of providing care will increase. The more people there are aged 75 or over, the more the costs of social care and healthcare will rise.

The primary aim of the study of long-term medication in later life (Bytheway et al, 2000) was to focus on how medication for people aged 75 or over living in their own homes was managed day by day. However, it also generated a number of case studies that cast light on the lives of people who live alone and who are supported by the health and social care services.

Our sample included 77 people aged 75 or over who were living in their own homes, and who had been receiving prescribed medication for 12 months or more. We identified 20 who either left their homes at most only twice during the two-week diary period, or who had severe problems with mobility. Of these, 10 lived alone, including Eric Farmer.

Our interviewer, Alison, described Eric as 'completely housebound, being unable to leave the house unassisted'. She visited him four times in March 1998 and agreed to keep the diary for him by phoning him periodically over the two-week period. He was 82, diabetic, registered blind (although he had some limited sight) and lived alone in a one-bedroom basement flat in Camden. He had lived in that area all his life and in his current flat for 28 years. He had never married and, for most of his life, had been a clock repairer. Recently, having fallen, he had been given a lifeline alarm connected to the social services office. He wore this round his neck. According to Alison, his hallway was 'stacked-out with boxes of incontinence pads, dressings, cans of sprays for his ulcers, a sharps box, clinical waste bags, etc.'

In his interviews he identified the following as people with whom he was in regular or occasional contact:

- David, his daily carer;
- a district nurse (not always the same person), who called every week to fill up a dosette box with his medicines (David, the carer, collected the prescription from the pharmacist);
- a chiropodist;
- a meals on wheels delivery person (meals were delivered each week, frozen and stored in a freezer that had been lent to him);
- a GP, who, he said, visited him once a month, but who had not been since the previous November (it was then March);
- someone who called to collect his clinical waste;
- Alan, a brother, who lived in Yorkshire and who phoned every day;
- Mr Jones, an old colleague, who visited him every four weeks or so to look after his financial affairs and to undertake tasks such as getting his dentures repaired.

David, the district nurses and the local social services office had keys to his flat.

The diary includes entries for every day of the fortnight (based on Alison's phone calls and visits) and these confirm that Eric was visited by David every day throughout, by the nurse on six of the 14 days, by the chiropodist on two days, once by meals on wheels and twice by the clinical waste collector. There were no other visitors noted. The diary records eight phone calls from his brother Alan and one from

Mr Jones. On one day, transport arrived to take him to the leg ulcer clinic. It was the only time he left his home.

In the first interview Eric mentioned recent dealings with the chiropodist and, in the course of this, he asked Alison to phone to make a new appointment. The interview was also interrupted by a phone call from the doctor's receptionist, advising him to reduce the dosage of one of his medicines. This led to Eric asking Alison to phone back to ask how he should do this. Alison was shocked when the receptionist suggested he should cut his tablets in half.

In the third interview Alison asked about his usual daily routine. She started in the following way:

> "Now tell me, I want you to think of your daily routine. Give me a typical or a usual day in your life, starting from when you get up in the morning. Not the out of the ordinary days but the usual day. So run through that for me just for a few moments."

> "Well I usually go and get up out of this chair because the bedroom is so cold, …"

> "So you sleep on the chair."

> "… and is facing north. It faces north and that room is so cold. Even when the heater is on, that room is so cold. I usually get up round about between seven or seven thirty to eight o'clock. And the first thing that I do, I make sure the light is on, that's the main thing. Usually, but not always now, because, as you know, now, … owing to the change in the time of the light, the light is coming up now between, well anything between seven and eight o'clock."

> "That's right."

> "I go into the kitchen and I switch the heater on for the kettle, to boil the kettle, for a cup of tea. I make a cup of tea for me with one teabag."

This response indicates that Eric had a clear idea of how his usual daily routine started. He adjusted this according to the season, and indicated that when it was warmer he would return to sleeping in his bedroom. Also, he was now no longer switching the light on first thing in the morning.

The time he woke and got up was variable, but not his immediate actions. His unqualified use of the continuing present tense in the above extract implies a lack of variation in this start to his day. Alone in the privacy of his home, he gets up and makes himself a cup of tea. Alison then asked about his medicines:

> "Then you take your medicines, do you?"

> "I take my medicine out with me. I take these tablets, this box, dose box. I take that out, take them tablets out, with me. Take my tablets, whatever they've allowed me to have in the first compartment."

Again there is confidence here in this first act in his daily routine of medication. Note, however, the potential variation implied in the phrase "whatever they've allowed me". He went on:

> "I take those and then I have something, either some biscuits or something. Because, normally now, being that David, my carer, is coming early, very often I don't hardly get a chance to have anything but the cup of tea, usually."

Thus a complete breakfast was normally not possible now, due to David's early arrival. In his experience, it was at this point that his daily routine was undermined. Alison asked when this happened and, although Eric wanted to be precise about time, he was unable to say when David normally arrived. Rather, he indicated that it might be anywhere between half past eight and half past nine and then, in some frustration, he referred to David's routines rather than his own:

> "It just depends where he is when he gets to this area, because he has to come from his area, where he lives, near the cricket ground at the Oval. He's got to come from the Oval, you see. Well, once he reaches this area where all his work is, if you can understand that …"

> "Yes."

> "Well, then he starts on … to look after the patients, and he likes to go to people who he's got to get up, cos some of them, he's got keys to get in. Some of them."

> "Yes."

"I don't think he's got many. I don't think he's got many keys. One or two of them where he's got to get in, to get the people up."

Eric shows here that he was aware of David's difficult and unpredictable work. He appears sympathetic with the needs of the few "patients who had to be got up". He conceded that they deserved priority over those like himself who were able to get up by themselves. Despite David having a key to his own flat, he was able to exclude himself from those in most need.

At this point, Alison turned Eric's attention back to his own routines. He pointed out that at present his ulcerated legs were bandaged and so he was unable to have an ordinary bath. David had to give him an "edge of the bath clean". He then described his usual breakfast and the interviewer asked what happened next. This was his response. Note how Eric started to answer the question but, almost immediately, had to abandon the idea that there was a usual routine:

"He does the breakfast. He puts things because – certain days, as you can understand – certain days I've got to keep everything warm while I attend to other people like, the nurse or whoever is coming to see me. And I tell him to – when he's finished with, with these things – I like to have hot milk in a bowl of cornflakes, you see. I have cornflakes in the morning."

So it was not just the arrival of David that complicated his early morning routines; he had to attend to other people like the nurse who came to see him. He had to "finish with these things" before he got back to his hot breakfast. At this point, his description returns to the pressures on David:

"And then he gets the machine out normally, that's if he isn't overworked, because they're pressurising him all the time, and he gets a call on my phone. I don't mind that. I don't mind that cos it's local. It's from Exeter Street, from his governor, and he calls him up, and he calls to David, and 'Is David there?' and I say 'Yes, David's here', and I pass the phone over to him, and then he gives him about four more or five more places where he wants him to call in at, you see, over and above what he's already got on his list, cos he's got a long list of names and addresses where he's got to call in at. See how things are worked out like, like planned out, you see."

So Eric recognised that David and the nurses were not just there to meet his particular needs; they were all involved in a world in which Eric was just one on a long list of names and addresses, a world in which he was expected to play an active role in assisting the home care service manage David's time.

Once again the interview moved back to his usual day. He explained how sometimes David did not have time to do the vacuum cleaning, and how sometimes he did not get his hot breakfast until around 10am. He described what was involved in preparing for the weekly trip to the leg ulcer clinic, and how on the previous Monday his name had not been on the transport list. As with his bath, he was bothered by such unexpected changes to normal arrangements.

His main meal was his dinner in the evening. His description of how this was produced again illustrates how he saw himself being caught up in the world of the care services:

> "How long does it take you to get all your dinner things prepared?"

> "Well, I'll get the dinner out of the freezer. I'll get the dinner and the sweet out of the freezer together either – cos I've got such a selection. You know what is coming up shortly, don't you?"

> "What?"

> "This Friday. This Friday. You know what's coming up, Friday?"

> "It's a Bank Holiday, isn't it? It's Good Friday."

> "I've got two whole weeks. The place is packed out solid and, do you know, there isn't even room for the spare packet of mixed veg."

> "Really? What do you mean, in your freezer?"

> "In the freezer."

> "Ah, so they've delivered all the meals for you?"

> "Yeah. For two whole weeks."

> "For two whole weeks."

"Cos don't forget … So I had to pay twenty, twenty, what was it now, twenty – two lots of ten fifteen. That's twenty, thirty something; twenty thirty pounds I had to pay this week. I said, 'Oh God, I've got to get some more money out of the float, get some more float money out.'"

In this instance, he has no interest or sympathy with the people who deliver the meals: where they are going over Easter, or the task of delivering twice as many meals as usual. Rather his concerns are where to put the mixed vegetables and how to get the money to pay for the meals.

Alison then asked him about the time he usually had his dinner and, once again, he described how his routine was threatened by interruptions:

"At about what, six o'clock, you eat? Or a bit earlier?"

"Er, seven o'clock usually. If nobody arrives and nobody comes and nobody interferes and there's no more phone calls, 'cos, usually my brother – he knows now what my routine is. And he'll ring me from Yorkshire and he'll say 'How are you going on then? Why haven't you rung me?'"

"What time does he usually phone?"

"Usually round about seven or half past seven, and he tries to get to me before I have my dinner, because I hate getting up when I'm eating my dinner."

There is evidence, possibly, in this description of changes and tensions in his lifelong relationship with his brother, Alan.

Finally the interview comes to the end of the usual day. Alison asks about switching the lights off. His reply typifies his commitment to the detail of the daily routine:

"Well, I don't switch the passage one off until I get into bed, until I've got a torch that I keep so that I can see my way about, so that I can get into bed, and then I switch the passage light off, cause that is a long-life lamp."

This case study illustrates how someone can develop a sense of inclusion in the world of care. However, rather than simply passively receiving care and support in order to continue to lead an allegedly 'independent' life, he has become a significant player in the worlds of those who support him. He is aware of the pressures and values inherent in their work and willingly helps by handling their phone calls.

In his description of his usual day, there is a constant tension between a desire for order, control and normality, and the unpredictable intrusion of callers. But, as Alison found, he knows how to deal with callers and how to take advantage of their presence. His description of his usual day, supported by the evidence of his diary, reveals the extent to which he is now isolated from neighbours and the local community. It may be that his old colleague, Mr Jones, and the chiropodist are active locally, helping others, but their contact with Eric is now limited to telephone calls and occasional visits. Similarly, it would appear that the chances that he might ever meet up again with his brother in Yorkshire are slim and that family life has been reduced to the routine evening phone call.

Important questions for the care services are raised by Eric's situation. As someone who represents the consequences of 'an ageing population' is he being provided with the kind of support that 'works'? There is no doubt that he depends on the regular support of David and the others, but, to what extent do they depend on him in order to gain some satisfaction from their work and in order to get through a long and busy working day? And to what extent is he dependent upon others of pensionable age: his brother and Mr Jones, for example? Undoubtedly, policy would claim that he is being kept out of hospital, living 'independently' in his own flat, but what kind of 'independence' does he enjoy? From what aspects of public life is he excluded, and into what has he become included? Finally, what does this case study tell us about the concept of dependency and, in particular, the interpretation of the dependency ratio?

Bureaucracy

Most organisations use chronological age for bureaucratic purposes. For example, when I visited my local health centre recently, the first question the receptionist asked me was 'What's your date of birth?' When I asked her how often there was more than one person on her list with the same date of birth, she replied 'Not often'. She then went on to explain that asking for a patient's date of birth is the easiest and quickest way of locating his or her records: it avoids possible complications in the spelling of names.

Bureaucracies need efficient ID systems and, typically, these are based upon such questions as 'What is your name?', 'Where do you live?', 'What is your date of birth?' In combination, they generate an identity that is unique in the vast majority of cases: how likely is it that there is more than one person with the same name, the same date of birth and living at the same address? There are, however, three problems with this line of argument. The first is that uniqueness is not guaranteed absolutely and bureaucracies prefer to be one hundred per cent sure. The second is that the space required to record each individual set of information is substantial. And the third is that mistakes and deception are easy. Personal names, for example are typically composites of at least two names, requiring over a dozen characters when spelt out, and frequently complicated by nicknames and changes in surname. Addresses have become simpler with the introduction of postcodes, but even then several people may share an address and perhaps a hundred or so the same postcode.

So it is easy to see why the receptionist prefers to ask for a patient's date of birth first: at a stroke it narrows the field. No matter how many times we change our address, or take on a new name, our date of birth remains the same. It is something that is easy to remember and difficult to forget. But bureaucracies also use date of birth to establish age and thereby potentially to control access to resources. No doubt, somewhere along the line, Eric Farmer was asked for his date of birth. In undertaking the RoAD project, we investigated one particular example of this, relating to breast cancer screening. In the March 2006 RoAD newsletter, posted to several hundred older people, we included the following item:

> There are approximately 41,000 women diagnosed with breast cancer each year in the UK, and approximately 290 men. Breast cancer predominately affects older women with 80% occurring over the age of 50 years. Many older women however are not aware that the risk of developing breast cancer increases with age. Very little is known about the breast cancer experience of older women or about their access to health care services, treatments and information and support services.
>
> So, over the coming year, the Policy and Research Team of Breast Cancer Care is focusing on older people and their experiences of breast cancer. They have contacted RoAD as they are very interested to hear about the concerns and experiences of older people, and the issues that people think Breast Cancer Care should take into account as part of their work. This will help inform their future research and campaigns, as well as helping them to develop their information and support services.

> RoAD is interested in hearing of your experiences or opinions about services relating to breast cancer.

There was a half-page box for comments in the reply-paid insert that was sent out with the newsletter and 47 were returned. Of these responses, 11 described personal experience of screening for breast cancer, and six drew on the experience of relatives or friends; 11 offered general comment on the issues raised.

The issue that was of most concern was whether women over a certain age are called automatically for breast cancer screening or whether they have to choose to book an appointment. Some linked their own experience specifically to policy and practice. For example, a 70-year-old woman wrote:

> In Nottingham, women have breast screening every three years until they reach the age of 70 years. If they want further x-rays they are responsible for remembering when another one is due as they will not be contacted by the hospital. Many women probably forget and – as the risk increases with age – it seems unfair not to notify older people.

And a 62-year-old in Milton Keynes wrote:

> After 65 or 70 we do not get a call for this service, we have to ask for it. Is this right when we are told it occurs in so many elderly people?

Another 68-year-old woman wrote to say she was worried, noting that:

> despite a family history of cancer + a (benign) lumpectomy in 1991, I was removed from the clinic's annual checklist at 65, but offered 3-yearly mobile unit screening until 70. After that I can request screening but will not be called automatically.

At least she was informed that she was being removed from the list. Others did not appear to have been so lucky. One woman, for example, aged 67 and living in Brighton, wrote:

> All I know is that I have tests every three years and receive the results ... At one point I thought the tests would cease at a certain age but I think I am allowed another one. Really they should go on as long as the person is alive, as should all kinds of routine care like eye tests, hearing, blood and so on.

A 70-year-old woman from Bristol agreed:

Free annual health checks (including breast screening) should be automatic for people over 65. Evidence shows that early health interventions lead to lower demands for intensive and critical care and reduces pressure on and cost to the NHS.

Another woman commented on changes in policy, and how this has left her uncertain about whether she could make arrangements to be reminded:

From age 50–65 we are called 3 yearly for mammograms. After this age we had to pay for screening and arrange our own screening. This has changed now, screening is free, but we arrange our own appointments when we think we need them. Alright for people able to organise themselves. I don't know if you can arrange for your surgery to 'remind' you.

Another 76-year-old woman, living in York, summarised her history extending back 15 years to the time when two lumps had been tested, and then reported:

Since then, 3 yearly, I have attended Breast Clinic for Mammogram and feel that this surveillance is necessary. I follow instructions on breast examinations and *on my own account* telephone every three years to ask for an appointment. Always this is forthcoming. I am 76 years of age and would be most unhappy if this service was unavailable. (emphasis as in original)

Although she did not comment directly on whether or not she considered this acceptable, it is significant that she emphasised the phrase 'on my own account'.

At that time, the Breast Screening Programme (BSP) of the NHS provided free breast screening every three years for all women in the UK aged 50 and over (NHSBSP, 2006a). Throughout the country, specialised screening units had been established in hospitals, mobile units and other locations such as shopping centres. Each unit posted an individual invitation to be screened to all eligible women in a defined local population. Initially the target age group was women aged 50 to 64. Following publication of the NHS Cancer Plan in 2000 (Department of Health, 2000), women up to and including the age of 70 also received routine invitations for screening. Coverage was measured by the percentage of women in a targeted population who had had at least one screening test over the course of the previous three years. In

March 2004, coverage was 75% for women aged 53 to 64 and 43% for women aged 65 to 69 (Government Statistical Service, 2005, Table 2).

The Programme explained that women under the age of 50 were not offered routine screening because it was not as effective and the incidence of breast cancer was lower in that age group (NHSBSP, 2006a). As women passed the menopause, however, interpretation of mammogram x-rays became more reliable. Moreover, breast cancer was more common in post-menopausal women and the risk continued to increase with rising age.

Once women reached the upper age limit for routine invitations, previously their 65th birthday, now their 70th, they could make their own appointments for screening. Although not routinely invited, they were encouraged to call the local unit to request breast screening every three years. The Programme produced cards to help them remember, to be handed out at their last routine breast screening appointment. Also, in association with Age Concern, the Programme issued a leaflet titled 'Over 70? You are still entitled to breast screening' (Department of Health, 2004). This stated that the risk of breast cancer increased with age and that it was important that women continued to be screened every three years because early detection reduced risks.

The statistics indicated that 24% of women aged 70, 11% of those aged 71 to 74 and 1.6% of those aged 75 or over had been covered by the Programme (Government Statistical Service, 2005, Table 2). Thus there was a marked decline in take-up with age over the age of 70. Nevertheless, as many as 176,500 women aged 70 or more were screened in the year 2003-04. In the large majority of cases this was as a result of their requesting an appointment: only 553 had received an invitation (Government Statistical Service, 2005, Table 4). Statistics on the outcome indicated that the rate of cancers detected per 1,000 women screened rose from 8.8 aged 60 to 64 to 11.8 aged 65 to 69 and 16.1 aged 70 or over (Government Statistical Service, 2005, Table 9). Thus the effectiveness of screening as a strategy for detecting previously undiagnosed breast cancer appeared to increase with age.

The Age Concern/BSP leaflet, although stating that it was 'important' that older women continued to be screened every three years, offered no explanation as to why they were not routinely invited to attend. The NHS Cancer Plan had commented: 'Evidence of the balance between the benefit and harm of screening is less clear in women over 70, but will be kept under close review' (Department of Health, 2000, para 3.5). There was no indication of what kind of harm might be caused by screening. The Advisory Committee on Breast Cancer Screening (NHSBSP, 2006b, p 36), in considering the benefits of screening for women over the age of 70, first drew on international research to argue that there was 'a benefit to women who wish to continue being screened after the age of 70'. It then commented:

> For women to benefit from breast screening, they must be in good health and have a life expectancy of at least about 10 years. For most women aged 50-70 years in England, this is a fair assumption. As women age, however, they become more heterogeneous in this respect, and attendance rates fall with increasing age. Therefore, at this stage it seems appropriate that a decision about whether or not to be screened is taken at an individual level, bearing in mind personal circumstances, rather than offering all older women a blanket invitation to attend for screening. (NHSBSP, 2006b, p 36)

The evidence supporting this argument can be challenged by asking why exactly was it considered appropriate not to offer older women a 'blanket invitation'? The rationale for issuing such invitations to a defined population is proactively to offer women an opportunity to be screened. In the case of the Programme, however, it was an invitation, not a direction: women aged 50 to 70 were free to decline. Indeed, there had been a shift over the years in the wording, from promotion of screening as an effective preventive measure, to the promotion of an informed choice (NHSBSP, 2006b, p 10). So a blanket invitation could be issued to older women, reminding them of the benefits of early detection and offering them an informed choice too. As a consequence, women aged 70 or over would be free to opt out of screening (as are younger women) rather than to opt in, as they were currently 'encouraged' to do.

The aim of the Programme was to reduce premature deaths – it was, after all, set explicitly in the rhetoric of 'saving lives' – and the evidence indicated that it was proving very successful. Given limited resources, few people would disagree with this aim. Indeed, there will be women in their 70s or 80s who have lost younger relatives through breast cancer who would argue that there are few more tragic experiences.

Nevertheless, as responses to the RoAD newsletter item indicated, many older women were left uncertain as to why the link they had with the Programme should change, what the risks were that they might yet develop breast cancer, and what they should do to prevent this happening. They saw the present arrangement as unfair, placing older people at unnecessary risk, particularly those who were not adept at 'organising themselves'. They were particularly anxious when there was a history of cancer in their family. One respondent spelt out the basic principle that the situation offended: 'all elderly people should have equal medical treatment to the young whatever their condition'.

However sensitively it might be done, being informed around the time of your 70th birthday that you are being removed from a mailing list must leave you feeling excluded. To then add that you are still free to request attendance seems rather like being told by an old friend that, although you are no longer on their Christmas card list, you are still free to send them one.

What I have attempted to demonstrate in this chapter is that even though chronological age, as a variable like social class, might be called a meaningless contrivance, it is extremely powerful as a predictor of more tangible life circumstances, so much so that research often has to be designed in order to remove its impact. Given this, it is hardly surprising that government and other agencies should pay so much attention to it, and that this attention in turn ensures that chronological age is 'made real'. However, policies inspired by alarmist headlines are always suspect. The increasing proportion of older people in the population has not happened suddenly or unexpectedly, and it should be one of the easier trends to adjust to. When full account is taken of the circumstances of people such as Eric Farmer, and of the issues entailed in providing access to services such as breast screening, then demographic trends will be set in their proper perspective. We can make appropriate adjustments to policy and cease to panic.

Questions for discussion

1   The last time you read about 'the ageing population', were you alarmed or did you feel that the issue was being exaggerated?

2   What's your reaction to the suggestion that the baby boom generation, born in the late 1940s, have had a charmed life?

3   What do you imagine is the weekly cost to the NHS and social care services of supporting people like Eric Farmer? In reflecting upon his circumstances and the alternatives, do you think this is money well spent?

4   Do you approve of chronological age being used to ration services such as breast cancer screening?

NINE

Gerontologists and older people

In this penultimate chapter I want to discuss the relationship between gerontologists and older people. There is in this a classic example of 'us and them'. As Margaret Simey commented a few years ago, when addressing the annual conference of the British Society of Gerontology:

> "For us, 'we' are older people and gerontologists are 'them'."

To overcome this harsh divide, there have been moves to promote 'participative research' through projects in which older people are actively involved in ways other than just as research subjects. The RoAD project is a good example, and I have little doubt that the outcomes would have been very different had the project not involved older people from the outset. It was funded according to a planned schedule and specific aims and it had a budget to cover the expenses of all the various participants. The entire project was undertaken jointly with Help the Aged and many (but not all) of the older people who took part were members of the local forums that Help the Aged supported.

One consequence of such collaboration is that as researchers we may find ourselves engaged in tasks and situations that cannot be easily justified in terms of the agreed contract. Nevertheless, they provide many insights into the wider context of the issues being researched. In addition, we may find the tables being turned and questions being posed about our involvement and commitments. Here is one example drawn from a long-running involvement that I had in the 1970s and 1980s with Age Concern.

In 1974, when at Keele University, I undertook a project for Age Concern researching the attitudes and priorities of its many local groups. A year later I moved to University College Swansea and, shortly after arriving, members of Age Concern West Glamorgan reminded me that they had responded to the Keele enquiry. When they asked me if I would join their committee I was pleased to accept. In 1978 a bid to the Welsh Office for the funding of a Hospital Discharge Scheme was accepted. I saw the setting up of this scheme as an opportunity to develop a proposal for funded research into hospital discharge and community-based care. While the newly appointed development officer for the scheme started meeting hospital staff and recruiting volunteers, I decided to pick a random sample of half a dozen streets and spend a day in each. The aim would be to find out what local residents knew about local hospitals and, in particular, what happened when older neighbours were discharged. I knocked on every door and told anyone who responded about the new scheme. I said that, in addition to recruiting new volunteers, we were interested in finding out something of what had happened to older neighbours in the past.

I learnt much about how neighbouring worked in West Glamorgan (Bytheway, 1979b, 1979c). For example, on one street there was a long-time resident of pensionable age who was severely disabled; she rarely left her house. Many of her neighbours knew this and, over the years, they had learned to trust her and to pass messages on through her. She was a key source of information for the informal care that went on in the street. In particular, she was the person who knew who was ill and who was coming home from hospital. As well as her being dependent on others, I realised that many of her neighbours were conversely dependent on her. In talking to her and to several of her neighbours, it was evident that the informal system of mutual care in that street would be at risk should she be admitted to hospital for any length of time. For example, she pointed out to me another house on the street and explained that another older person lived there, someone who had moved recently in order to be nearer her daughter. She told me that the family saw to her needs and warned me that I wouldn't get an answer when I knocked on her door. True enough, I had not got an answer when I had knocked earlier in the day. For me, this was valuable evidence of the substantial difference between systems of care based on neighbours and those based on families.

In 1982, I found myself unemployed between contracts. Coincidentally, the Hospital Discharge Scheme's development officer had obtained a new job and, while the post was being advertised and filled, I agreed to take it on temporarily. This was the only time in the whole of my career when I was employed as a 'care worker', and it left me with a fund of anecdotes and a wealth of experience. After six months, I returned to the university to undertake the research with the steelworkers and their families. My links with Age Concern proved to have significant consequences, as the following case study demonstrates.

Reacting to need

In Bytheway (1989a) I published a case study of one of the steelworker families. In 1984 I had interviewed Tom Wilson. He lived with Gwyn, his 24-year-old son who suffered from epilepsy. Doris, Tom's older sister, lived with Martin, their father, a hundred yards or so down the road, in a village near Port Talbot. Doris had serious heart disease and Martin, born in 1901, was rapidly losing his eyesight. I had returned to see Tom in April 1985 to give him a copy of a report on the redundancy study and to ask him about his father. He agreed to me returning a week or so later when he would introduce me to Doris and Martin. It was a pleasant sunny day when I returned and both Doris and Martin appeared phlegmatic about their health problems as they talked about how they managed from day to day.

Two months later, I was visiting the local Age Concern office when they had just received a call for help from Doris. As a result of my work for the Hospital Discharge Scheme, I was familiar with the local services and so I volunteered to go round to see her. This is my account of what happened:

> when I arrived in the mid-afternoon I found Doris looking very tired and weak. Martin had been ill in bed for three days. [... she] asked me if I could get a urine bottle for Martin from the health centre. She told me that the doctor had been that morning and had said he would arrange for a consultant to come to see Martin. She thought I might have been him.
>
> It was not appropriate to press her with questions, but I was prepared to sit there whilst she talked. She described with some exasperation how the doctor had called, had asked Martin how he was doing. Martin had answered 'not too bad', the doctor had said 'that's alright then', and that had been about it. Typical of men, she said. In the course of this, a car drew up, and she suggested this might be the consultant. I looked out of the window and saw a man getting out of his car with an open-necked shirt and large medallion round his neck. Not the consultant, he was George, the secretary of the club that Tom would take Martin to two or three times a week. George sat down opposite Doris and did what he could to raise her spirits.
>
> She had said, in passing, that Martin's bedding needed changing because he had spilt his coffee. As George talked, it occurred to me that this was probably the best chance of the bedding being changed that week. It might be that others would be calling in, but it might also be that Martin would be left in damp sheets for several days, Doris growing more and more depressed. I had the time whilst George talked to savour what I was about to propose: two virtually

strange men going upstairs to strip and change the old man's bed. When I put it to Doris, she thought long, looking at the two of us, doubting I suspect our competence, but realising that this might indeed by the only opportunity. She and George went upstairs to see Martin. She then called down that it was all right. So the three of us, in a crowded bedroom with precious little leg-room, managed to strip and remake the bed, Martin rolling from one side to another to save him having to get up. George remained upstairs to do what he could to cheer up Martin, and, assured that there was no more to be done, I set off to get a bottle from the health centre. Unfortunately, by that time it was 4.30 and the centre was closed. I left a message asking the nurse to call round as soon as possible. (Bytheway, 1989a, pp 97-8)

A little over two years later, I returned again to give Tom and Doris a copy of the report I wrote for the Joseph Rowntree Foundation on family care. Doris gave me a long account of how Martin had died nine days after George and I had called and changed his bed. Much of what she said was critical of the GP. He always explained Martin's condition, she said, as being due to old age: 'Everything was old age to him'. She also described her own deteriorating condition and her struggle to obtain effective treatment. In particular she said that her own age, 'only 62', was held against her: she was 'too young' to be eligible for the help she needed.

I decided that I should write the 1989 paper because, although I had come into contact with Martin's family in a convoluted way, originally it was through Tom being included in the systematic sample of older steelworkers, rather than through my links with Age Concern. At that time, no one had referred Doris or Martin to the health or social services. Rather, I claimed, they represented – in a statistical sense – 'a minority of between 5 and 20 per cent of the population' and that the family had had the kind of experiences that many will have when the eldest member comes to die (1989a, p 103).

Older people and involuntary retirement

In thinking through the relationship between gerontologists and older people, it is as well to recognise, not only that older people can participate in research, but also that gerontologists grow older. How do we make sense and good use of our own hard-earned first-hand experience? It is a fact that from time to time gerontologists tell anecdotes that are intended to indicate some kind of recognition of their age. All too often this is done in a self-deprecatory way that, unintentionally no doubt, appears to reflect an ageist belief that there is nothing good about growing older. Are there different ways in which we can make use of our personal experiences? The case study described earlier is an example of how I have been able to look back at a particular experience and make sense of it in terms of my own unfolding career as an empirical researcher.

In planning the RoAD project, it was decided that although older people had to be involved in the project 'at every level', we would not impose any age bars: no one would be 'too old' and no one would be 'not old enough'. As explained in Chapter One, all participants would be asked to draw on their experience as an 'older person'. Some participants, however, were below pensionable age and still active in the labour market and, arguably, they had less experience to call upon. Even so, one of the youngest, aged 44, felt able to participate because she was a grandmother, and others made similar claims to 'older' status.

The RoAD fieldworkers were key to the success of the whole project and they agreed to identify themselves as 'older people' when working with the diarists. Having identified certain experiences in the diaries as potential examples of age discrimination, we wanted the interviews to move into a more conversational mode. We wanted the fieldworker to discuss these selected experiences and to compare notes with the diarist/interviewee on their respective experiences of age discrimination. Overall this strategy worked well but occasionally it spilled into exchanges outside the confines of the recorded interview. Here, for example, is what Anna French, one of the fieldworkers, wrote about her second visit to Mike, one of the diarists. She called to go through his diary and to talk to him about it:

> I left behind my jacket after the second interview, and Mike phoned me to tell me so. I felt quite embarrassed, because earlier that day I had mistakenly gone to the block of flats adjacent to Mike's. I was *sure* I was at the right place, but I couldn't find his name and number on the outside door. I phoned him on my mobile. "You're having a senior moment," he told me. Later, when he recounted to me his fears of the 'beginning of the end', I realised I had had a similar feeling. "I hope you find your way back to your car," he said jokingly, as I left. So when he phoned me to tell me I'd left my jacket, I felt doubly mortified. He brought my jacket to me in a carrier bag at my place of work in town

(he was passing there anyway). When I got home I found an unknown umbrella in the bag. To my shameful pleasure, I phoned him back to tell him. "Oh, yes, I'd brought an umbrella with me because it might have rained. Please keep it as a gift." We both had a laugh. But I woke in the night, worrying about the whole business.

Compared with some RoAD participants, Anna and Mike were relatively young: he was just turned 60 and she in her late 50s. The joke about 'a senior moment' suggests that both felt rather self-conscious in finding themselves engaged in a project on age discrimination, being undertaken in association with 'Help the Aged'.

There were many moments for all of us, when we were unsettled by our age and our relation with the RoAD project. For me, a particularly disturbing event was the publication in *The Oldie* of a small item suggesting that it was ironic that the Open University should be hosting the RoAD project when it was also imposing involuntary retirement on several hundred members of staff. I wrote a response pointing out that the OU was not alone in enforcing age-specific retirement policies and that a 'vigorous debate' was under way within the University. We on the RoAD project, I wrote, considered such policies to be 'ageist, discriminatory and unacceptable, and should be made illegal'.

The fact is that when the Employment Equality (Age) Regulations were implemented in the UK in October 2006 many older workers were led to believe that their employment rights would be strengthened. For example, in March 2006 Alan Johnson, then Trade Secretary, had commented: 'It's all about choice – not work till you drop but choose when you stop'.[1] So it was a shock for many to discover that the new regulations invited employers to set the 65th birthday as the national 'default retirement age'. Drawing on my own experience and that of various colleagues, the following is an account of how this worked out at the OU.

The OU has a well-earned reputation for 'lifelong learning', and older graduates are frequently used to represent the University's slogan of 'open as to people'. It is itself a large-scale employer and, in particular, for many years it provided satisfying work for many retired teachers and lecturers. Most had been part-time 'associate lecturers' (ALs) whose job it was to tutor OU students in their local area. In 2006, there were approximately 1,000 ALs over the age of 65.

Around that time, a 69-year-old OU graduate contacted the RoAD project to let us know that he had been told that he was 'too old to

be considered' for an AL post. Similarly, an AL complained to RoAD
as follows:

> In 1999 I was given a contract for only two years – I was
> then 63 – to take me up to the age of 65. Younger tutors
> were given a contract for the duration of the course. Now
> I have to apply regularly every year in order to continue
> tutoring – younger tutors do not.[2]

These experiences indicated that in 2006, before the new regulations
came into force, the OU was employing many people over the age of
65, but in ways that were less secure and satisfactory than for younger
employees.

In September 2006, the University issued a memorandum regarding
the implementation of the new regulations, explaining first that it
was now illegal to discriminate on grounds of age, and that it aimed
to become 'free of discrimination'. There then followed a section on
retirement age which started:

> The University has decided that the normal retirement age
> for *all* employees will continue to be age 65 [...] However,
> requests [...] to stay on beyond this age will be considered
> and extensions will be granted *exceptionally* [...] (emphasis
> as in original)[3]

Elsewhere on the website it stated that staff would be treated solely
on the basis of merit, ability and potential, regardless of a long series
of characteristics including age. On the 'Equality and Diversity' page,
there were further reassurances: a truly inclusive organisation, differences
respected and valued, everyone able to fulfil their potential, and so
on. It stated that the University recognised that people with different
backgrounds, and diversity of experiences 'bring fresh ideas and
perceptions which enrich the experience of all those who participate'
in the life of the University.

In February 2007, the University issued a new strategy document.
This stated that a priority would be to 'review policies and procedures to
enable the OU to abolish the retirement age'. This appeared to reverse
an earlier decision and implied that no one would be involuntarily
retired on reaching a specified age. The rationale for this began
positively. It said that this would fit well with the University's values
and that there were good business reasons to do so. However, it ended
negatively: 'Reviewing the age profile and conducting an equality
impact assessment is a priority because our academic staff is markedly
older than the rest of the sector and we need to understand the reasons

for this'. It appeared that the retirement age would only be abolished once a strategy had been agreed for changing the age profile and that, in the meantime, the retirement policy would remain in place.

Over the following months, ALs and other members of the academic staff continued to inform RoAD of their anger and distress. One wrote:

> Prior to 1st October 2006, the OU showed some discrimination against over 65s, but very much less than that shown now.

And another:

> I've only this week had an email from a staff tutor and a course team chair apologising for their very long delay (and silence) and apologising also for not being able to invite me for interview because I'm 'too old' (and saying how appalling they think it is for them to have to say this).

These colleagues were bitter that retirement was being forced on them as a result of 'age equality'. They were disappointed knowing that in former years the University had led the way on many other access and equality issues.

Since that time, along with a number of colleagues, I have endeavoured to persuade the University to abandon its retirement policies, and to adopt more sensitive practices regarding retirement from employment. We have argued that it should offer continuing support for those who wish to maintain a productive association with the University.

The disintegration of age-related social worlds

This section is based on a paper I presented in October 2008 to the Sixth International Symposium on Cultural Gerontology, *Extending Time, Emerging Realities, Imagining Response*, held at the University of Lleida in Catalunya, Spain. My paper was dedicated to the memory of Mike Hepworth.[4] I decided that I wanted to feature ways in which social worlds began to disintegrate as we grow older and to attempt to illustrate this with evidence ranging from national statistics to personal experience. A photograph of Mike was displayed on the screen as people entered the lecture theatre. It was a touching moment, not only because he was a good friend to me, but also because he had supported the development of Dedal-Lit, the research group based in the Department of English and Linguistics at Lleida, which was hosting the Symposium.

Cultural gerontology is not yet recognised as an 'established branch' of gerontology and some would argue that this is how it should remain. Lars Andersson, for example, describes it as an umbrella covering 'many disparate academic, political and social issues' (Andersson, 2002, p vii). The current interest in cultural gerontology, I argued in Lleida, reflects a reaction against research that has consolidated rather than challenged popular beliefs about old age (Bytheway, 2002). In contrast, there is comparatively little research that has revealed the lived experience of growing older (rather than that of 'being old') and of the drift in time from earlier to later life. The focus on 'the elderly person with needs' has also meant that little attention has been given to change in the much more general social worlds of later life (Gubrium, 2005) and, in particular, to the impact that death has upon these worlds. It is significant that Daniel Cole, anticipating the demise of his mother, wrote the following in his diary for the TOG project:

> ... A project to do with the over-75's and their lives would
> be lacking without some real-time account of the last days
> of life, no matter how subjectively reported or recorded.

Death is seen in gerontology – if at all – as the end of the ageing person's life rather than as a feature in the lives of those who continue to survive.

The aim of the paper, I declared, was to draw on readily available evidence in developing a broader understanding of finitude in later life. I began with some national statistics.

'When am I likely to die?' On the face of it, this is a simple question and most of us, for most our lives, assume we will have our three-score years and ten and perhaps a few more. Setting aside the diagnosis of terminal illness, falling under the ubiquitous bus or the possibility of homicide, the expected answer to the question will refer to chronological age: 'You are likely to die between ages X and Y'. Most demographic indicators of mortality, however, measure risk per unit of time, often (as discussed in Chapter Eight) 'controlling for age'. In this way, different populations can be compared and trends over time monitored. But an age-standardised mortality rate does not answer the question of when I am likely to die. To attempt this, Table 9.1 lists the single-year age groups with the highest number of deaths in England and Wales in 2007. This shows that the 'top six' for men cover the age range 81 to 86 inclusive and for women the range is 82 to 87. The numbers decline on either side of these ranges; for example, at the age of 50 there were only 1,156 and 840 deaths of men and women respectively, and likewise only 246 and 1,366 for those aged 100. Infant mortality is no longer as high as it used to be: only 1,889 male and

1,456 female deaths before the first birthday. Clearly it is reasonable, for most of us for most of our lives, to expect to live for 80-odd years.

Table 9.1: The single-year age groups with the highest number of deaths in England and Wales in 2007

Male		Female	
Age	**Number of deaths**	**Age**	**Number of deaths**
82	8,790	86	12,527
86	8,744	87	12,297
85	8,710	85	11,637
81	8,682	84	10,724
83	8,677	83	10,065
84	8,651	82	9,398

Developing the argument for Table 9.1, the analysis presented in Table 9.2 begins with the total number of deaths in England and Wales in 2007, halves this number, and then identifies the *narrowest* age range with more than this number. Table 9.2 indicates that over half of all male deaths were of men aged 72 to 87 inclusive, and that over half of all female deaths were of women aged 80 to 93. Given the data upon which the table is based, it is reasonable to answer the question 'When will I die?' with 'between 72 and 87' for men and 'between 80 and 93' for women. Statisticians might call these the 'modal ranges' of the age at death distribution.[5]

Table 9.2: The narrowest age ranges with over 50% of all deaths in England and Wales in 2007

	Male	Female
Total number of deaths of all ages	240,787	263,265
50%	120,394	131,632
Narrowest age range with more than 50%	72-87	80-93
Number of deaths in this age range	123,560	134,396

I compared this statistic for 12 European countries. Table 9.3 shows significant differences that have important implications for public health, but the point I made in Lleida was that the differences in Table 9.3 could have been greater. Regardless of where we live in Europe, we can all expect to live at least 60 years. But having done so, we can then expect to die within the following 35 years and, depending upon our sex and where we live, within a range of ages that is less than 20 years in extent. These simple statistics are evidence of the predictability of mortality in the modern world.

Table 9.3: The narrowest age range with over 50% of all deaths in 12 European countries

	Men	**Women**
Country with the highest mortality rate	61-80	73-87
Country with the lowest mortality rate	75-90	81-94

When, as older people, we are urged, as we often are, to think positively about 'twenty, thirty or even more years of active life!' we should be alert, as was George Hillman, to the possibility of the opposite. No sooner have we settled into a risk-reducing, age-defying post-60th-birthday activity, than we hear of the sad, but no longer demographically tragic, news of the death of a contemporary, such as that of Mike Hepworth.

The significance of the concept of 'natural' death is well brought out by Gilleard (2008). He reviewed the case of Harold Shipman, a family doctor practising in a suburb of Manchester, England, who became 'one of the twentieth century's most prolific mass murderers' (pp 88-9). In 2000, Shipman was convicted on 15 counts of murder and the subsequent inquiry concluded that he had murdered a total of 215 of his patients (Smith, 2002). Noting that over 90% of Shipman's victims were aged 65 years and over, Gilleard argues that the primary reason why he was able to kill so many and not be noticed, was because his killings mirrored the actuality of death in contemporary British society: 'unlike most mass murderers, his victims were almost entirely "old" people' (p 90). Most deaths of people of that age are seen as 'deaths that conform to the natural order, and so need not be prevented' (p 91).

A similar illustration can be found in the aftermath of Hurricane Katrina. Well over 1,000 people died in Louisiana in 2005 as a result of the hurricane, and the number of deaths has been widely used to emphasise the scale of the disaster. Although the popular assumption is that the victims were primarily poor and black, the fact is that over half the deaths were of people aged 70 or more (Bytheway, 2007a). Arguably the real scandal was that the authorities provided so few resources for the effective evacuation of older people, particularly those in care homes and hospitals, at the time of the hurricane.

These two examples confirm how death over the age of 60 is seen as 'natural' and not in itself newsworthy. Arguably this is why, in debates about euthanasia, age is so often bracketed with terminal illness. The statistics of the two disasters reflect the national picture of age-specific mortality. Does the same interpretation apply at the rather more personal level? I decided, in preparing my Lleida presentation, to offer an example of a formally constituted group, of whom all but one were dead. This was the sibship of four sisters and four brothers to which my mother belonged.

Regarding marriage and parenthood, all except the youngest brother had married and had children. The third brother, widowed in 1950, had remarried in the 1950s. In total the seven siblings became parents to 21 children (including myself). With their spouses, there were 16 members of this sibship and only one was still alive in 2008. She is my aunt, Moira Chadwick, born in 1905, a centenarian like Frances Partridge and May Nilewska.

To what extent does the history of this sibship reflect the typical course of family life? Between 1957 and 1975 there were no births to, nor deaths of, the 14 surviving siblings (and spouses). They were all married, all parenting and they all, in time, became grandparents. Then, between 1975 and 1995, 12 died. The only survivors of the group were my aunt and her brother's second wife (who subsequently died in 2004).

Reinterpreting the same facts in terms of age rather than dates, two of the 16 siblings died before the age of 65, and 13 died between the ages of 65 and 91: a 26 year range. Only Moira has lived beyond 91. The narrowest age range that contains half of these deaths – eight – is 75 to 87 years.

I can't say when or how I first learned that most people live to the age of 70 or 80 – it may have been when learning of the biblical prediction of three-score years and ten – but, as I and my cousins grew older during the second half of the 20th century, the fate of our parents, uncles and aunts, confirmed the validity of this knowledge. It is interesting for me, now in 2010, to compare the above with the analysis of the network of people associated with Frances Partridge (see Chapter Six).

For me, and for other participants, the Lleida Symposium on Cultural Gerontology was extremely stimulating and productive. That said, it was similar, organisationally, to many other conferences: several months in advance the event had been announced and papers solicited. Abstracts were submitted, a programme compiled and participants had booked their places. In these ways, the event was systematically documented and thereby made 'real'. In total, 140 people arrived and registered as participants at the opening on 16 October 2008, approximately 70 papers were presented and six plenary addresses delivered.

As the final plenary speaker on the Symposium's programme, I began my presentation by remembering Mike Hepworth and, reflecting back on the symposium, I noted how several speakers had acknowledged Mike's work and their debt to him. I suggested that this demonstrated that the event itself, the symposium, was not external to 'the real world'; rather it was – and would remain – of it. We, the participants, (I continued) were constituents of the symposium: we had come to Lleida to discuss the cultural significance of age. I noted that several participants had revealed their chronological age in the course of discussions. Revealing one's age is done deliberately and can serve various purposes. Not least it provides a link with past historical events: older people can say 'I was there' or 'I remember that' in a way that younger people cannot, and this event, the symposium, I suggested, was no exception.

At this point, taking a lead from the title of the symposium, I invited the audience to 'extend time' in the context of the ongoing history of cultural gerontology, to speculate about 'realities' that might yet emerge, and to imagine their future 'responses'. First I guessed that the difference in age between the oldest and youngest persons present (as I was speaking) might have been 30 to 40 years. I then said:

> Thirty or forty years from now, the youngest person will be as old as the oldest is now. Thirty years from now, survivors might reminisce about what has gone on this week. Think about the people you've met here. Imagine meeting them in the year 2038, and reminiscing about 'Lleida'.

Having issued this challenge I continued with the following account of a past conference:

> Thirty-one years ago, in September 1977, I went to Ystad, on the southern coast of Sweden, to take part in a colloquium organised by the European Social Sciences Research Committee of the International Association of Gerontology. It cost me £263, a considerable sum of money, and when I boarded the plane at Heathrow I was unsure whether this would be covered by my employer. I was the only participant from the UK. I arrived on a Monday and left the following Saturday morning. It was a long and memorable experience. Although little in the programme

would now be called 'cultural gerontology', it was in Ystad that I first discovered 'the cultural' in age.

At the time, I wrote a report on the colloquium and I have kept a copy of this. As a result, in Lleida in 2008, I was able to display the names of the 29 participants. What had become of them? I named some who have remained well-known in gerontology: Margaret Huyck, Kees Knipscheer, Nan Stevens and Lars Tornstam, for example.

I then reported that the week before setting off for Lleida, I had 'googled' the names of the others. When I came to Margret Dieck I found a report on her death in 1997. I remembered that she had spoken in Ystad about the policy of the then West German government to maintain a population of two million people living in West Berlin. To achieve this, many government employees such as Margret herself were required to live there. She talked about the impact of this, not just for people such as herself who were not 'Berliners', but also for the older residents of West Berlin, people who had lived there through much of the 20th century. This was a good example of what I referred to earlier as learning about the cultural in age.

To illustrate some of the consequences of this pattern of mortality, I turned at this point in my presentation, to the writing of Julian Barnes, and in particular to his book *Nothing to be Frightened of* (2008). In interviews, Barnes had described himself as an 'amateur in life' but a 'professional writer'. Like many readers I had been curious to know more about the origins of a book that claimed to be non-fictional and truthful. Here, in an interview, was how Barnes described his relationship with his reader:

> I like to think of the writer and the reader sitting together, not face to face, but side by side, looking out in the same direction, through something like a café window. (Baron, 2008)

Let's begin, I suggested, 'sitting side by side' with Barnes, with the fact that he reveals his age ('now over sixty') and discusses its relevance to what he writes. However, he neither specifies the date of his 60th birthday nor offers any account of how the day was celebrated or marked, other than to mention having lunch that day with one of his friends (Barnes, 2008, p 128). That he accords it some significance is evident in an interview where he said the fear of death 'doesn't seem to have diminished after the age of 60 as my friend G assured me it would' (O'Connell, 2008). He dates the writing of the book as

'2005–07' (Barnes, 2008, p 250) and it is not difficult to discover from other sources that his 60th birthday was 19 January 2006.

While writing the book he had an email correspondence with his older brother, Jonathan, a philosopher. This was an important resource that he drew on in several places in the book. Here is how he raised the matter of age:

> My brother and I are now both over sixty, and I have only just asked him – a few pages ago – what he thinks of death. When he replied, 'I am quite content with the way things are,' did he mean that he is quite content with his own personal extinction? And has his immersion in philosophy reconciled him to the brevity of life, and its inevitable ending for him within, say, the next thirty years?
>
> 'Thirty years is pretty generous,' he replies (well, I had inflated it, for my comfort as much as his). 'I expect to be dead within the next fifteen. Am I reconciled to that fact? … I know it's going to happen, and there's nothing I can do about it.' (pp 61-2)

The difference between the two brothers in how they view the prospect of death is one of the main themes of the book. In this quote, Julian provides direct evidence of how, in passing our 60th birthday, we can be alerted to the prospect of death, and how this expectation is, in turn, often couched in temporal terms (in other words, 30 years for Julian and 15 for Jonathan). These markers directly echo the demographic facts presented above in Table 9.2.

A few pages further on, Julian writes that Jonathan admits that nowadays he thinks of death more than he used to 'in part because old friends and colleagues are dying off' (p 65). Julian himself does not recount any such experiences. Rather, the accounts of death in his book are limited to those of his grandparents and parents, and of various celebrated writers, artists and musicians. But there is an echo of his brother's experience in the following affectionate story of a group of writers:

> Another week, another meal: seven writers meet in the upstairs room of a Hungarian restaurant in Soho. Thirty or more years ago, this Friday lunch was instituted: a shouty, argumentative, smoky, boozy gathering attended by journalists, novelists, poets and cartoonists at the end of another working week. Over the years the venue has shifted many times, and the personnel diminished by relocation

and death. Now there are seven of us left, the eldest in his mid-seventies, the youngest in his late – very late – fifties.

It is the only all-male event I knowingly, or willing, attend. From weekly it has slipped to being merely annual, at times it is almost like the memory of an event. Over the years, too, its tone has shifted. It is now less shouty and more listening; less boastful and competitive, more teasing and indulgent. Nowadays no one smokes, or attends with stern intention of getting drunk, which used to seem worth doing for its own sake. We need a room to ourselves, not out of self-importance, or fear that our best lines will be stolen by eavesdroppers, but because half of us are deaf – some openly so, thumbing in their deaf aids as they sit down, others as yet unadmittedly. We are losing hair, needing glasses; our prostates are swelling slowly, and the lavatory cistern at the turn of the stair is given a good workout. But we are cheerful on the whole, and all still working. (pp 78-9)

This is an account of how a group experiences its ageing: it is full of references to the passage of time, and changes in arrangements, capacities, appearances and expectations. The fact that some past members have died is indicated only by his noting that the group has 'diminished', partly through death. However, he returns to the group, 30 pages on, and writes:

… as the Friday lunchers were saying – or rather, never saying, though perhaps occasionally thinking – in that Hungarian restaurant: either I'll be going to your funeral, or you'll be coming to mine. Such has always been the case, of course; but this grimly unshiftable either/or takes on sharper definition in later years. (p 108)

So, although death is not often spoken about, it is there in later life, and there is some recognition that an unpredictable sequence of deaths diminishes groups and networks of older people as a result. Mellor argues that when death strikes, it causes people to 'question the meaningfulness and reality of the social frameworks in which they participate, shattering their ontological security' (1993, p 13).

Although chronological age might not have any biological significance over and above its statistical associations, the analysis above demonstrates that it is the dominant popular predictor of mortality. Barnes is not alone in the contemporary world in expecting a long life – and death in 'extreme old age' – as 'a right' (Barnes, 2008, pp 39-40). Over the first 60 years of life (or so), we become acquainted with many people in many social worlds. And, over time, the 'normality' of death between the ages of 60 and 95 is repeatedly confirmed, first among older generations and then eventually within our own. As our 60th birthday approaches, we begin to abandon the idea that death is a temporally distant event. Rather we begin to see ourselves entering a time in life when death becomes 'natural', and no longer 'tragic'.

At this point I offered the testimony of a contributor to the MO Archive, writing anonymously in 2002 about her most recent birthday (Bytheway, 2005):

> Growing older – I don't know if it makes a difference. I'm still at the stage of being slightly surprised by how old I seem to be getting. I don't look 55 so other people are often very unbelieving when I say how old I am, and I feel the same inside as I did when I was about 20. Sometimes I wonder how many more birthdays will I have but I don't wonder it much because my family is very long lived. We all hang by a thread anyway so not a very useful piece of wondering. (Z2276)

So, as with Julian Barnes and his brother, a birthday had led her into thinking about age and finitude: she still resists the idea that age makes a difference, she is reassured by the demography of her own family, but she ends with a fatalistic acknowledgement that death is inevitable.

On page 108 of his book, Barnes teases us with the suggestion that either he, the author, or we, the reader might die at that point on that page, and the paragraph ends: 'Perhaps right in the middle of a wo'. At the start of the next paragraph, he explains that:

> I've never written a book, except my first, without at some point considering that I might die before it was completed. (2008, p 108)

How do we cope with such uncertainty? In drafting a title for the Lleida paper, I decided I would work on the idea that the answer might lie in the two words 'still' and 'same'. Briefly I reminisced about meeting old friends at Mike Hepworth's funeral in February 2007. Despite signs of age, the claim to be 'still the same old me' was not far from our lips. Beneath the mask of age – an idea that 'the two Mikes' had astutely brought into gerontology some years earlier (Featherstone and Hepworth, 1991) – there lurks the 'same old me'. The power of the argument is not that behind the mask there is 'a younger me', but rather 'the same old me', and in this context 'old' is the antonym of 'new' not 'young'.

The word 'same' also figured in Chapter Three, where I drew on Marie White's diary, kept for *'The Last Refuge' Revisited* project. Marie indicated there that her life was characterised by a daily 'sameness'. Julian Barnes also uses the word in telling a story about the way he lives his life:

> A biographer friend once suggested she [...] write my life. Her husband argued satirically that this would make a very short work as all my days were the same. 'Got up,' his version went. 'Wrote book. Went out, bought bottle of wine. Came home, cooked dinner. Drank wine.' I immediately endorsed this Brief Life. That will do as well as any other; as true, or as untrue as anything longer.' (2008, p 131)

As with Marie, the story of Barnes' life rested in the basic daily routine, not in the 'truth' of actual events and experiences. The sameness of everyday life is evident when another MO panellist writes: 'My birthday is April 20th and this last one was the same as any other day' (F1634). Equipped with this kind of cyclical view of life, we are able to imagine that we can resist age and change, by remaining the same, day by day and year by year, just so long as we keep doing the same activities, and maintaining the same relationships. With each and every reunion, we endeavour to present an image of sameness – still the same old me.

The effort to sustain, share and enjoy unchanging sameness, is also evident in Margaret Goodchild's account of her return to the Alps (see Chapter Three). Here is how she describes walking into the village, rucksack on her back:

> I'd got back to my beautiful 'Nowhere'. A place where I had had such a wonderful way of living, far removed from the mechanical march of so-called progress ... the old houses which even at close quarters seemed totally unchanged ... all as if I had left the day before. I had the extraordinary feeling of permanence, of enduring. (Bytheway, 1996b)

Sameness is also evident in rediscovering old objects. I described how in 2006 I had visited Moira Chadwick, my aunt, shortly after her 100th birthday. We spent time looking at her old photographs. She had been a family photographer and I thought it would be good to bring my digital camera into play. She was interested in it, but did not have the strength to hold and use it. Jennifer, my cousin, her daughter, found her old, much lighter, camera and immediately she responded positively to it, an old 'friend', and she was still able to use it in 'the same old way'. I concluded my presentation in Lleida by showing a photograph of my aunt taking a photograph of Jennifer. I felt it brought together – admittedly in a rather forced way – the complex contradictions implicit in finitude and sameness.

In summary, in the Lleida paper I explored two phenomena: first, the relationship between age and finitude in the context of various social worlds (the conference, the sibship and the national population); and second, popular resistance to the idea that we might change as a result of age: in later life we prefer to remain 'the same'. How are these two issues related? Statistically, mortality can be expected to occur within a range of ages that is comparatively narrow relative to the expected length of life as a whole. The consequence of this, certainly in Europe in the 21st century, is that people are expected to live for 60 (or so) years, and then to die within the following 40 years (or so). These expectations are universal in the sense that they apply to the population in general and are reflected in, and confirmed by, the demise of older generations.

What I hoped to do in the Lleida paper was undermine the implication of so much gerontology that it is produced by ageless gerontologists researching their 'age-ful', 'elderly' subjects. Without wishing in any way to see gerontologists turn in on themselves and become preoccupied with their own ageing, I was equally concerned to balance the testimonies of 'older people' who might be participating in gerontological research, with those of the participating gerontologists, and that methodologies are developed which ensure that self-deprecatory ageist humour is minimised.

Questions for discussion

1   Some scientists would argue that participative research inevitably compromises the objectivity of the data and the rigour of the analysis. Would you agree?

2   Bearing in mind the situation I faced when visiting Doris and Martin, what moral dilemmas should fieldworkers anticipate in undertaking participative research?

3   What insights into how age is experienced did you gain from the extracts taken from Julian Barnes' *Nothing to be Frightened of*?

4   We all have a fund of anecdotes to tell. Is it possible for social researchers to share and analyse these and then draw authoritative conclusions about the impact of age on personal lives?

TEN

Getting real

In writing this book I have tried to focus on the concept of age and to examine critically how it is used in social research and gerontology. Is age real? Of course it is: it is clearly evident that our bodies age in fairly standard, predictable and visible ways. As Mike Hepworth has argued:

> ... sociologists do not deny that ageing is a process of biological change; rather they wish to draw attention to the social and personal implications of the ways in which the meanings of biological change as 'decline' are culturally constructed and interpreted through discourse. (2003, p 90)

And it is not just the assumption of decline that we might challenge. The reasoning that starts with the various physical signs of age and ends in the conceptualisation of 'age' is essentially the result of a history extending over many nations and centuries, a history that has engaged many disciplines and occupations as well as biologists. Out of much observation, listening, reading and thought about how individual lives change with time, age has emerged: it now occupies an undisputed position in popular conversation as something that is real, something we all have to live with. So my overall aim involves examining how this belief is sustained. In believing that age exists, are we simply facing up to the reality of our ageing bodies? Are we recognising hard facts and their consequences? Or are we setting up ways of institutionalising assumptions and tensions, and making life all the more difficult for ourselves as a consequence?

I set about answering these questions by reflecting on the state of gerontology, by drawing on my recent, and not-so-recent, experiences of researching age, and by tapping into some other sources of insight. As a social researcher, my objective has been to collect evidence that casts light on age as it affects and is experienced by human populations, preferably from different angles, posing challenges to the 'received wisdom'. This entails the deployment of various methods, acquiring access to different sources of information and undertaking original analyses. At the end of this chapter, I will reflect on how social research in the future might develop in ways that increase our understanding of age.

Behind the mask

The mask of ageing, as articulated by Featherstone and Hepworth (1989), is a powerful metaphor. A real mask, something that a person wears, is seen by the viewer to be concealing a hidden face, but who is it? Who is wearing this mask? The mask is preventing us from identifying this person. As claimed in the Age Concern poster discussed in Chapter Four, all we see is 'age'.

Our age is made manifest in two very different and distinct ways: chronological age (based on our date of birth), and signs of age evident in our appearance (based primarily on the sight of our bodies). The experience and recording of time passing contributes to our sense of increasing age. Initially our parents number our birthdays, perhaps with symbols such as candles on a cake. Most of us are free to decide how to mark the occasion as we leave childhood, but by this time we have learnt how to count the years, never mind the candles. Occurring on a set date every year our birthdays are difficult to ignore. The examples presented in Chapters Three and Five offer evidence of how we use chronological age to articulate comparisons, sometimes attempting sophisticated arithmetic deductions based on dates and ages. Whether we are simply working it out on the basis of our date of birth and today's date, or attempting more complicated calculations, as is sometimes required when making decisions about insurance or pensions, the fact is that the arithmetic of chronology is something with which we acquire some familiarity in our everyday lives.

J.B. Priestley's reaction to seeing himself in the shop window illustrates well just how sensitive most of us are to the image we present when out in public. It is one thing to address our bodily selves first thing in the morning in the privacy of a bathroom, quite another to unexpectedly see ourselves in a shop window. The Couplands' research, discussed in Chapter Four, is important because we know comparatively little about how, in everyday life, we recognise and interpret 'the signs of age'. Rather, gerontologists have become a little beguiled by the continuing struggle of the media and commerce to construct effective and acceptable images of age: typically we are appalled by the way clothes, for example, are displayed by youthful models, conforming to normative ideals of beauty, rather than by more realistic representatives of potential customers. Nevertheless, gerontologists go shopping too, and the question remains: what sense do we make of the idealised images around us, as we try on clothes and examine what we see in a shop's mirror?

Reconciling chronology and visual image is perhaps the most striking problem we face in attempting to capture the reality of age as one meaningful concept. Even though they overlap in the simple question 'How old do you think I look?' they are two very different elements in our individual make-up. But, as I have argued in earlier chapters, age figures in other ways too. First, there is past, present and future: a categorisation of time rather than the quantification that is achieved through chronologisation. A sense of age develops as, over time, we reflect (in the present) more on the past and less on the future. The grammar of communication changes in the use of tenses. For example, on his 23rd birthday in 1948, Tony Benn was worrying about what to do with his life; 59 years later, in a postscript to his latest volume of diaries, he reminisces about taking his sons to Parliament in 1958 to hear their grandfather speak (Benn, 2008, p 368).

Age reflects identity. You remain 'the same person' with a continuing identity and your date of birth is a key element in this. This locates you in a particular generation and a particular age category. Do you remember rationing? Are you old enough to see this film? Are you old enough to have a concessionary fare on the railways? An eye may be run over your appearance as a judgement is reached. Standards are set on the basis of chronological age and these generate anxieties over potential inconsistency: whereas Kenneth Williams wanted to act 'his age', Audrey Wise felt she had to lie in order to further her career.

While children may be impatient to grow up and acquire full adult status, as adults we tend to resist age and we prefer to think of ourselves as remaining the younger person we have 'always' been. With each reunion, we are happy to be teased as 'still the same old you'. Each day includes familiar routines, and the same is true of the annual cycle: the seasonal rhythms of domestic life (as evident in the dairies of Adam Arthur and Alice Watson featured in Chapter Five), work and education, and the anniversaries that are celebrated in the 'usual' way (as in Tony Benn's diaries). If we are convinced that we have 'settled down' then age becomes incidental, and, if age does not matter, then we may feel free to ignore age or to lie about it. Chips Channon, for one, claimed that he regularly lied about his age. In our everyday lives we can ignore the fact that, through age, change is constant, complex and slow.

Things happen that transform life: school-leaving, parenthood, migration, new jobs, retirement and widowhood are just some of the more obvious transitions. New daily routines are set up and, in retrospect, these turning points are seen to mark distinct phases in life. Potentially new anniversaries come to be celebrated. The interview with Angela Rammell revealed a series of events that would mark out phases in her life. It is in this individual way that the concept of stage becomes relevant, not through a series of universally prescribed stages of life. Through the experience of surviving such changes, we each accumulate a distinctive biography. In her diaries Frances Partridge provides a telling account of how the death of her husband was both devastating and transforming. Similarly, at a different age, Katherine Moore's letter to Joyce Grenfell told of her 'great loss' when her husband died. The experiences of Martha Gellhorn and Daniel Cole illustrate how the loss of a parent can be just as traumatic. And there are other experiences which can transform lives: Pat Moore, for example, described how her experience of donning the mask of age left her 'forever changed, both as a person and a professional'.

So, simply as a feature of the individual, age is a complex phenomenon that is best thought of in terms of chronology and appearance.

Relations, groups and divisions

In one-to-one relationships, age underpins and occasionally threatens differences in seniority. The parent–child relationship sets a standard against which other age differences can be judged. The tensions that can arise between parents and teenage children (as described, for example, by Carol Shields and Linda Grant; see Chapter Six) are reflected in inter-generational relations outside family life, as Julian Barnes shows in describing Gregory's experience of having his hair cut by Kelly. With time and age the balance between the generations changes and perhaps mellows. A sense of attachment is consolidated (as for Jean Rhys and her daughter), and as parents fall ill (as Tom Courtenay found) or become frail (Chapter Seven), positive aspects of the relationship may emerge. In particular, towards the end of life, children may find themselves providing regular care for an ailing parent. On this basis, broader understandings regarding inheritance and succession develop. Seniority is also a feature of many relationships within the same generation. An example of this, the election of Ed Miliband as leader of the Labour Party, provided a timely example of how seniority can change hands at a turning point in the careers of two politicians. The simple fact, however, is that within any one-to-one relationship, the person who is older, chronologically, can reminisce about how things were when they were the other's age and, conversely, the latter can declare ambitions about where they will be when they are as old as the former.

Many institutions such as schools and day centres group people according to chronological age and, as a direct consequence, we occasionally encounter school parties or buses of day-tripping pensioners. Sometimes such groups dress in distinctive ways (school uniforms, for example) and, when viewed in large numbers, the sight can reinforce stereotyped thinking about people of 'that age'. Thinking about age groups rather differently there are many opportunities for people to form, or to identify with, groups of age peers. We age as members of a birth cohort (Ryder, 1965) with a shared experience of growing older. At any point in time, the survivors of a birth cohort constitute an age group defined loosely by upper and lower chronological ages: the 'baby boom' generation is a classic example of how demography and the media can combine forces in establishing a new understanding of the position of a cohort in history. People who think of themselves as 'baby boomers' are able to follow (and perhaps participate in) debates about their continuing impact upon the wider society.

As a cohort grows yet older and the end of life approaches, social networks based on age peers begin to disintegrate, as is evident in the biography of Frances Partridge. There are echoes of this in The Oldest Generation project, where accidents, illnesses and the deaths of contemporaries occasionally figure in diary entries. Funerals provide opportunities for reunions in which, despite possible jokes about 'who will be next', old friendships can be revived. We may be tempted, like Margaret Goodchild, to return to remembered places 'while we are able' or, like Josie Shaw's parents, to visit distant friends or relations 'one last time' before it is 'too late'. We may be tempted like George Hillman to spend our life savings on one final big celebration. Within each cohort, however, a few will end up as 'survivors', reaching a great age and seemingly defying the odds.

Much sociology is based on an interest in the social divisions within society (Anthias, 2001). The overall conceptual framework is, of course, subject to continuing debate, but the fact is that age is increasingly recognised by sociologists as one of the basic divisions. For example, in their introductory textbook Macionis and Plummer argue that the original interest in social and economic stratification has been extended in recent times and now gender, ethnic and age stratification 'can be introduced' into such theorising (1997, p 241). Social divisions are often associated with conflict and, insofar as this might arise over access to scarce resources, then generational differences, and thereby age, can be easily invoked. The historical balance between what different generations 'put in' and 'take out' over the course of their lives can be estimated and compared. Complex and emotional arguments can follow over what is 'fair', and 'generational equity' has become the subject of international conferences and political campaigns. Although much of this hangs upon generational identities, age may play a part in the ensuing debates and struggles. Insofar as the oldest generation is represented by a declining number of survivors, the question of how the end of their lives should be resourced is open to discussion. At one extreme, we may invest, or be urged to invest, in ways of 'looking after ourselves', deploying various techniques in 'keeping fit' and 'self-health care', the aim being to live longer, more independently and in a better state of health; in short, to age 'successfully' (Bowling and Dieppe, 2005). At the other extreme, there is a moral panic over the rising number of very old and frail people, prompting extensive public discussions of dementia, assisted death and euthanasia. Much of this conflates age and terminal illness. In this context, Michael Bury's comment on the overlap between images of age and chronic illness is telling:

> The significance of age requires underlining. The image of arthritis as a disease of the elderly is common. On the one hand it makes the possibility of a straightforward process of recognition remote. Arthritis was seen, initially, by those I interviewed as a 'wear and tear' disease, a consequence of becoming old with inevitable disabling consequences, particularly expressed in fears of seizing-up and becoming crippled. Individuals, even in their forties and fifties, did not think of arthritis as occurring in the way experienced, and this was even more true for the women in their twenties. The emergence of the condition implied a 'premature ageing' for the individual [...] As such, it marked a biographical shift from a perceived normal trajectory through relatively predictable chronological steps, to one fundamentally abnormal and inwardly damaging. (Bury, 1982, p 171)

There is a commonly understood vocabulary associated with age. We can be confident that in talk about age there is no risk of serious misunderstandings. We might argue about the significance or meanings of words, but in doing so we do not doubt that we are talking about 'the same thing'. So, when Bury refers to arthritis being seen to be a 'disease of the elderly', this rings true. 'The elderly' represents a division in society, one that creates a sense of distance and difference; it is 'the elderly' who have arthritis, we are led to believe, not 'us'.

Social research

Much of the evidence upon which this book is based is drawn from empirical social research. There has been a long and sometimes sterile debate in gerontology about the balance between theory and data. As a 'practitioner' of social research, I have not needed to be unduly concerned with this, believing that the job in hand (literally) required me to collect data, analyse it and draw appropriate conclusions. The general aim has been to contribute to the development of a better understanding of what is going on 'out there'. Accessing an appropriate source may entail opening closed doors or even 'gate-crashing' institutions. It may involve travelling long distances or spending long periods of time watching what happens. There is a growing literature on the experience of undertaking research (McLeod and Thomson, 2009, p 7) and it is becoming clear that theorising the world 'out there' increasingly requires researchers to understand better and more critically what they themselves are doing and, in particular, the strengths and weaknesses of the methods they use and the material they collect and analyse.

For many people, age is a sensitive topic, and when they are interviewed, rather than think hard about what age means to them, there is a tendency to fall back on various standard tropes. Of course, how tropes are used can be revealing, as, for example, when Vera Griffiths claimed that the notion of 'mutton dressed as lamb' is 'instilled into us'. But I would want to check her claim that her daughters 'whizz' her past shops for older people, by observing this happening or, at the very least, by interviewing her daughters. As Laud Humphreys (1970, p vii) has argued, 'empirical study of sensitive areas of human conduct calls for enterprising methods'.

Without empirical social research, there can be little doubt that gerontology would return to a heavy dependence upon clinical practice and institutional rhetoric. Government policies, for example, would be increasingly geared to 'maintaining independence' and helping older people 'remain in their own homes for as long as possible'. The training of health workers and care providers would be increasingly based on anecdotes and stereotypes gleaned from within the narrow worlds of medical treatment and care provision.

Despite advocating investment in empirical research, however, I acknowledge there are obvious weaknesses that are difficult to overcome. Many of these arise from the simple fact that good systematic research is labour intensive and time consuming. All too often the immediate goal of securing funds leads to projects being based on inadequate resources and, subsequently, to the use of short-cuts in methods and analysis. Consider, for example, the simple issue of gaining access to an appropriate sample of older people. The easiest way of achieving this is through agencies servicing large numbers of older people. The cooperation of such organisations is most easily achieved if the proposed research is likely to cast the organisation in a good light or, at the very least, not reveal aspects of its work that might prompt public criticism. The alternative, gaining access to a random sample of a local population of people over a certain age, is not so easy. Nevertheless, it is manageable either through agencies that have appropriate lists or through cold calling to houses or telephones. The weakness here is that the researcher has a brief moment in which to persuade the prospective subject to agree to participate. However the encounter is managed, there will always be a number who refuse or who are unable to take part. What the researcher ends up with is a sample biased towards older people who have the time, capacity and inclination to take part. Gerontology is left with a huge gulf between these capable, articulate and (largely) positive older people and those encountered through service providers in various care settings.

What this implies is that social research should indeed be enterprising: searching out relevant data from a wide variety of sources, triangulating findings and undertaking secondary analyses of archived material. There is a constant tension between consolidating knowledge and understanding on the one hand, and questioning the received wisdom and the dominant stereotypes on the other. Often the best way forward is for contested issues to be checked against lived experience, and it is here that realist fiction and biography can make a significant contribution. But so too can gerontologists, not just by undertaking in-depth and sensitive research, but also by drawing on their own personal experience of age and ageing, not in a self-deprecatory way, but through serious reflection on the course of their lives and their reactions and interpretations of age-related events. We need a way of theorising anecdote in a rigorous and productive way.

Theorising age

Having nearly completed this book, how do I now, in 2010, theorise age? The following argument is based upon conclusions drawn from the evidence presented in this book, evidence that reflects where and how age is made manifest in everyday social life.

Essentially age is about the ways in which the ongoing life of the individual person is plotted and observed: it is about time and the body. Age is made real through chronological records, visual images and the biological state of the body. Defined narrowly, this is all that gerontologists need be concerned with: studying the slow and complex ways in which people grow older and the ways in which language is used to describe the age and ageing of the individual.

But age is also evident in social relations and groups and in how social divisions complicate the ways of the world. It may be, for example, that the reason why the idea of old age is so easy to accept is not because individuals 'enter' old age by crossing some threshold, but because old age is a concept that helps to identify and justify social divisions. This was why I titled the last chapter of Bytheway (1995) 'No more "elderly", no more old age': age prejudice and discrimination exist because these divisive concepts are accepted and used as if they were real. In other words, old age is only indirectly a feature of the individual life course. As a result, the extensive work of critical gerontologists over the last 30 years has contributed to our understanding of how the idea of old age fits into contemporary ideologies and inter-generational tensions. Townsend's theory of structured dependency (1981), for example, helps us understand better the backdrop rather than the course of individual lives, and to appreciate that people are 'made' old and dependent primarily by well-meaning caring policies and practices, rather than by physiological change. So, more generally, age can be recognised, not only in the life and identity of the individual person, but also in relationships between people, in social groups and in some of the divisions in society.

In what forms do we recognise age? Materially the chronological age of a person can be deduced from the birth certificate or estimated from the sight of the ageing body, either 'in person' or in images such as photographs. With regard to everyday practices, including those of social researchers, age is specified in numerical answers to the question about age, combined with the appearance of visible parts of our bodies: face, hand and posture. Age is a sensitive matter, however, and precision is often avoided. It need not be revealed through a specific number of years; reference may be made to less direct indicators. In this respect, the concept of stage is helpful and people may be happier to be described simply as 'middle-aged', supplementing this perhaps with the ages of parents or children, or perhaps dates such as the year they started work. Not only are such responses less divisive and perhaps stigmatising, but words such as 'middle-aged' help validate a staged view of the life course. We are happier to think of ourselves as being in a stage in life, rather than the state of constantly growing older. But stages can be just as divisive, and the debate over the third age, for example, has unsettled many assumptions about the course of later life.

The concepts of seniority and relative age are a further complication. The former is rather broader than chronological age and it may be that the scope of gerontology would be extended and somewhat reorientated if seniority were given more attention. It is significant, for example, that the word appears in neither the index of Bengtson et al (2009) nor that of Johnson (2005), both key handbooks aimed at the further development of gerontology. The data we obtained from the Timescapes siblings project reveal the ways in which relative age is associated with size: 'big sis' and her 'little sis'.

This theorisation and, in particular, the clear distinction between chronological age and the appearance of the older body, parallels similar approaches to the study of other social divisions such as class, gender and ethnicity. While there is much to be learnt from research that compares the impact and consequences of these basic divisions and how they are inter-related, it is important to avoid assumptions of direct conceptual equivalence. As is often pointed out, age is the only characteristic that is universal and constantly changing. It is the simple fact that we are *all* growing older *all* the time that makes the study of age and ageing so important.

Questions for discussion

1 The mask of age: is it real?

2 Do we grow old or are we made old?

3 Having virtually reached the end of the book, what one question about age would you now like to embark on researching?

Postscript

I never expected that the two people who would feature most prominently in this book would both become centenarians. In very different ways, the lives of May Nilewska and Frances Partridge have been highly revealing for me, and it has left me wondering why. The reason, in my opinion, is that the evidence demonstrates how the lived experience of growing older is one of slow but constant change, change that continues for as long as there is life. Undertaking research with centenarians is not easy and much of what exists has been largely epidemiological, aimed at discovering their 'secrets', the predictors of longevity (Yong, 2009). An unintended consequence of this curiosity has been the idea that they are in some way 'freaks' who have escaped the fate of the ordinary person.

As I was drafting the concluding chapter, Remembrance Day 2010 approached, and some attention was given to Harry Patch, the last surviving British soldier who fought in the trenches, who had died in July 2009. In 2008, Andrew Motion, then Poet Laureate, was invited by the BBC to visit him. Motion's grandfather had fought in Flanders and he himself had edited an anthology of poetry from the First World War, and so he was pleased to take up the invitation. The staff at the nursing home where Harry lived told him that Harry was 'amazingly robust' for someone aged 110 years, 'but, nevertheless', they said '110 is 110' (Motion, 2008a). Talking to them, Motion began to realise that for several years Harry had been regularly visited by media people and well-wishers. Although Harry insisted he was 'just an ordinary chap', he'd come to be seen as a hero: he felt awkward about this as well as pleased. In media interviews he had stuck to the same few stories, so what Motion hoped to do was 'surprise Harry back into his old self'.

When they met, Harry was in a wheelchair, 'little and frail but, given his great age, astonishingly spry-looking'. On his 'sparrow-body' there were medals on his chest:

> I shook his hand, then held it for a moment. I had expected to be moved, but not this much. The fingers felt fragile as twigs; 91 years ago they had picked up a machine gun and aimed it across No Man's Land. For a moment I couldn't speak. Harry was grinning at me. He'd seen this kind of thing before. (Motion, 2008a)

Harry's voice was 'very low, almost worn out' and Motion had to bend close to catch what he said. He tried to understand why there were lengthy pauses. He wondered if they were to allow Harry to collect his memories or because some memories still appalled him. Motion was moved by Harry's recollections and felt 'completely drawn into his world'. This world revolved around his experience of the war: 'One way or another, the few months Harry served in France now entirely dominate the 1,300 months he has lived elsewhere'.

> Before we said goodbye, Harry breathed me a joke: he thought that because he'd been alive for such a long time, he might as well go on for ever. What he meant, in all modest seriousness, was that he knew his own value as one of the very few who are still able to say, 'The war was like this; I was there.' (Motion, 2008a)

Motion commented: 'To sit in his company is to feel the flow between "then" and "now" is unbroken'. It was an 'intimate' experience, he wrote. Despite this, he argued that come the time that Harry was 'no longer with us', the war would keep 'its eagle-grasp' on our imaginations: we would simply have to work harder to find it elsewhere.

Motion's account provides a vivid illustration of the social consequences of living to a great age. Harry Patch was in the care of a nursing home, and visitors were guided in how to engage with him. Amazingly, such is the power of chronological age, that someone seemingly felt it appropriate to remind Motion that '110 is 110'. Motion recognised the challenge of conversing with someone of such an age, and that he was just the latest in a long line of visitors. Nevertheless, he felt it was possible that Harry might remove the public mask and return to 'his old self'. How Motion related to Harry's body is important: the 'sparrow-body' with the twig-like fingers. He shook his hand, felt his fragile fingers and recognised the link with history: this was the same hand that had held a gun 91 years previously. Reflecting the importance of mirrors for age, the poem that Motion wrote about Harry includes the line: 'You grow a moustache, check the mirror, notice you're forty years old, then next day shave it off, check the mirror again – and see you're seventy' (Motion, 2008b). This is a poetic way of conveying a common timescape: that of time rushing by.

There are many similarities between this account and what can be learnt from the diaries of Frances Partridge and Viv Mackie: how the 'achievement' of centenarians in surviving for so long galvanises social networks and the media into organising ceremonial celebrations and visits, and how centenarians have mixed feelings about how their success is celebrated. More generally, what their experiences demonstrate is that, regardless of the detail, later life is characterised by a dynamic that is much more complex than either a general decline or some kind of end-of-life success, as promoted by competing gerontological theories. Age, and the ageing that goes with it, is a much more diverse and complicated phenomenon.

Three years ago, I visited my Aunt Moira, then aged 101, and, as we toured the garden, she turned to me and said, quite clearly, 'I'm not different'. At that moment my mind was on other things, moving the wheelchair perhaps, and it was only that night that I pondered over what she might have meant by this simple but clearly expressed claim. There were a number of possibilities but, whatever, I felt it was an important statement about age and a sense of continuing personhood. The accounts that we have of Frances Partridge's relationship with her biographer Anne Chisholm, May Nilewska's with her interviewer Joanna Bornat, and Harry Patch's with his visitor Andrew Motion, provide powerful evidence of the continuing drama of age, ageing and age differences.

Notes

Chapter 1

[1] http://www.ons.gov.uk/about/who-we-are/our-services/omnibus-survey/index.html [accessed 1/10/2010]. I used the ONS Omnibus Survey in the course of the Birthdays Project.

[2] As with all research subjects presented in this book, these are pseudonyms (see the Appendix).

Chapter 2

[1] www.iagg.info [accessed 10/10/2010].

[2] http://www.randomhouse.co.uk/offthepage/guide.htm?command=Search&db=/catalog/main.txt&eqisbndata=0099449285

Chapter 4

[1] These five words were: antiquity, eld, senility, vale of years and years.

[2] A photograph of the sign, including these words, appears on the cover of the UK edition of Katz (1996).

[3] I selected this advertisement for a lecture I gave to the Institute for Age and Health (Bytheway, 2001).

Chapter 6

[1] http://www.nhs.uk/conditions/IVF/Pages/Introduction.aspx

[2] http://bellybelly.com.au/forums/post-94185.html

Chapter 9

[1] http://news.bbc.co.uk/1/hi/business/4791238.stm (see Bytheway, 2007b).

[2] OU courses are presented for a number of years, perhaps as many as ten.

[3] http://www.open.ac.uk/tutors/employment-info/pages/policy/employment_equality_age_regulations_2006.htm [accessed 27.09.2006].

[4] See Bytheway (2005) for an appreciation of Mike's contribution to the study of ageing.

[5] This conclusion should be qualified since it does not take account of differences in the size of birth cohorts. It may be that deaths among the post-war baby boom generation, for example, will come to distort these age ranges. But, at most, this is unlikely to be more than two or three years. The analysis of mortality data for birth cohorts would provide more precise statistics.

Appendix

The following is a complete list of the people whose personal experience of age I draw upon in this book. They are either real people – (p) indicates pseudonyms – or fictional characters (f).

Case	Source	Medium	Pages
Aggie (f)	Barfoot (1985)	novel	100-1
Decca Aitkenhead	Self	newspaper article	104
Alix (f)	Grant (2002)	novel	96-7
Pete Allen (p)	Retirement through Redundancy project	research	133-4
Anssi (p)	Nikander (2002)	research	47, 94
Adam and Marion Arthur (p)	The Oldest Generation (TOG) project	research	17, 66-71, 74, 209
Diana Athill	Self	newspaper article	95
Julian Barnes	Self (Barnes, 2008)	book	17, 36, 92-3, 100, 135-6, 200-5, 210
Simone de Beauvoir	Self	book	92
Tony Benn	Self	diaries	17, 107-9, 112, 209
Mr Bergstein (p)	Nikander (2002)	research	47, 94-5
Ken Blakemore	Self (Blakemore, 1998)	book	48-9, 60
Vera Brittain	Self (Brett, 1976)	anthology of diaries	101
Bill Bytheway	Self	own experience	2-5, 9-18, 37, 47-8, 135, 159, 180-1, 187-8, 198-200, 203-4, 219
Deborah Cavendish	Self	newspaper article	137-8
Moira Chadwick	Self	conversation	198, 204, 219
Chips Channon	Self (Brett, 1987)	anthology of diaries	102, 209

Case	Source	Medium	Pages
Iris Chase (f)	Attwood (2001)	novel	96
Daniel Cole (p)	TOG project	research	17, 112-13, 144-7, 155-6, 158-9, 195, 210
Tom Courtenay	Self (Courtenay, 2000)	autobiography	17, 121-2, 210
Imogen Cunningham	Self (Cunningham, 1979)	book	17, 84-6
Eustace and Hilda (f)	Hartley (1979)	novel	45, 54-5
Eric Farmer (p)	Long-term Medication and Older People project	research	13, 174-80, 186
Margaret Forster	Self	online interview	36-7
Anna French and Mike (p)	Research on Age Discrimination (RoAD) project	research	16, 191-2
Martha Gellhorn	Moorehead (2006)	biography and published letters	34, 95-7, 112, 210
Margaret Goodchild	Self	unpublished document	17, 71-4, 111, 204, 211
Gregory and Kelly (f)	Barnes (2004)	novel	135-6, 210
Joyce Grenfell and Katherine Moore	Selves (Grenfell and Moore, 1981)	published letters	35, 210
Vera Griffiths (p)	RoAD project	research	98, 213
Peter Hall	Self (Brett, 1987)	anthology of diaries	102
Jeremy Hardy	Self	newspaper article	94, 97
George Hillman	Unknown reporter	newspaper article	111, 197, 211
Barbara Hulanicki	Self	newspaper article	94-5
Olive Jamieson (p)	Siblings project	research	124-6, 136
Freda Jones (p)	RoAD project	research	98-9, 100, 116
Millicent King (f)	Falconer (2003)	book review	37
Martha (p)	Grenier (2007)	research	138
Ed and David Miliband	Wheeler (2010)	newspaper article	123-4, 210

Case	Source	Medium	Pages
Pat Moore	Self (Moore, 2005)	magazine article	92, 210
Jane Neal (p)	Long-term Medication and Older People Project	research	13, 58-60, 74
Harold Nicolson	Self (Brett, 1987)	anthology of diaries	102
May Nilewska (p)	TOG project	research	17, 144-61, 198, 217, 219
Mrs Owen (p)	Long-term Medication and Older People project	research	58
Frances Partridge	Self (Partridge, 1990; Chisholm 2009)	diaries and biography	17, 20, 42-4, 113-16, 129-32, 139-43, 159, 161, 198, 210-11, 217-19
Harry Patch	Motion (2008)	newspaper article	217-19
Muriel Pawson (p)	Siblings project	research	124
J.B. Priestley	Self (Featherstone and Hepworth, 1989)	book	94-5, 208
Angela Rammell (p)	TOG project	research	16, 62-4, 74, 209-10
Jean Rhys	Self (Rhys, 1985)	published letters	120, 136, 210
Saleem Sinai (f)	Rushdie (1981)	novel	60
Jean Serjeant (f)	Barnes (1986)	novel	92-3, 100
Josie, Alan and Beat Shaw (p)	TOG project	research	16, 39-41, 211
Ryan Sidebottom	Self	newspaper article	49, 134
Margaret Simey	Self	conference presentation	187
Daphne Smith (p)	RoAD project	research	15, 56-7, 74
Caro Spencer (f)	Sarton (1973)	novel	5
Alison Steadman	Self	newspaper article	94
Queen Victoria	Self (Brett, 1987)	anthology of diaries	101

Case	Source	Medium	Pages
Connie Watkins (p)	RoAD project	research	99, 116
Alice Watson (p)	TOG project	research	17, 66-71, 74, 209
Evelyn Waugh	Self (Brett, 1987)	anthology of diaries	102
Marie White (p)	Johnson et al (2010)	research	57, 74, 204
Kenneth Williams	Self (Davies, 1994)	diaries	1-2, 6, 8, 205, 209
Tom and Martin Wilson (p)	Early Retirement and the Care of Older Relatives project	research	11, 188-90, 205
Reta and Christine Winters (f)	Shields (2003)	novel	119
Audrey Wise	Mullin (2010)	diaries	48, 209
Kathleen Woodward	Self (Woodward, 1997)	article	45, 47
11 anonymous contributors to the Mass Observation Archive	Birthdays in Adult Life project	research	103-6, 117-19, 203
3 anonymous participants	Coupland et al (1991)	research	46
7 anonymous participants	RoAD project	research	182-3

References

Achenbaum, A. (1995) 'Images of old age in America, 1790–1970: a vision and a revision', in M. Featherstone and A. Wernick (eds) *Images of Ageing: Cultural Representations of Later Life*, Routledge, London, pp 19-87.

Adam, B. (1995) *Timewatch: the social analysis of time*, Polity Press, Cambridge.

Adam, B. (1998) *Timescapes of Modernity: the environment and invisible hazards*, Routledge, London.

Adam, B. (2008) 'The Timescapes challenge: engagement with the invisible temporal', in R. Edwards (ed) *Researching Lives through Time: time, generation and life stories*, Timescapes Working Paper Series, No 1, University of Leeds, Leeds, pp 7-12.

Aitkenhead, D. (2005) 'The things left unsaid', *The Guardian*, October 29.

Alaszewski, A. (2006) *Using Diaries for Social Research*, Sage, London.

Alheit, P. (1995) 'Everyday time and life time: on the problems of healing contradictory experiences of time', *Time & Society*, vol 3 no 3, pp 305-19.

Andersson, L. (2002) 'Introduction', in L. Andersson (ed) *Cultural Gerontology*, Auburn House, Westport, CT, pp vii-x.

Andrews, M. (1999) 'The seductiveness of agelessness', *Ageing & Society*, vol 19, no 3, pp 301-18.

Anthias, F. (2001) 'The concept of 'social division' and theorising social stratification: looking at ethnicity and class', *Sociology*, vol 35, no 4, pp 835-54.

Antonucci, T.C., Birditt, K.S. and Akiyama, H. (2009) 'Convoys of social relations: an interdisciplinary approach', in V.L. Bengston, D. Gans, N.M. Putney and M. Silverstein (eds) *Handbook of Theories of Ageing*, Springer, New York, pp 249-60.

Attwood, M. (2001) *The Blind Assassin*, Virago, London.

Baars, J. (2007) 'Introduction. Chronological time and chronological age: problems of temporal diversity', in J. Baars and H. Visser (eds) (2007) *Aging and Time*, Baywood Publishing Co, Amityville, New York, pp 15-42.

Baltes, P.B. and Meyer, K.U. (eds) (1999) *The Berlin Aging Study: Aging from 70 to 100*, Cambridge University Press, Cambridge.

Barfoot, J. (1985) *Duet for Three*, The Women's Press, London.

Barnes, J. (1986) *Staring at the Sun*, Picador, London.

Barnes, J. (2004) *The Lemon Table*, Picador, London.

Barnes, J. (2008) *Nothing to be Frightened of*, Cape, London.

Baron, S. (2008) 'An interview with Julian Barnes', *The Oxonian Review of Books*, vol 7, no 3 (http://www.oxonianreview.org/issues/7-3/baron.shtml).

Bengston, V.L., Gans, D., Putney, N.M. and Silverstein, M. (eds) (2009) *Handbook of Theories of Ageing*, Springer, New York.

Benn, T. (1995) *The Benn Diaries*, Hutchinson, London.

Benn, T. (2003) *Free at Last: Diaries 1991–2001*, Arrow Books, London.

Benn, T. (2008) *More Time for Politics: Diaries 2001–2007*, London: Arrow Books.

Berger, P.L. and Luckmann, T. (1967) *The Social Construction of Reality*, Doubleday, London.

Blaikie A. (1999) *Ageing and Popular Culture*, Cambridge University Press, Cambridge.

Blakemore, K. (1998) *Social Policy: An introduction, 1st edition*, Open University Press, Buckingham.

Bond, J., Peace, S., Dittmann-Kohli, F. and Westerhof, G. (2007) *Ageing in Society*, Sage, London.

Bornat, J. and Bytheway, B. (2008) 'Tracking the lives of the oldest generation', *Generations Review*, vol 18, no 4.

Bornat, J. and Bytheway, B. (2010) 'Perceptions and presentations of living with everyday risk in later life', *British Journal of Social Work*, vol 40, no 4, pp 1118-34.

Bowling, A. and Dieppe, P. (2005) 'What is successful ageing and who should define it?', *British Medical Journal*, vol 331 (7531), pp 1548-51.

Brett, S. (1987) *The Faber Book of Diaries*, Faber and Faber, London.

Bryar, R. and Bytheway, B. (eds) (1996) *Changing Primary Health Care*, Blackwell Science, Oxford.

Burke, J. (1955) *Burke's Peerage, Baronetage and Knightage*, Burke's Peerage, London.

Bury, M. (1982) 'Chronic illness as biographical disruption', *Sociology of Health and Illness*, vol 4, no 2, pp 167-82.

Bury, M. (2005) *Health and Illness*, Polity Press, Cambridge.

Bytheway, B. (1970) 'Aspects of old age in age-specific mortality rates', *Journal of Biosocial Science*, vol 2, no 4, pp 337-49.

Bytheway, B. (1973) *The Dynamics of Family Structures*, Unpublished PhD Thesis, University of Keele, Staffordshire.

Bytheway, B. (1979a) 'Ageing and sociological studies of the family', in G. Dooghe and J. Helander (eds) *Family Life in Old Age*, Martinus Nijhoff, The Hague, pp 15-29.

Bytheway, B. (1979b) 'Care in the street', *MSRC Report*, University of Wales, Swansea.

Bytheway, B. (1979c) 'The rota: a case study of an informal good neighbour scheme', *MSRC Report,* University of Wales, Swansea.

Bytheway, B. (1980) 'Is ageism just a joke?' *New Age,* vol 12, pp 29-30.

Bytheway, B. (1981) 'Variation with age of age differences in marriage', *Journal of Marriage and the Family,* 43, 923-7.

Bytheway, B. (1982) *Exposing Myths,* Report to the SSRC.

Bytheway, B. (1986) 'Redundancy and the older worker', in R.M. Lee (ed) *Redundancies, Lay-offs and Plant Closures: Causes, character and consequences,* Croom Helm, London, pp 84-115.

Bytheway, B. (1987) 'Care in the families of redundant Welsh steelworkers', in S. di Gregorio (ed) *Social Gerontology: New directions,* Croom Helm, London, pp 177-87.

Bytheway, B. (1989a) 'Poverty, care and age: a case study', in B. Bytheway, T. Keil, A. Allatt and A. Bryman (eds) *Becoming and Being Old,* Sage Publications, London, pp 93-103.

Bytheway, B. (1989b) 'Beginning with life histories: interviewing in the families of Welsh steelworkers', in D. Unruh (ed) *Current Perspectives on Aging and the Life Cycle* (vol 3), JAI Press, Greenwich, CT, pp 119-26.

Bytheway, B. (1990) 'Age', in S.M. Peace (ed) *Researching Social Gerontology: Concepts, methods and issues,* Sage, for British Society of Gerontology, London, pp 9-18.

Bytheway, B. (1993) 'Ageing and biography: the letters of Bernard and Mary Berenson', *Sociology,* vol 27, no 1, pp 153-65.

Bytheway, B. (1995) *Ageism,* Open University Press, Buckingham.

Bytheway, B. (1996a) 'The experience of later life', *Ageing & Society,* vol 16, no 4, pp 613-21.

Bytheway, B. (1996b) 'At the point of return', *Generations Review,* vol 6, no 1, pp 7-9.

Bytheway, B. (2000) 'Youthfulness and agelessness: a comment', *Ageing & Society,* vol 20, no 6, 781-90.

Bytheway, B. (2001) 'Images of age', *Ageing and Health,* vol 7, pp 4-6.

Bytheway, B. (2002) 'Positioning gerontology in an ageist world', in L. Andersson (ed) *Cultural Gerontology,* Auburn House, Westport, CT, pp 59-76.

Bytheway, B. (2003) 'Visual representations of late life', in C. Faircloth, (ed) *Aging Bodies: Images and everyday experience,* Alta Mira Press, Walnut Creek, CA, pp 29-53.

Bytheway, B. (2005) 'Age-identities and the celebration of birthdays', *Ageing & Society,* vol 25, no 4, pp 463-77.

Bytheway, B. (2007a) 'The evacuation of older people: the case of Hurricane Katrina' (http://understandingkatrina.ssrc.org/Bytheway/).

Bytheway, B. (2007b) 'Choose when you stop? Retirement and age discrimination', *Policy & Politics*, vol 35, no 3, pp 551-5.

Bytheway, B. (2009) 'Writing about age: birthdays and the passage of time', *Ageing & Society*, vol 29, no 6, pp 883-901.

Bytheway, B. and Bornat, J. (2010) 'Recruitment for The Oldest Generation project', in F. Shirani and S. Weller (eds) *Conducting Qualitative Longitudinal Research: fieldwork experiences*, Timescapes Working Paper Series No. 2, University of Leeds, Leeds.

Bytheway, B. and Bornat, J. (2011) 'The oldest generation as displayed in family photographs', in V. Ylänne (ed) *Representing ageing: Images and identities*, Basingstoke: Palgrave Macmillan.

Bytheway, B. and Johnson, J. (1990) 'On defining ageism', *Critical Social Policy*, vol 29, pp 27-39.

Bytheway, B. and Johnson, J. (1998) 'The sight of age', in S. Nettleton and J. Watson (eds), *The Body in Everyday Life*, Routledge, London, pp 243-57.

Bytheway, B. and Johnson, J. (2003) 'Every day's the same? A study of the management of long-term medication', in B. Bytheway (2003) (ed) *Everyday Living in Later Life*, No. 4 in The Representation of Older People in Ageing Research Series, Centre for Policy on Ageing, London/Centre for Ageing and Biographical Studies, The Open University, Milton Keynes, pp 34-48.

Bytheway, B. and Johnson, J. (2005) 'Cataloguing old age', in G. Andrews and D. Phillips (eds) *Ageing and Place: Perspectives, policy, practice*, Routledge, London, pp 176-87.

Bytheway, B. and Johnson, J. (2009) 'An ageing population and apocalyptic demography', *Radical Statistics*, vol 100, pp 4-10.

Bytheway, B. and Johnson, J., Heller, T. and Muston, R. (2000) *The Management of Long-Term Medication by Older People*, Report to the Department of Health, The Open University, Milton Keynes.

Bytheway, B., Ward, R., Holland, C and Peace, S. (2007) *Too Old: Older people's accounts of discrimination, exclusion and rejection*, Help the Aged, London.

Bytheway, B., Bornat, J., Edwards, R. and Weller, S. (2008) 'Sisters and brothers: results of a UK-wide postcard exercise', *ESRC Festival of Social Science 2008* (www.lsbu.ac.uk/families/brothersandsisters/ Postcard_findings_for_web_report_%20final.pdf).

Carrigan, M. And Szmigin, I. (2000) 'Advertising in an ageing society', *Ageing & Society*, vol 20, no 1, pp 217–33.

Charcot, J-M. and Loomis, A.L. (1881) *Clinical Lectures on the Diseases of Old Age*, William Wood, New York.

Cheung, E. (2007) *Baby Boomers, Generation X and Social Cycles*, Long Wave Press, Toronto.

Chisholm, A. (2009) *Frances Partridge, the biography*, Phoenix, London.

Chudacoff, H.P. (1989) *How Old are You? Age consciousness in American culture*, Princeton University Press, Princeton, NJ.

Coupland, N., Coupland, J. And Giles, H. (1991) *Language, Society and the Elderly: Discourse, identity and ageing*, Blackwell, London.

Courtenay, T. (2000) *Dear Tom: letters from home*, Black Swan, London.

Cumming, E. and Henry, W.E. (1961) *Growing Old: The process of disengagement,* Basic Books, New York.

Cunningham, I. (1979) *After Ninety*, University of Washington Press, Seattle.

Cunningham, M.R. (1979) 'Weather, mood, and helping behavior: quasi-experiments with the Sunshine Samaritan', *Journal of Personality and Social Psychology*, vol 37, November, pp 1947–56.

Davies, R. (1994) *The Kenneth Williams Diaries*, Harper Collins, London.

de Beauvoir, S. (1977) *Old Age*, Penguin, London.

Department of Health (2000) *NHS Cancer Plan: A plan for investment, a plan for reform,* Department of Health, London.

Department of Health (2004) 'Over 70? You are still entitled to breast screening', NHS Cancer Screening Programme/Age Concern, Department of Health, London.

Department of Health and Social Security (1981) *Growing Older*, HMSO, London.

Department of Work and Pensions (2008) *Preparing for our Ageing Society: A discussion paper*, The Stationery Office, London.

Elder, G. (1977) *The Alienated: Growing old today*, Writers and Readers Publishing Cooperative, London.

Essed, P. (1988) *Understanding Everyday Racism*, Sage, London.

Faircloth, C. (ed) (2003) *Aging Bodies: Images and everyday experience,* Alta Mira Press, Walnut Creek, CA.

Fairhurst, E. (1998) '"Growing old gracefully" as opposed to "mutton dressed as lamb": the social construction of recognising older women', in S. Nettleton and J. Watson (eds) *The Body in Everyday Life*, Routledge, London, pp 258-75.

Falconer, H. (2003) 'A life less ordinary', *The Guardian*, 19 April.

Featherstone, M. and Hepworth, M. (1989) 'Ageing and old age: reflections on the postmodern life course', in B. Bytheway, T. Keil, P. Allatt and A. Bryman (eds) *Becoming and Being Old: Sociological approaches to later life*, Sage, London, pp 143-59.

Featherstone, M. and Hepworth, M. (1991) 'The mask of ageing and the postmodern life course', in M. Featherstone, M. Hepworth and B.S. Turner (eds) *The Body, Social Processes and Cultural Theory*, Sage, London, pp 371-89.

Featherstone, M. and Hepworth, M. (1995) 'Images of positive ageing: a case study of *Retirement Choice* magazine', in M. Featherstone and A. Wernick (eds), *Images of Ageing: Cultural representations of later life*, Routledge, London, pp 29-47.

Fletcher, A.E., Jones, D.A., Bulpitt, C.J. and Tulloch, A.J. (2002) The MRC trial of assessment and management of older people in the community: objectives, design and interventions [ISRCTN23494848], *BMC Health Services Research*, vol 2, no 1, p 21.

Forster, M. (2003) *Diary of an Ordinary Woman*, Chatto & Windus, London.

Gilleard, C. (2008) 'A murderous ageism? Age, death and Dr. Shipman', *Journal of Aging Studies*, vol, 22, no 1, pp 88-95.

Golinski, J. (2000) 'Putting the Weather in Order: narrative and discipline in eighteenth-century weather diaries', Paper given at the William Andrews Clark Memorial Library, UCLA, Los Angeles, 16 May 1998. (www.unh.edu/history/golinski/paper3.htm)

Government Statistical Service (2005) 'Breast screening programme', *Statistical Bulletin*, February, Government Statistical Service, London.

Graham, H. (1984) 'Surveying through stories', in C. Bell and H. Roberts (eds) *Social Researching*, Routledge and Kegan Paul, London, pp 104-24.

Granovetter, M.S. (1983) 'The strength of weak ties: a network theory revisited', *Sociological Theory*, vol 1, pp 201-33.

Grant, L. (2002) *Still Here*, Abacus, London.

Grenfell, J. and Moore, K. (1981) *An Invisible Friendship*, Macmillan, London.

Grenier, A. (2007) 'Constructions of frailty in the English language, care practice and the lived experience', *Ageing & Society*, vol 27, no 3, pp 425-45.

Gubrium, J. (1986) *Old Timers and Alzheimer's: the descriptive organisation of senility*, JAI Press, Greenwich, CT.

Gubrium, J. and Holstein, J. (2001) *Handbook of Interview Research*, Sage, London.

Gubrium, J. (2005) 'The social worlds of old age', in M.L. Johnson (ed) *The Cambridge Handbook of Age and Ageing*, Cambridge University Press, Cambridge, pp 310-15.

Gubrium, J. and Wallace, B. (1990) 'Who theorises age?', *Ageing & Society*, vol 10, no 2, pp 131-50.

Hall, S. (1997) 'The work of representation', in S. Hall (ed) *Representation, Cultural Representations and Signifying Practices*, Sage, London.

Harris, C.C. (ed) (1987) *Redundancy and Recession in South Wales*, Blackwells, Oxford.

Harrison, K. and McGhee, D. (2003) 'Reading and writing family secrets: reflections on mass–observation', *Auto/Biography*, vol XI, nos 1 & 2, pp 25-36.

Hartley, L.P. (1979) *Eustace and Hilda*, Faber and Faber, London.

Health Advisory Service (1982) *The Rising Tide: Developing services for mental illness in old age*, Sutherland House, Sutton, Surrey.

Healy, J.D. (2003) 'Excess winter mortality in Europe: a cross country analysis identifying key risk factors', *Journal of Epidemiology and Community Health*, vol 57, pp 784-89.

Hepworth, M. (2000) *Stories of Ageing*, Open University Press, Buckingham.

Hepworth, M. (2003) '"The changes and chances of this mortal life": aspects of ageing in the fiction of Stanley Middleton', *Ageing & Society*, vol 23, pp 721-37.

Hepworth, M. (2004) 'Images of old age', in J. Nussbaum and J. Coupland (eds) *Handbook of Communication and Aging Research*, Lawrence Erlbaum, Mahwah, NJ, pp 3-30.

Hockey, J. and James, A. (1993) *Growing Up and Growing Old*, Sage, London.

Hockey, J. and James, A. (2003) *Social Identities across the Life Course*, Palgrave, London.

Holden, U.P. and Woods, R.T. (1988) *Reality Orientation: Psychological approaches to the confused elderly*, 2nd edn, Churchill Livingstone, Edinburgh.

Hughes, E.C. (1971) *The Sociological Eye*, Aldine Atherton, Chicago.

Humphreys, L. (1970) *Tearoom Trade: Impersonal sex in public places*, Aldine, Chicago.

Jamieson, A. and Victor, C. (2002) *Researching Ageing and Later Life: The practice of social gerontology*, Open University Press, Maidenhead.

Johnson, J. (2004) *Writing Old Age*, No 3 in The Representation of Older People in Ageing Research Series, Centre for Policy on Ageing, London/Centre for Ageing and Biographical Studies, The Open University, Milton Keynes.

Johnson, J. and Bytheway B. (2001) 'An evaluation of the use of diaries in a study of medication in later life', *International Journal of Social Research Methodology*, vol 4, no 3, pp 183-204.

Johnson, J., Rolph, S. and Smith, R. (2010) *Residential Care Transformed: revisiting 'The Last Refuge'*, Palgrave, London.

Johnson, M.L. (2005) 'Preface', in M.L. Johnson (ed) *The Cambridge Handbook of Age and Ageing*, Cambridge University Press, Cambridge.

Katz. S. (1996) *Disciplining Old Age: The formation of gerontological knowledge*, University Press of Virginia, Charlottesville, VA.

Kaufman, S.R. (1986) *The Ageless Self: Sources of meaning in later life*, The University of Wisconsin Press, Wisconsin.

King, N. and Calasanti, T. (2006) 'Empowering the old: critical gerontology and anti-aging in a global context', in J. Baars, D. Dannefer, C. Phillipson and A. Walker (eds) *Aging, Globalization and Inequality: The new critical gerontology*, Amityville, NY: Baywood Publishing, pp 139-57.

Kitwood, T. (1997) *Dementia Reconsidered, the person comes first*, Open University Press, Buckingham.

Laurance, J. (2005) 'Demand for IVF treatment among older women soars', *The Independent*, 22 January.

Litwin H, and Shiovitz-Ezra S. (2006) 'Network type and mortality risk in later life', *The Gerontologist,* vol 46, pp 735-43.

Livingstone, G., Cooper, C., Woods, J., Milne, A. and Katona, C. (2008) 'Successful ageing in adversity: the LASER-AD longitudinal study', *Journal of Neurology, Neurosurgery and Psychiatry*, vol 79, pp 641-5.

Macdonald, A.M. (1973) *Chambers Twentieth Century Dictionary*, Chambers, Edinburgh.

Macionis, J.J. and Plummer, K. (1997) *Sociology: A global introduction*, Prentice Hall, London.

Marks, K. (1998) 'Go on, show us your bra', *The Independent*, 4 February.

Matthewman, S. (2000) 'Reach for the skies: towards a sociology of the weather', *New Zealand Sociology Journal*, vol 15, no 2.

McAdams, D.P. (1993) *The Stories We Live By: Personal myths and the making of the self*, The Guilford Press, New York.

McDonald, B. and Rich, C. (1983) *Look Me in the Eye: Old women, aging and ageism*, The Women's Press, London.

McGoldrick, A. and Cooper, C.L. (1980) 'Voluntary early retirement and taking the decision', *Employment Gazette*, pp 859-64.

McLeod, J. and Thomson, R. (2009) *Researching Social Change: Qualitative approaches to historical and personal processes*, Sage, London.

Mellor, P. (1993) 'Death in high modernity: the contemporary presence and absence of death' in D. Clarke (ed) *The Sociology of Death*, Blackwell, Oxford, pp 11-30.

Mitchell, M. (1977) 'Introduction', in I. Cunningham, *After Ninety*, University of Washington Press, Seattle, pp 9-23.

Moore, P. (2005) 'Designed for life', *SGI Quarterly* (www.sgiquarterly.org/feature2005Jly-8.html).

Moorehead, C. (2006) *The Letters of Martha Gellhorn*, Chatto & Windus, London.

Moss, S. (2010) *The Guardian G2*, 13 September.

Motion, A. (2008a) 'Meeting Harry', *The Guardian*, 5 November.

Motion, A. (2008b) 'The five Acts of Harry Patch', *The Daily Telegraph*, 8 March.

Mullin, C. (2010) *A View from the Foothills: The diaries of Chris Mullin*, Profile, London.

Nascher, I.L. (1919) *Geriatrics: the diseases of old age and their treatment*, 2nd revised edn, Kegan Paul, London.

Neale, B. (2008) 'The timescapes of personal lives and relationships: the temporal turn in social enquiry', Paper presented at *Human Development and the Life Span: Antecedents, Processes and Consequences of Change*, Institute for Society, Culture and Environment, Virginia Tech, Riva San Vitale, Switzerland, September.

Newton, E. (1980) *This Bed My Centre*, Virago, London.

NHSBSP (2006a) (www.cancerscreening.nhs.uk/breastscreen/#how-org).

NHSBSP (2006b) *Screening for Breast Cancer in England: past and future*, Advisory Committee on Breast Cancer Screening, NHSBSP Publication no 61.

Nikander, P. (2002) *Age in Action: Membership work and stage of life categories in talk*, The Finnish Academy of Science and Letters, Helsinki.

O'Connell, J. (2008) 'Julian Barnes: interview', *Time Out London*, 13 March.

ONS (Office for National Statistics) (2008) 'UK population approaches 61 million in 2007', News Release, 21 August 2008 (www.statistics.gov.uk/pdfdir/popest0808.pdf).

ONS (Office for National Statistics) (2009) 'Excess winter mortality in England and Wales', *Statistical Bulletin*, November (www.statistics.gov.uk/pdfdir/ewm1109.pdf).

ONS (Office for National Statistics) (2010a) *Cancer Statistics Registrations, registrations of cancer diagnosed in 2007*, England, Series MB1, no 38 (www.statistics.gov.uk/downloads/theme_health/MB1-38/MB1_38_2007.pdf).

ONS (Office for National Statistics) (2010b) *Cancer Registration Statistics England 2007* (2007cancerfirstrelease.xls).

ONS (Office for National Statistics) (2010c) *Marriages in England and Wales 2008* (www.statistics.gov.uk/pdfdir/marr0210.pdf).

Partridge, F. (1990) *Hanging On*, Collins, London.

Plummer, K. (2001) *Documents of Life 2: An invitation to critical humanism*, Sage, London.

Randall, W.L. (1995) *The Stories We Are: An essay in self-creation*, University of Toronto Press, Toronto.

Registrar General of England and Wales (1973) *Statistical Review of England and Wales, 1971*, HMSO, London.

Rhys, J. (1985) *Letters 1931–1966*, Penguin, London.

Robb, B. (1968) *Sans Everything: A case to answer*, Nelson, London.

Rolph, S., Johnson, J. and Smith, R. (2009) 'Using photography to understand change and continuity in the history of residential care for older people', *International Journal of Social Research Methodology*, vol 12, no 5, pp 421-40.

Ross. D. (1972) *G. Stanley Hall, the Psychologist as Prophet*, University of Chicago Press, Chicago.

Rosser, C. and Harris, C.C. (1965) *The Family and Social Change*, Routledge and Kegan Paul, London.

Rowe, G.P. (1966) 'The developmental conceptual framework to the study of the family', in F.I. Nye and F.M. Berardo (eds) *Emerging Conceptual Frameworks in Family Analysis*, Macmillan, New York, pp 201-9.

Rushdie, S. (1981) *Midnight's Children*, Picador, London.

Ryder, N. (1965) 'The cohort as a concept in the study of social change', *American Sociological Review*, vol 30, no 6, pp 843-61.

Sacks, H. (1992) *Lectures on Conversation, Vols 1 & 2*, Blackwell, Oxford.

Sarton, M. (1973) *As We Are Now*, W.W. Norton, New York.

Sawchuk, K.A. (1995) 'From the gloom to boom: age, identity and target marketing', in M. Featherstone and A. Wernick (eds) *Images of Ageing: cultural representations of later life*, Routledge, London, pp 173-87.

Shegog, R.F.A. (ed) (1981) *The Impending Crisis of Old Age*, Nuffield Foundation/Oxford University Press, Oxford.

Sheldon, S.H. (1948) *The Social Medicine of Old Age*, Oxford University Press, Oxford.

Shields, C. (2003) *Unless*, Fourth Estate, London.

Silverman, D. (2005) *Doing Qualitative Research*, 2nd edn, Sage, London.

Smith, J. (2002) *The Shipman Inquiry: first report*, HMSO, London.

Sontag, S. (1972) 'The double standard of aging', *Saturday Review*, 23 September, pp 29-38.

Sontag, S. (1977) *On Photography*, Farrar, Strauss and Giroux, New York.

Sussman, P.Y. (2006) *Decca: The letters of Jessica Mitford*, Phoenix, London.

Symonds, A. and Holland, C. (2008) 'The same hairdo: the production of the stereotyped imager of the older woman', in R. Ward and B. Bytheway (eds) *Researching Age and Multiple Discrimination*, in The Representation of Older People in Ageing Research Series, Centre for Policy on Ageing, London/Centre for Ageing and Biographical Studies, The Open University, Milton Keynes, pp 26-44.

Thane, P. (2000) *Old Age in English History: Past experiences, present issues*, Oxford University Press, Oxford.

Thomas, W. I. and Thomas, D. (1929) *The Child in America*, 2nd edn, Alfred Knopf, New York.

Thomas, W. I. and Znaniecki, F. (1958) *The Polish Peasant in Europe and America*, vols 1 and 2, Dover, New York.

Thomése, F., van Tilburg, T, Broese van Groenou, M. and Knipscheer, K. (2005) 'Network dynamics in later life', in M.L. Johnson (ed) *The Cambridge Handbook of Age and Ageing*, Cambridge University Press, Cambridge, pp 463-8.

Tomassini, C. (2005) 'Demographic profile', in A. Soule, P. Babb, M. Evandrou, S. Balchin and L. Zealey (eds) *Focus on Older People*, Office of National Statistics, London.

Townsend, P. (1957) *The Family Life of Old People*, Routledge and Kegan Paul, London.

Townsend, P. (1962) *The Last Refuge*, Routledge and Kegan Paul, London.

Townsend, P. (1981) 'The structured dependency of the elderly: the creation of social policy in the twentieth century', *Ageing & Society*, vol 1, no 1, pp 5-28.

Turner, B. (1995) 'Aging and identity: some reflections on the somatization of the self', in M. Featherstone and A. Wernick (eds) *Images of Ageing: Cultural representations of later life*, Routledge, London.

Twigg, J. (2006) *The Body in Health and Social Care*, Palgrave, London.

Twigg, J. (2007) 'Clothing, age and the body: a critical review', *Ageing & Society*, vol 27, pp 285-305.

Twigg, J. (2011) *Fashion and Age: Dress, the body and later life*, Berg, Oxford.

Uhlenberg, P.R. (1969) 'A study of cohort life cycles: cohorts of native born Massachusetts women, 1830–1920', *Population Studies*, vol 23, no 3, pp 407-20.

Vincent, J. (2007) 'Science and imagery in the "war on old age"', *Ageing & Society*, vol 27, pp 941-61.

Walker, A. (1982) Evidence submitted to the House of Commons Social Services Committee, *Age of Retirement*, HMSO, London.

Walker, A. (2009) 'Aging and social policy: theorizing the social', in V.L. Bengston, D. Gans, N.M. Putney and M. Silverstein (eds) *Handbook of Theories of Ageing*, Springer, New York, pp 595-613.

Ward, R. and Holland, C. (2011) '"If I look old, I will be treated old": hair and later-life image dilemmas', *Ageing & Society*, vol 31, no 2, pp 288-307.

Weiss, R.S. and Bass, S.A. (eds) (2002) *Challenges of the Third Age: meaning and purpose in later life*, Oxford University Press, Oxford.

Wheeler, B. (2010) 'The Ed Miliband story' (www.bbc.co.uk/news/uk-politics-11316855).

Wilkinson, P., Pattenden, S., Armstrong, B., Fletcher, A., Kovats, R.S., Mangtani, P. and McMichael, A.J. (2004) 'Vulnerability to winter mortality in elderly people in Britain: population based study', *British Medical Journal*, vol 329 (7467), p 647.

Woodward, K. (1997) *Telling Stories: Aging reminiscence and the life review*, Occasional Paper No 9, Doreen B. Townsend Center for the Humanities, University of California, Los Angeles.

Woodward, K. (1999) *Figuring Age, women, bodies, generations*, Indiana University Press, Bloomington, IN.

Worsfold, B. (ed) (2010) *Acculturating Age: Approaches to cultural gerontology*, Grup Dedal-Lit, Lleida, Spain.

Ylänne, V., Williams, A. and Wadleigh, P.M. (2010) 'Ageing well? Older people's health and well being as portrayed in UK magazine advertisements', *International Journal of Ageing and Later Life*, vol 4, no 2, pp 33-62.

Yong, E. (2009) 'Secrets of the centenarians: life begins at 100', *New Scientist*, 7 September.

Young, M. (1988) *The Metronomic Society: natural rhythms and human timetables*, Thames and Hudson, London.

Young, M. and Willmott, P. (1957) *Family and Kinship in East London*, Routledge, London.

Ziman, J. (1994) *Prometheus Bound: Science in a dynamic steady state*, Cambridge University Press, Cambridge.

Index

See also the Appendix.